FATE AND DESTINY

THE TWO AGREEMENTS OF THE SOUL

Illustration for Cover

Originally, "pity" and "piety" were very close with each suggesting aspects of affection, duty, and kindness. The idea of "having pity" on some poor soul came much later. William Blake considered Pity to be a divine attribute in the eternal realm; but on earth, like many other things, pity becomes divided. Here, the image of Pity represents the distinction between fate and destiny, for those two energies can also be seen as unified in eternity, but fatefully divided once the soul is born on earth.

FATE AND DESTINY

THE TWO AGREEMENTS OF THE SOUL

Revised and Expanded
Edition

MICHAEL MEADE

GREENFIRE PRESS
An Imprint of Mosaic Multicultural Foundation

GREENFIRE PRESS
An Imprint of Mosaic Multicultural Foundation

Contents

Stories

EX MALO BONUM
Out of bad comes good; but also out of fate can come a destiny.

INTRODUCTION

Ancient notions of fate include an invisible thread woven through all the things of the world and throughout all the events of time. Fate appears as the original web of life, but also as the fine thread that weaves each soul into the world of time and space at birth. *Fate* comes from the Latin, *fata*, which can mean a "thing spoken by the gods" at the beginning of each life. And *fate* carries the sense of *fatality*, the presence of death waiting at the end of every life journey.

As divine pronouncement, *fate* carries the sense of oracular speech, a prediction made at the beginning of life. Each soul begins a life sentence at birth; for the basic agreement for receiving the gift of life involves accepting the inevitability of death. Life itself is fatal and can seem to be fatalistic, until we understand the deeper intimations of our individual fate. Our fate is there at the very beginning. It waits for us at the very end, but it also tries to surface and become conscious to us at each critical juncture of our lives.

Throughout our lives an invisible thread pulls us along. Novalis wrote that "fate and the soul are the same thing;" while Plato was reported to have said that "fate and love are the same thing." Our soul is wedded to a fate secretly inscribed within it. This original life-thread of the soul was there before the umbilical formed. It ties us to the eternal realm and sets us upon the plot line of the soul's unique adventure in life.

Upavita is an old Sanskrit term for the eternal thread and fine filament of golden imagination that makes each life unique, inherently noble, and meaningful from the beginning. This indelible thread involves the measure and inner shape of our lives; yet it cannot be measured even by fine instruments. It cannot be found through scientific experiment or be proven to exist in logical ways. Yet it is there, woven within us and felt in fateful moments and at critical turning points in life.

Without a sense of fate, life seems more random and accidental and we tend to feel less purposeful, less convinced that our souls could be leading us somewhere. In times of trouble we can sense the delicate nature of the life-thread and know that all of life hangs by but a thread. In moments of awakening we can feel its subtle presence and learn how we are woven within and mysteriously entangled with the life-threads of others and with the great skein of life.

Fate is the inner *Koan*, the archetypal pattern and enigma of each soul; it is the puzzling question that one's life secretly desires to answer. Denying the sense of inherent limitations set by fate also means denying the essential uniqueness of one's soul. Our individuality was shaped and seeded within us before we were born and our fate involves those exact things which give us an "intended personality." The "twist of fate" that twines us to the world makes each soul unique and each life unrepeatable.

The Territories of Fate

Fate is a mysterious presence found within each life and encountered in all serious undertakings. Fate refers to our deepest sense of subjectivity, where we become subject to mysterious limitations, yet open to surprising potentials. Whenever we try to change or grow a greater life we encounter our inner limitations as well as outer obstacles; both can be seen as the inevitable presence of fate in our lives. Fate appears as whatever limits, restricts or even imprisons us; yet fate is the territory where we must go if we are to awaken to our inner destiny.

Our fate includes the dark nights of the soul where we feel most lost; yet fate also holds the key that can unlock the area of life that is our true destination. Fate seeks the unfolding of itself and the revealing of the inner purpose and meaning of our lives. Our very mortality hides within it a divine seed, planted at the beginning, waiting throughout each life to be enlivened and flower forth. Taken together, fate and destiny are an archetypal pairing within each soul; they form a dynamic tension that makes each life meaningful and purposeful.

Fate appears in those issues and events that we don't directly choose yet can't simply refuse. The paradoxical nature of fate includes both the sense of the inevitable and the shock of the unexpected. Fate involves what could have happened at any time, yet seems so fated once it does occur. Fate is the accident that isn't fully accidental; the coincidence that is more than coincidental. It is the synchronistic, paradoxical occurrence where the expected and the unexpected coincide.

Fate can be fortunate or fatal, a blessed or a cursed event. Fate is what imprisons us from within; yet the territory of fate is where we must go if we would awaken to our purpose in life. Our divinely inscribed destiny hides exactly where we are least likely to look for it-- in the fateful issues and darkest areas that most of us try to avoid, outwit or outrun. Fate is that to which we must at times surrender if we wish to find the life purpose set within us. As James Joyce put it, "Think you're escaping and run into yourself. Longest way round is the shortest way home."

Our longings for home are also a desire for awakening to the destiny hidden within the soul from the beginning. Destiny is the most hidden aspect of one's life; at the same time, it involves one's original destination. In avoiding the fateful issues in our lives we miss our appointments with destiny. Fate ties us to the world and keeps us in it, while destiny calls us to a divine errand set deeply within us.

Fate inscribes an area or territory that we are bound to enter. Our fate places us in specific contexts where meaning and purpose can be explored. Wherever we brush against the limits of our fate we also stand near the doors of our destiny. When not considered as something predetermined, fate implies both an innate destiny and the hidden unity of the soul.

Fate and destiny are opposing energies, but also complementary threads woven closely in our souls that secretly foreshadow and shape our lives from within. When we face our fate in life we also begin to move it and when fate moves destiny moves closer to us. The threads of destiny allow us to find a way through exactly those areas and issues that constrain the vitality of our lives. Only when seen from the ground of destiny do the suffering and restrictions of an individual life make sense. Fate is purpose seen from the other end of life.

We each have an appointment with destiny but must suffer the disappointments of fate in order to arrive there. Fate would stop us in our tracks and strip us to the bone so that we might discover the essential imagination and sense of meaning and purpose that lies at the core of our lives. Attempting to escape one's fate not only removes one's destiny, but can threaten sanity and survival. When we refuse the limits of fate and ignore the hints of destiny we tighten the unconscious web of our lives. We make our lives fixed and settled and insulated from the soul's great calling. Thus, we seal our own fate and rescind our hidden destiny.

The Call of Destiny

Although *fate* can mean "it has been written," the elements of fate present an unfinished inner story trying to unfold, a living text that is open to interpretation and subject to change. Fate shapes the particular plotline through which each soul tries to awaken and enter the great drama of life. When accepted and attended to, our fate functions more as an oracle needing interpretation than a narrow plot with a fixed outcome. Facing the elements of one's fate and seeking the destiny hidden within it are part of the art of truly living and of living truly.

Fate may involve the earthly limitations of our "lot in life," but *destiny*, from the Latin, *destinare*, implies that we are also "of the stars." The sense of each soul being star-born appears in ancient astrology, but also surfaces in modern astrophysics. Theories of the Big Bang include the notion that we all carry within us a bit of the original exploding star. Each of us is secretly tied to the stars, both star-born and star-bound, and a bit of a star in our own way.

Destiny can mean "to stand out, to stand apart;" especially to be seen standing in a visible relation to one's inner genius. Destiny involves an irreversible process of becoming from within. Becoming one's true self means revealing one's innate genius. Our destiny sets us apart from others and places us in proximity of our natural genius. The old meaning of *genius* refers to the "spirit that is already there," the inborn spirit that enters the world with each child born.

The native genius residing within us bears the innate gifts and talents we bring to the world and it intends to give them. The soul must be limited by fate, but it arrives gifted and aimed and dedicated to fulfilling its original agreement to contribute meaningfully to life. The primary agreement our souls have made before birth is to deliver our unique gifts to the world. However, the labor of being born and the necessity of entering the realm of time and expediency cause us to forget the divine errand that the soul has agreed to undertake.

We are each woven into the common world of time and space; yet we are also secretly tied to things eternal. We each have a foot in time and a toehold in eternity; we have a foot in each world and a responsibility to both. We are made of the warp and woof of fate and destiny which taken together comprise that which is truly weird and inherently unique about us. Each life has its own weirdness, its indelible inner pattern and essential uniqueness that allow it to truly stand out from others.

Weird or *wyrrd* comes from old roots that include the German *werden*, meaning "to become, to grow." The wyrrd is the way we are spun from within, the way we are shaped and styled and aimed at life. The wyrdd refers to that which we must become if we are to become our true selves. Our inner weirdness is also our divine connection. Our essential task in life is to awaken to the way that the eternal would speak through us, to learn to live out our intended personality and the inner weirdness that makes us a unique torchbearer of the flame of life. Only from this ground of destiny can an individual life truly make sense in the end.

Without a sense that we are aimed by fate and uniquely formed, we can fail to live the adventure our souls came to life to live. We can become pawns in the hands of whatever outside authority happens to be in our lives. Instead of finding where we best fit into the mysterious scheme of life, we try to simply "fit in." We simply accept the life being handed to us and live within the ideas and expectations of others. We live within a collective fate and fail to find the unique path our souls would have us walk.

Fame and Fortune

In modern, mass societies the uniqueness of the individual is increasingly in danger of being lost amidst the pressure to conform to collective ideas. Whereas the soul would have us find and live the unique and sacred purpose that brought us each to life to begin with, mass culture tends to deny the individual and promote the same goals for everyone. Vague modern notions of "fame and fortune" tend to replace the essential idea of becoming ourselves from within. Increasingly, people seem willing to trade the possibility of a life of purpose and meaning for "fifteen minutes of fame."

There is an old connection between fate and fame that is preserved in the words themselves. The Latin root, *fata*, reminds that each soul is "spoken of by the divine." "In the beginning was the word…" as each soul is touched by the divine and breathed into life. On the other hand, *fame* comes from *fama*, meaning "to speak and to tell of," but especially to "tell rumors and report on the reputation of others." Our fate involves what the gods first said about us, while any fame we might acquire refers to what others see in us and say about us during our lives and after our death as well.

Destiny is the hidden thread that connects the sense of fate with old ideas of fame. Living out one's inner destiny reveals the divine word set within the soul and that causes others to recognize our innate value and speak well of us. In this older, deeper sense, becoming famous meant something closer to being "known well," rather than simply becoming "well known." The true sense of fame relates more to the unique quality of one's life than to the simple quantity of one's renown.

Fame and fortune can be worthy goals when seen as extensions of the soul's inner story. *Fortune* comes to us from the Latin *fortuna*, meaning "chance or fate." Fortuna is also the name of an ancient goddess who turns the "wheel of fate" and gives each soul its lot in life. Life is the original lottery in which we each have a chance to stand out and stand for something meaningful. Being famous in that way makes us exemplary, unique, and irreplaceable; living proof of the underlying meaning of life. In the end, all else is pretense, mistaken identity, and *infamy*.

Infamy is the opposite of fame, being "not famous" or more often, famous for the wrong reasons. Infamy involves a subversion or perversion of the true spirit in one's life, a reversal and undermining of the aims of one's inner star and the purpose of one's innate genius. Infamy suggests being seen standing away from the true spirit and original aim of one's life. The infamous become famous for the wrong reasons and become well-known in the wrong ways.

Modern mass cultures seem to produce new forms of infamy as brief flashes of fame substitute for the genuine discovery of the inner spirit and true destination of people's lives. People succumb to notions of general fame and literal fortunes. Through modern technology anyone can suddenly "be a star" and go from being an unknown to becoming world-famous in a moment. More and more people seem willing to become famous for no good reason as if sudden infamy has replaced meaningful notoriety. They desire their fifteen minutes of fame and by virtue of modern technology and mass communications, they may get it.

The greater meaning of individual life is still found where destiny calls each soul to a unique adventure, where each person takes the chance to become who they already are in essence. Throughout life the soul seeks to grow and unfold its inner story and reveal the destination it was aimed at from the beginning. When we tolerate the growing pains and trust in something as yet unseen, the constrictions of fate can open in ways that allow us to give the innate gifts carried by the soul. In doing so the individual soul becomes reconnected to its divine origins and others are encouraged to become themselves. The older sense of fame depends upon moments of revelation in which the inborn spirit of one's life becomes evident and can be celebrated.

About this Book

This book is about the first agreement of the soul and the divine errand that forms the inner meaning of each life. It is about the mystery of fate speaking everywhere and the possibility of destiny appearing anywhere. It is a collection of stories both personal and mythical, for those are the twin texts that give texture and shape to the mysteries of fate and destiny.

Although I have considered the ideas of fate and destiny for many years, the timing of the book has to do with the increasing rattling of the world around us. For it seems to be our mutual fate to be living during a time of great upheaval and sweeping change. An old mythological image-idea refers to nature and culture as the "two great garments of life." At this time the fabrics of both cloaks of being have become frayed and torn, leaving us more exposed to the unknown and less woven into the world.

There are many ways to view the dramatic changes that are well underway, but no easy way to see where life is going and how things might end. There is no way to avoid the current crises in culture and the radical changes in nature. There is no sudden remedy for the tragedies and losses that characterize the modern era. However, there may be no better time to learn the inner story that our souls carry and find the ways we are intended to be in this increasingly uncertain world. What we each have to contribute has already been sown and seeded with us.

When the story of the world becomes less clear, it is the unfolding of the inner life of the soul that might provide the best guidance for how to proceed. It has always been on the ground of uncertainty and in the face of the unknown that the inner story of our souls must unfold. The soul is ancient and knowing and it knows both the nature of change and the necessity of drama for the continuance of life. The soul requires an outer drama so that it can reveal its inner myth, its full imagination for life and its surprising capacity for renewal.

As the book makes clear, I had my first conscious connection to the mysteries of fate when I was barely a youth. Since then, I have learned that all of us have at least one experience in which the inner pattern of our souls becomes revealed to us. Unfortunately, modern life tends to overlook, miscast or diminish the ways in which the soul tries to awaken us early in life. The stories gathered here are of the kind that people used to use to bring the essential experiences of the soul into greater awareness.

Myths, folk tales, and fairy tales most often depend upon great obstacles and impossible tasks to call forth the inner resources of the heroines and heroes of the soul. Fairy tales were once called "fated tales" as if to drive home the point that fate is waiting for us to enter the drama of life and learn what we are truly made of. Mythic tales can act as vessels of meaning that help people find the ways that the threads of fate hold them and aim them at the ground where destiny and meaning can be found.

For the past thirty years, I have worked with at-risk youth and overlooked elders, with prisoners and homeless youth, with battle veterans and homeless refugees. One thing they all have in common is that there can be no denying that they are in trouble and facing great obstacles. Of course, those are the exact conditions for generating change and for bringing the soul's inherent genius and deep resources closer to the surface of life. I am not wishing trouble on anyone, but I have noticed how trouble comes knocking at every door and how it knocks harder on our lives if it is simply ignored or denied.

This is a book about trouble and trouble is another word for fate; what troubles us the most is what we are fated to one day face. What troubles us in youth has significance for our lives and will return at each crossroads we face because it secretly seeks to provoke a deep awakening to the unique way that we are intended to live. The stories gathered here are full of troubles and trials and threaded through with the surprising ways that the genius of life opens the way to change and healing and wisdom.

Some of the stories are "wisdom tales" that try to return genuine wisdom to a world that prefers information or the kind of knowledge that can be captured as data. Wisdom involves a darker knowledge of life as well as ways of finding uncommon illumination. The wise are those who find the inner thread and true gradient of their lives and learn the ropes from following the line of their own destiny. The last section of the book is titled "The Return of

Wisdom," as if wisdom is trying to return to us through the impossible tasks we face and the deep troubles we find ourselves in collectively.

Of necessity, the return of wisdom involves the presence of love. In the old sense of things, love is a secret part of wisdom as well as a necessary condition of the soul. Learning and love both require that the heart remain young and that we remain foolish enough to follow the dream of our own soul and in doing so become wise within ourselves. Only those who have followed the dream of their soul become wise enough to help others on the surprising road of life and death.

The middle section of the book bears the title "The Dream of Life." Without fully intending it, I have put a dream in the middle of the book. Then again, there is a dream in the middle of each life; each of us being a dream seeded in a soul around which the body is wrapped. The first agreement of the soul can be viewed as the dream that keeps calling us to a greater life. An old idea holds the place of awakening to be in the space between sleep and the waking world, as the awakened soul serves both worlds and connects them together.

The first section is titled "The Book of Fate." It refers to the book of myths that I received by mistake on my thirteenth birthday. Of course, it was less of a common mistake and more an act of fate that was inevitable in its own way. Fate appears when life needs to change and in the mistakes that turn out to be fortunate and purposeful. I take aim at critical events in my own life in order to offer a sense of how fate has shaped and informed it. Along the way, the personal tales keep slipping into myth, perhaps in the same way that myth keeps slipping back into life.

Aspects of the Self

Another way to view the sections of the book involves the way it considers certain aspects of the deep self. I use soul and the "deep self" almost interchangeably as I imagine each to be an inner depository of the exact knowledge that we need for our lives to become purposeful. Under the old notion that each person is born with their own inner medicine, the deep self can also be seen to carry the antidote for what truly ails us in life.

Throughout the book I contrast the deep and knowing self with the little-self or ego self. Seen from this view, the first section focuses on the Gifted Self, how it tries to awaken during youthful encounters with fate, but also how it tries to become known at each stage of later life. The initiations of youth involve an awakening of the inner sage and the rites of the elders require a renewal of the dream of life first encountered in youth. There are stories of the struggles of youth trying to find and use the god-given gifts of the soul. And there are tales that describe the weird and wise ways of genuine elders.

The second part of the book focuses upon the Golden Self as it tells tales of the birth of the soul and the origins of the "callings" that try to bring the inner gold to the surface of one's life. The First Agreement of the soul is described and contrasted with all other agreements that life requires. Tales of following the dream of the soul serve to remind that the treasure hard to attain and the inner gold are within us all along. However, a genuine calling must be followed to uncover the golden self and learn the purpose it would have us serve. Here, the intimate relationship between our gifts and our wounds becomes critical for healing and growth as well as for understanding both what we fear and what we love.

The Awakened Self becomes the focus of the third part of the book as we move deeper into the territory of myth and take up old ideas from both the West and the East regarding the "inner disciple" of our lives. The search for the deeper self becomes a pilgrimage that leads to the pearls of wisdom, the pains of awakening, and the power of truth to counteract all that can poison the soul. Distinctions are made between "big death" and the "little deaths" that take us to the middle of life and make rebirth and renewal possible. While following the path of the disciple we learn of the brilliance of the tiger-self, the "roar of awakening," and the many ways that difficult fates unwind into realizations of wisdom and destiny.

Taken together, these tales open the territory of the initiated soul and awakened self and serve as a ground for considering the necessary troubles and essential callings that affect all young people. At the same time the stories mark the paths along which people of any age can find threads of meaning and hints of purpose.

The text is populated by images of the wily teachers and wise guides that exemplify the soul's instinct and ability to serve both this world and the otherworld. There's an old thief who instructs misguided authorities, an old prostitute with critical truths to tell, a young woman who must approach a tiger to preserve love, a foolish dreamer who learns the alchemy of the heart, a holy man who falls in love and forgets his errand for god, and a village where the rotten aspects of life are cleansed and the inner gold of the self is polished.

The great marketplace of life appears in several forms and is populated by terrified servants and wandering disciples, lost dreamers and saintly thieves. Death makes an appearance in the middle of life as do Brahma, the Buddha, and the ancient river goddess Saraswati. All have something to say about the conditions of the soul, the importance of dreams, the dance of fate and destiny, and the secret unity that dwells within each of us and holds the two worlds together.

I

The Book of Fate

We are hunting our fate and we are pursued by it.

CHAPTER 1

THE BOOK OF FATE

In refusing fate we also deny destiny.

Our fate marks us from the beginning, it makes us and shapes us from within; it ties us to the world with hidden threads that aim us at life and pull us in certain directions. I began to learn about fate on my thirteenth birthday when I received a book that indelibly marked my life. It was my first conscious experience of fate and it involved a hint of destiny as well. It was the first hard-cover book I ever received that wasn't a school book or a church text. In some ways it turned out to be both of those things for me, yet also more than either of them. The book was a gift, but was also given to me by mistake. A twist of fate can work that way, turning one thing into another in order to reveal the inner shape of one's life.

My closest aunt had noticed that I read a lot and asked what most interested me. I told her that history intrigued me, how the stories of the past seemed to continue to affect the present. In order to support my interests and encourage my education, she went looking for a history book for me. She was kind-hearted and generous and she looked out for me and my sisters. She was also a notably short woman and that may have affected what happened next.

In the bookstore she spotted a history book on an upper shelf. Reaching high above herself, she must have taken down the book next to the one she aimed at. Unaware of the mistake, she purchased the wrong book and had it wrapped as a gift for me. As I began removing the wrapping paper, my aunt could see that she had come away with the wrong book. Saying that it was all a mistake, she insisted on returning it. Meanwhile, I was having a completely different experience. For, partially revealed behind the torn paper I could see the image of a winged horse with an archer riding bare-back upon it. Holding fast the book and pulling off more of the wrapping, I could see that he had released an arrow aimed at something behind him. Following the flight line of the arrow led me to the spine of the book. There I found a stark mask emblazoned with a tangled array of snakes for hair and wild staring eyes glaring at me.

Compelled by the images and already caught in the tension between them I turned back to the cover to see the title of the book. It was simply stated: *Mythology* by Edith Hamilton. Through an accident or an unintentional accuracy, history had become mythology and I was instantly changed. No way would I exchange this surprising gift; not for a history book, nor for any other book, not for any other gift either. The arrow loosed on the cover struck something deep inside as something in me leapt to the image of the flying horse and understood the language of images immediately. In one glance I found something I was looking for without even knowing that I sought for it.

Looking back, I cannot recall anything about that birthday other than the remarkable book and the effect it had upon me. It is as if a part of me still stands with that book in my hands, time having stopped still as something timeless took hold of me. In reading history, I had really been seeking something older, something deeper, and more mysterious. Looking back, it makes sense that a book that contained many mysteries of life would arrive in a mysterious way.

My aunt bought the book by accident and gave it to me by mistake or else we were both pulled to a moment of meaning by the unseen hand of fate. Seen from the deeper angle of fate, it was the right book that fell into her hand and it fell to her in order to find its way to me. Given the way my soul was inclined, the accident was not accidental at all. It was a fortunate gift as well as a mistake, the kind of accurate error that occurs when fate takes a hand in things and someone's life is about to change.

Many years passed before I could see how elements of fate and destiny were present in that moment that remains a living memory. Unnoticed by my family, unseen by my friends and only partly conscious to me, I had been touched by fate and had found a thread of my own destiny. What I am calling fate has to do with the way a person's soul is seeded and shaped from within, like a story trying to unfold and become known. What I am calling destiny has to do with the inner arc and arrow of one's life. For each soul is secretly aimed at the world and inclined towards a destination that only becomes revealed in crucial moments and at turning points in life.

The elements of fate and destiny are intimations of the story our soul would have us live, both the limitations that must be faced and the destination that would be found. As fate would have it, they are often found through what seems like a big mistake, a strange accident or a surprise. Fate brings the outer world and the inner realm of the soul in contact in order to reveal underlying realities that make life both mysterious and meaningful. Before it happens our fate seems unlikely; yet once it appears it seems that it was bound to happen to us.

That night I read almost the entire book. Time stood still and the timeless realm of myth kept opening before me and growing deeper like the night. I pored through the stories and felt the world around me expand as if I had stepped into a remarkable territory that had been nearby all along. It was as if a void in my life suddenly became filled with stories and mythic images that turned the unnamed emptiness into a newfound abundance. I had received a true gift, something beyond anything I expected, yet something I seemed bound to encounter.

Years later, when I thanked my aunt for that gift, she could not recall the occasion. Yet that night, in the blind confines of New York City and amidst the confusion of my youth, I found something of my own purpose for being alive. The image of the flying horse, the arrow launched from it and the word *mythology* all entered me together and altered me entirely. I later learned that symbols and myths work just that way; they grab one's psyche and fill it with images and sudden ideas and newfound energy as well. Mythic images defy rational explanation and open areas beyond and within the usual limits of time and space. Myths and symbols affect each person differently as they draw inner meanings and our deepest feelings up to the surface of life.

I felt invited and drawn into an inner world that was intensely alive and brimming with living imagination. Early in the text I encountered the idea that the ancient tellers of myth "transformed a world of fear into a world of beauty." I wanted to be part of such a transformation. I was standing at the end of childhood feeling caught in the uncertainty of my unformed identity. I feared I might become trapped in life the way most grown people around me seemed to be. I worried that the same forces that made my family and my neighborhood feel confined and narrow would somehow capture and entrap me.

I knew that my father felt burdened and drained from the dull repetition of days and years spent driving a truck through the narrow streets of Manhattan. Each day consisted of loading and unloading freight like Sisyphus pushing rocks up a mountain only to find them waiting at the bottom again the next day. I knew that my mother dreamed of some other life, one more comfortable and less encumbered by the needs and troubles of five growing children. I could see the hidden anguish behind the brash façades of the neighborhood taverns where all our parents socialized, either soothing their souls or else troubling them further.

Most of the time I liked the intensity of New York City, the palpable sense of life's rough and tumble, the feeling that we knew what hard reality was and could handle it as well. Yet, there was something diminished about the reality we shared and there was a persistent meanness in our lives. It wasn't just the dangers and edginess of the "mean streets," but a hollowness that could be felt just under the bare-boned surface of everyday life. At times I could identify this other kind of meanness as a "demeaned life," a kind of fallen state where people give up on their genuine dreams and replace them with a chip on their shoulder, or worse with a cynical shrug of dull acceptance.

People around me talked knowingly of having to face the facts of life and deal with harsh realities like poverty as if that was the only reality of life. Meanwhile, I found that many people seemed mean-spirited whether they were impoverished or not. Despite the local bravado, we seemed to live under a mean rule, within a poverty that included the emptiness of actual hunger, but just as often a spiritual hollowness as well. By the age of thirteen I feared that what I observed in those around me was what I had to become. I loved my family, yet there was a double bind that went with the bonds of that love. Part of me was already looking for a way out of the family fate and out from under the collective weight of collapsed dreams.

The Glam and the Gloom

The rule of fate causes each soul born to enter an ongoing story that includes threads that reach back into the mists of time. Both sides of my family came from Ireland, driven forth by the hungers and pains of poverty, yet also carrying an unseen inheritance. There is an old notion of "the gloom and the glam" deeply seeded in the Irish soul, the long shadows and recurring brightness that attend things Celtic. The sense of Irish gloom plays out in the great tragedies of the land and its people, in the ongoing "troubles" that trouble both politics and religion. For there is a dark side to Irishness, a rough music and heavy gloom that slips shadowlike down the back stairs of time passing from family to family, from parents to child, like an old lament.

The other side of the gloom appears in the "glam," shorthand for the old word *glamour* that meant not so much superficial beauty as the natural magic and essential love for the mystery and enchantment of life. The glam involves the very "spell of life" that combines the beauty and wonder of nature with the inspiration and art natural to any genuine culture. The glam appears in the grandness of the poets and musicians; it speaks in the "blarney" that turns everything into a story and in the tendency to seed common speech with mystical and philosophical notions. At its best the glam provides an imagination and an instinct to make anything and everything tragically beautiful and wondrous at the same time; to make each thing encountered seem to be living proof of the blessed, mythic, calamity and enduring song of life.

My family had its share of both the glam and the gloom as well as a mixed attitude towards our Irish ancestry. My mother could wear her heritage like a badge; she was Irish and proud of it. She spoke of the Emerald Isle with a great longing, yet we knew next to nothing of relatives back in the old country. Irish songs dominated the juke boxes in the local pubs, but we had no idea where we actually hailed from. Like so many ethnic immigrant groups, there was an intense desire to leave the dramas and confusions, the tragedies and misfortunes of the past behind in order to hopefully join the American quest for a redemptive future. There was enough inner pride to claim some of the glam of Irishness, but plenty of remembered gloom that caused the immigrants to join the hordes of Americans voting to be all future with no past.

There was an edgy humility as well as a potential for humiliation about the immigrant background that lingered like an indelible ring pressed into the blue collar of an old shirt. There was a conspicuous lack of education and some shadowy mysteries hidden behind the lace curtains intended to put a genteel veil over family things. "Lace curtain Irish" was a term used for those who lived in the old "shanties" yet sought to rise socially in American life. The lace of the curtains allowed those within to keep watch on the outside while keeping others from seeing all the way in. The curtains both hid and revealed elements of our family fate and the ethnic threads that tied us back to history, but deeper yet to the mysteries and fateful myths of ancestry.

The recent past of my family involved a crowd of quarry-workers and dock hands, longshoremen and horse handlers. They were teamsters and union men, many of whom married waitresses and seamstresses, laundry maids and nannies. If you listened carefully and asked the right uncles, you could learn that there were also some gangsters and hooligans that figured into the mix. My father was born and raised in Hell's Kitchen and something of those fires also burned behind the lace curtains and smoldered inside the family and inside me as well.

My mother made sure that her children felt the Irish bones within us. She held her grandmother in great esteem as if the woman had brought the sod of the old country over and spread it here for us to walk on. In my mother's eyes, the Irish-speaking grandmother always walked on holy ground. She had raised ten sons here, all the while dreaming of the rolling, green hills of mother Ireland. At times it was as if my mother clung to the earth of that story more than to the ground beneath her feet. A sense of loss rested uneasily right under my mother's skin and could be provoked by an odd word or an Irish song, or by a sudden shift of her inner mood. For she was taken to sudden and extreme moods and the mood of "dear old Ireland" was one I preferred as a child.

I liked the sense that we came from somewhere unseen that had magical and mythical proportions that were still worth seeking for and returning to. I liked it less when the mood changed from the longing for mystical, mother Ireland to my mother's painful lament for the mother she never knew. My mother was the first-born child with her sister coming along less than a year later. During the second labor something went seriously wrong. The new daughter arrived well enough, but as fate would have it, the young mother failed to survive the birth of her second child. My mother never told many details of that story, but she carried the felt sense of a tragedy along with a fear of the world only barely covered over by her own bravado.

She would tell repeatedly how the two tiny sisters not only became motherless, but were soon abandoned by a father who never recovered from the devastation of losing the young wife he loved. Because the presence of the daughters only served to remind him of the wife he had lost, he gave the little sisters over to their Irish grandmother, the one already burdened with ten growing sons. Apparently, she loved having the little daughters after producing the long line of sons; but she was already worn to the bone with the work of nursing and nourishing so many. The old grandmother did her best to love them, but her own heart longed more than anything to return to the green hills in the West of Ireland and rest herself near the holy waters and wells of Saint Brigid.

Having lost her own mother early and lacking the love she needed as a child, my mother absorbed the longing for mother Ireland as if it were breast milk. Inside herself, she mixed the loss of one mother with the longing for the other. It was in the mood of mother longing that she would talk of the old country as if she knew it firsthand. What she did know firsthand was the fear that she and her sister shared of being lost in the commotion or else smothered by the heavy coats that their uncles would toss in a pile each evening when they came home from work.

I could picture my mother and aunt terrified, like children in a fairy tale huddling close in a dark house of giants. As I grew older, I realized that although the story of the orphan sisters was in the past, the effects of it were frequently present. My mother, who could be a force of nature and could erupt with volcanic intensity, was also afraid of many things. At times she became childlike in her fears and desperate to find something preserving and stable to believe in.

My mother also sought for her missing mother in the Catholic Church. She went to mass each morning and prayed to Mary, Mother of God and keeper of all children. She insisted that her children attend mass regularly and go to Catholic schools. In trying to fill a hole she felt within herself she took the church with all its doctrines and dogmas as whole cloth, and she expected me and my siblings to do the same. It was as if any new thing had first to be passed through the unsteady womb of the family; it had to be doused in the waters of loss and then be approved by the mother church in order to be considered real or acceptable.

I consider it part of my own fate in life to have been born into the womb of my mother's loss of her mother. I feel that I was nurtured on longings that couldn't be fulfilled and often mothered by "mother-loss." I call it fate because I was born into it, because I had no control over it, and because I felt constricted by it. While growing up, I too felt smothered by something from the past, as if there was no way to escape the shades and glooms, no way to compensate for the lost lands, no way to restore the missing mothers and disappearing fathers.

My mom never recovered from her lack of direct mothering and fathering. At times she referred to herself as a "street orphan" who was left alone and on her own as a child. She roamed the streets of New York learning to look out for herself. One side of that orphan feeling involved a deep sense of loss and abandonment. The other side grew tough and independent, becoming resourceful, unless it was being resentful and punishing. She married my father despite and because her own father threatened to disown her forever if she chose an uneducated, rough-neck from Hell's Kitchen.

My father was himself the youngest of ten children and something in him secretly resonated with my mother's feelings of being overlooked and undernourished. He left school after the third grade to help support his family. There were hungry mouths to feed and his father was never known to have taken a job. He was at school just long enough to learn to read and write, but not long enough to learn what his own capacities might be or what his destiny might entail. Throughout his life he continued to perfect the cursive script he learned in school. He would pen the address on bills as if he were completing school lessons or carefully signing important documents. He had an elegant and careful hand with a pen, even if his fists were most often grasping freight or imitating the jabs of his favorite boxer.

Inside, he longed to be a writer and carried western novels by Zane Grey in his freight truck. He had a photo of himself wearing a suit and holding a pen to paper while sitting at a copy desk at the New York Times. Once someone had seen some latent quality in him and offered him an entry level job at the great newspaper. You could see his inner smile of delight in the photo, as clearly as the part in his slicked back hair. And if you didn't know about the Second World War that killed the career before it began or the gloomy periods of joblessness that followed after, you would think he was a bright young writer settling in at his destined vocation.

My father worked two and sometimes three jobs that kept him away from home a good deal of the time. He never spoke of the dreams he had for his own life and only rarely revealed the level of disappointment he carried within. Yet a longing for heaven and an affinity for hell seemed to grow behind the lace curtains and set the stage for me and my siblings. We were born into a fateful arrangement of missing mothers, distant fathers, street orphans and lost lands all waiting for some divine intervention or magical release.

Each family has its own inheritance of fateful themes and inner woven stories that are passed down along with the DNA sewn into the body's cells and the bones that give us familiar and familial shapes. Each family has its own womb of fate with a specific mixture of glam and gloom through which each child born must pass. Despite the modern obsession with the future, the past is never quite over; it clings to us and secretly asks us to solve and resolve the essential questions about life that we have inherited. Each family harbors particular issues and shared qualities that can pull everyone together when they aren't driving us all apart. Family acts as a vessel of fate, as a necessary drama and inherited plot that begins all over again each time a child is born.

My Lot in Life

I was born a year after my sister and after my father had been drafted into the Second World War. His departure left my mother and my aunt with two infants in a one-bedroom, fourth-floor, walk-up flat. My younger sister was also born during the war and my mother and aunt had to manage on food stamps and rations while caring for three young children. My brothers arrived much later, so for a time I was the only boy in a flat full of women and girls.

I was born between my two sisters who in many ways seemed reflected images of my mother and her sister. Being the second child born also meant that I fell into a particular shadow of disaffection. As my aunt told the tale, my impending birth triggered an array of fears and anxieties in my mother. It was winter and wartime; times were hard and throughout the pregnancy she feared that she would miscarry. More than that however, she dreaded that she would die while giving birth to me as her own mother had failed to survive giving birth for a second time. My mother carried her deep fears of death and disaster as certainly as she carried each child God chose to give to her. She particularly feared for the child trying to enter the world amidst the storms of winter and the winds of war.

Later, she would tell whoever might listen how I was her most difficult pregnancy and the cause of great uncertainty and trouble from conception to birth. She would describe her long night of laboring through a winter storm with icy winds and driven snow and an entire city shaken with bolts of lightning. She feared that night would never end and that the pains of labor would never stop. Finally, at dawn or sometime after it depending on the version she was telling, I was born and she could rest. She would tell the tale with me in the room, all the while acting as if I were not there at all. I was left with a shadowy feeling of being unwanted, but also a strange sense of power as a child heralded by lightning and delivered by storm.

According to my aunt, my mother would hesitate to respond when I cried and sometimes not respond at all. Of course, that caused me to cry all the louder and may have pushed her further away. Apparently, I continued to be a fearful reminder of her early life loss, leaving me with little choice but to feel somehow at fault and somewhat rejected for a mysterious error. Later on, my Catholic education would serve to deepen that sense of guilt with the notion that I was also somehow responsible for an "original sin."

Reflecting upon the history and stories of my family makes clear why my aunt took a caring and kind interest in me and how she would later become an agent of fate and destiny on my birthday. The truth was that I had rarely received what I asked for on birthdays and holidays. As a child I often asked for too much, being as yet unaware how poverty and the necessity of survival can make gifts a secondary consideration. The simple act of asking can bring up too many family shadows; it can stir too many ghosts and threaten to reveal the despair of broken dreams.

When there are too many mouths to feed and the next paycheck may not come, you learn not to ask for much. When the desired gift was unlikely to appear anyway, saying that I didn't know what I wanted seemed to counteract the inevitable depths of disappointment. Eventually, I learned not to ask for what I really wanted. Of course, learning not to ask for what you want can all too easily lead to not knowing what you most desire.

My aunt was naturally sympathetic and tried to fill in the gaps for me and my siblings. She knew that we lacked certain things and that I felt overlooked. Throughout our childhood she brought us special treats and caring gifts. But the gift of the mythology book introduced something of a different order. Something greater than avoiding childhood disappointment had occurred. I had received something that I truly wanted without even knowing that I wanted it. I had requested one thing, but received something better and more exactly meaningful than anything I could have asked for. The wrong-right book fell into my hands just when I was becoming old enough to imagine a life of my own.

The fact that the book of myths arrived mysteriously hinted at a separate element of fate, a previously hidden life-thread that did not originate within my family. It was as if I was secretly tied to something outside the confines of history and beyond the family fate. I could not dismiss the surprising gift as a mere accident or a fluke, for the myths themselves informed me that to scorn fate was an unwise thing to do. Remember old Oedipus? On the night of my own fateful birthday I read the tale of his birth and of the oracle that announced that the child about to be born would one day slay his father. In order to avoid that terrible fate, the fearful father ordered that his newborn son be taken to a lonely mountain and be left to die.

Yet each fate has its own twisting path and the servant given the task of exposing the child could not simply abandon it to death. The unwanted child is given to a humble family to be raised in obscurity. Later, when the boy had become a youth, a second oracle predicts that Oedipus will slay his father and also sleep with his mother. Unaware that the adoptive parents were not his natural mother and father, the worried son quickly leaves home in order to avoid fulfilling the dark fate. Of course, in running away from what appeared to be his fate he has a fatal run-in with his actual father. Soon after that he falls in bed with his birth mother and the oracle has been proven.

Like oracles, myths are open to many interpretations; but it is noteworthy that Sigmund Freud founded modern psychology on this myth of inescapable fate. Oedipus fulfills the oracle blindly, slaying his father unknowingly and sleeping with his mother unwittingly. In thinking that he will escape the issues of fate, he runs right into them. Not understanding his true origins and being aware of the story he was born into, he succumbs to the darkest aspects of his fate. Afterwards, he becomes literally blind and only then begins to see the story he was in all along. As people used to say, we live our lives forward, but only understand them backwards.

We are each blind to our fate in some way and like Oedipus only encounter the mysteries of our fate once we set out on the road of life. Trying to run from the fate woven within us only leads us back to it; for we cannot run from our fate any more than we can completely escape from our family. Fate involves aspects of life that aren't freely chosen and plot lines that were well underway before we each came crying and needy upon the scene. We are each styled from within and woven into a story already underway in this world. Each occasion of fate reveals something that was in us all along and something that might distinguish us from others. In the crucible of life we can choose to learn about the fated elements and hidden qualities within us or else live our fate unwittingly, encounter it blindly, and act it out unconsciously.

Myths often include oracles and prophecies as if trying to remind us all that each soul is oracular, both imbued with inner speech and seeded with an inner story that intends to be discovered and become uncovered. Fate is a kind of inner oracle that cannot be completely denied; it can intensify and even harden the longer it is denied or avoided. Fate involves the inevitable and indelible threads of family heritage as well as the unique and oracular inner voice of our own lives. Only in facing the specific limitations of our fate can the blindness within us be penetrated and the intended story and potential destiny become revealed.

The Sisters of Fate

The book of mythology caused me to see the world in a new way. I read the tales voraciously and could see them vividly in my mind's eye. It was as if I entered the stories as they entered me. I wandered amidst them often forgetting all else. The felt sense of an array of gods and goddesses secretly populating the earth as well as the heavens stirred a feverish imagination in me. Rather than the church's depiction of a single god in a distant heaven I could imagine the divine anywhere. There might be one god above it all, but the sense of immortals nearby and semi-divine figures like tree sprites and river nymphs made the world more immediate, more mysterious, and more meaningful.

Through the lens of stories and the eye of myth, I found a surprising world of meaning and true imagination. For me, the mythic stories offered more truth than anything else I had heard or read. It wasn't that my youthful troubles went away or that I knew exactly what to do with the rest of my life; far from it. It would be years before I could grasp what so suddenly had grasped me. Yet for the first time I felt not just meaningfully connected to the world but somehow centered in my self. I did not understand it, could not have described it, and did not express to anyone what I felt. But the encounters with myth marked me indelibly and remain a sign post that stands out brightly whenever I look back over the path my life has taken.

The realm of myth seemed both brighter and darker than the world around me and more full of insights and understanding. In the procession of surprising figures depicted in the text there were several sets of divine sisters. The first to appear were the Graiae, three gray-cast sisters who had but one eye among them. In order to see anything they had to pass the single eye from one to the other. As one began to see, the other two went blind. Somehow that made sense to me. It seemed to reflect the amount of blindness in so many situations and the way that most people tried to insist that the world be seen a certain way.

The shaded sisters were said to dwell on the "farther bank of the ocean." There was no explanation of what the farther bank might be, but on the way there you might encounter another set of sisters called the Sirens. They lived on a rocky island in the open sea experiencing some great longing that made them sing endlessly. The Sirens had beautiful and enchanting voices; but the Sirens' song most often lured people to their death upon the rocks of their lonely island. The Sirens were only known by their song; no visual descriptions of them were given. They couldn't be described in any detail because no one who had seen them had returned to tell the tale.

As I imagined this wild geography of the unseeing and the unseen, the three Sisters of Fate were introduced as "very important but assigned to no abode whether in heaven or on earth." Their importance did not involve where they resided unless you considered that they lived unseen within people. The Fates were within us, and each sister held a part or portion of a person's life. Each contributed to the allotment of good and bad things that each soul receives at birth. According to this mythic view, each soul born is in the hands of fate before ever being held in human arms. Our fate in life includes inherited aspects of our family, but it also involves unique qualities that were present before we were born into the world of time and place.

The Sisters of Fate were named and briefly described as if the great skein of mythic tales could not ensue without their presence. Clotho was "the spinner" who first pulls into existence the invisible thread that secretly runs through each person's life. Lachesis was called the "disposer of lots;" she gave each person positive and negative characteristics and assigned each a potential destiny. Atropos was "she who cannot be turned." She came last and carried the "abhorred shears" that cut one's life-thread when the end of life had been reached.

The Fates appeared as formidable and essential to the beginning as well as the end of each life. They held the threads of continuance and continuity and were not to be discounted or scorned. The Fates represented the feminine side of the mystery of life; they were a "mysterious power, stronger even than the gods." To resist or refuse one's fate could bring forth Nemesis, a fierce, dark spirit who could cancel all good fortune and bring in its place dire retribution. The fateful sisters wove each soul's inner story with limitations that must be encountered but also set within each soul capacities that could transcend those limits.

I felt compelled by this trio of sisters, so nearby as to hold parts of one's life, so strong that even the gods must bow to their presence. For me they represented an alternative mystery to the doctrines of the church and they provided a sense of hidden potentials that could also be a destiny beyond one's inherited conditions.

Hell on Earth

From a young age I had been frequently warned that I could wind up burning in hell for my sins. Now, I learned that in Greek mythology hell was called Hades, a mysterious territory that was always nearby. It was not simply a terrifying region you might be sentenced to at the end of your life, but a place that you might fall into at any moment. I knew that kind of sudden slip or eerie fall into a dark place of confusion or inner pain. I felt it in moods I suddenly fell into, in vague feelings of not wanting to go out of the house, but not knowing exactly why. Living in a big city I had seen familiar streets suddenly turn into hell. A person could be attacked and beaten just for being in the wrong place at the wrong time. I saw troubled people living on the streets as if trapped in a personal hell, physically present, yet also out of reach. It seemed that the pitfalls in life could easily become a living hell and that Hades could open wide and swallow a person whole.

One day I saw a person running through the streets, completely on fire. I was on my way to school when the man, engulfed in flames, burst screaming out into the street. He came burning and howling through the doors of a little car-repair garage next to the store at the end of our block. He must have lit a cigarette while standing too close to a gas can and it exploded. By the time people caught him and knocked him down, he was charred beyond recognition. I never saw him again, but I thought of him whenever I passed the garage doors. I could see the men working in there covered in grease and oil and smoking away. I thought of Hades, how close it could be, how its fires could suddenly engulf a life.

A few blocks away there was a junk yard with rusted old cars and piles of metal and deep shadows that didn't seem to move. It was guarded by a fierce dog kept on a heavy chain that only allowed him to prowl the perimeter of the place. It was clear that the dog was intentionally underfed and only barely held back by the links of the chain. You could not go near the place without it going wild with barking and snarling and spitting. My friends would stand just at the point where the chain held the dog back and taunt it as it drooled and lunged and snapped at them. I thought of Cerberus, the three-headed hound of Hades that could trap and hold a person in the shades and shadows of the underworld, and kept my distance.

I had begun to see that there was a darker side to everything and that the Fates and Sirens could represent the shadows and uncanny elements that might erupt into the daily world at any moment. When one dark night it turned out that the dog had slipped its chain, I was way ahead of everyone else when the race to outrun the hound of hell began.

For me, there was an increasing overlap between the common world of facts and the uncommon realms of myth that could give meaning and gravity to each event and each encounter in life. I became fascinated by the god Janus who stood at the beginning of each year and at the start of every enterprise. I was born in January and it was a birthday in that dark month that brought the book of fate to me. Statues of Janus had two faces with one being youthful and the other old. That's how I felt when sitting with the myths. I felt young like a child whose eyes were opening wider than ever before; yet also older somehow and more able to see behind the scenes and into the shadings and shadows of life.

The temple of Janus had two doors. One faced East where each day began, while the other looked to the West where each day ended. Janus looked both ways and held beginnings and endings together. He was entreated as the "god of good beginnings" and I began to understand how New Year's Eve had to be celebrated even if people had forgotten the mythic origins of the feast. Life continually renews itself from a light hidden within the darkest time of the year. In the same way, destiny could be a light hidden within each person, often found in the darkest moments of life.

When I later learned that the candles on birthday cakes derived from an ancient Roman practice of honoring the light inside each person, I thought back to the book that fell into my hands and lit a flame inside me. Birthday celebrations began as a way of recognizing the spirit that comes to life with each soul born. Originally, a single candle represented the invisible fire at the core of each life no matter what the age of the celebrant might be. The single flame symbolized the shining genius within each soul that would light a path through this uncertain world. Birthday gifts were not given to the person, but to the spirit born within them.

In this old sense, birthday celebrations and gifts served as reminders that each person is already gifted; each having an inner genius and god-given gifts intended to be brought to life and be given to the world. One's birthday served as a reminder of the inner flame of one's life. The point was not simply to make a wish, but also to consider what the candle of each life burns for. If the candle was blown out it was in order that the rising smoke could carry prayers for the spirit of the celebrant to the heavens above.

On that momentous thirteenth birthday, I felt that I had received a gift secretly intended for something that already existed within me. I could almost feel that this was not just another birthday, but was also another birth. It wasn't simply that I received the right birthday gift, but also that a kind of gift already existing within me became more present and palpable, even if it was only apparent to me. The stories seemed to speak directly to me as I stood at the edge of life where childhood retreats and the blessed turmoil of youth arrives with stirring dreams, sudden drives, and burning questions.

Unexpectedly, I had found a way out of the purely local story and a pathway into the greater drama and ongoing mystery of the world. I was repeatedly struck with wonder and transported beyond anything I had seen or heard before. I may as well have taken off on a flying horse myself, for I was carried back before time as it said in the book, back where "imagination was vividly alive and not checked by reason." The ancient stories arose from someplace before the march of history began and for me they opened the doors of mystery and meaning.

For a time, I felt that the world was an open book trying to reveal itself to me, to anyone, to everyone. What I experienced wasn't an escape *from* reality; more of a case of finding what reality was to be for me. I felt fully connected to life for the first time in my life. I felt able to see in a new way and invited to learn what was behind the confusing foreground of life. For me, this was "it," a way of seeing and thinking that made immediate, intuitive sense of the chaos and confusion and vacancies of the world around me.

The gift within the gift involved the opening of an inner eye that changed how I looked at life. That was the point, the opening up of an entire way of seeing and being present in the world. I didn't have to qualify to receive it because it was already tuned to something trying to awaken in me. I didn't have to wait until I was older or pass a test; somehow I was already qualified. In the midst of the tales of gods and goddesses, in the heroic adventures of love and danger, I was no longer too young or too small or too poor to be fully involved in life. I didn't even have to believe in the tales. Believing wasn't the point, for I could imagine it all. That was the point; a radical awakening of an imagination for life that somehow was waiting to be discovered within. Our fate involves moments of awakening to gifts and aims set within us trying to become known.

By the hand of fate, I had become a disciple of myth and, strangely, a devotee of the notion that the soul is threaded from the beginning with a plotline that aims at a destiny that might be possible to find before the end. I felt truly pulled into the story of life and sensed that I had a meaningful role to play in it. I felt in touch with something essential and artful, although I would struggle for years to properly possess and learn to express what had been given to me.

Like so many young people I experienced no outer confirmation or even recognition of what had been ignited within me. When I tried to offer a mythic image or tell part of a story, people did not get it. Yet something inside me took a deeper root and began to grow, however slowly. There was an inward branching that continued whenever I returned to the reflection and musing that the stories caused in me. I felt more rooted in the world and able to aspire to a life beyond the life I had been given. I imagined that there were adventures that I could undertake and that could take me to places of meaning and beauty.

My life may have gone differently if someone had confirmed what I was experiencing. Yet again, I have always tended to go my own way and rarely have taken direction from others. If someone had suggested I look into mythology, I surely would have resisted. Having the mythic world suddenly and accidentally appear in my hands seemed to be a right thing; it seemed similar to the surprises and sudden appearances that were essential to the mythic tales themselves. Looking back upon it, I can see that the die had been cast and the future path indicated even though decades would pass before I found a way to tell stories and live with them more consciously.

Meanwhile the book of myths seemed to flip a switch that gave me a genuine interior life. Whatever might be happening in the outside world, I could enter the stories and a light would go on. Not only did they "speak to me," they seemed to offer spontaneous guidance and alternative ways to view all aspects of my life. Secretly, yet potently, I felt related to, even descended from mythic heroes. In the "wine-dark seas" of imagination I followed the adventures of wily Ulysses who escaped so many dangers, and courageous Theseus who survived the dark labyrinth. I followed into the underworld where Orpheus searched for his beloved Eurydice and saw the strange fate of Psyche whose beauty caused great envy and left her exiled in darkness. Like Theseus following a thread through the maze, I had to find my own way through each tale and learn to find my own way of being in the world.

The notion that the soul was shaped from within and possibly aimed from the beginning cracked something open in me. I didn't know it then, but know it better now, that all of us receive at least one revelation of the core pattern woven within our life. The human soul is shaped in such a way that it carries in seed form something meaningful and valuable that cannot remain completely hidden. Our shared human birthright includes at least one intuition of the innate gifts and natural orientation of our soul. The revelation may be brief and may make no sense to other people. The inner pattern may conflict with the expectations of one's family and may be disturbing to the one having to carry it. Yet the pattern would be known and, if possible in any way, would have us follow where it leads.

Urth's Well

Myths are full of sudden changes and after a long survey of Greek tales, the book's backdrop shifted from the orderly pantheon of ancient Greece to a wild creation story from northern Europe. The section on Norse mythology began with a vivid cosmology in which the world was divided between a realm of fire and another of ice. After the extremes of fire and ice became separated from each other, the middle ground of the earth appeared and along with it came the first humans. In this creation story the original ancestors were not shaped from mud and bone but were created directly from trees with the first man coming from an ash tree and the first woman from an elm.

The entire cosmos also formed around a wondrous, eternal tree that supported the entire universe and everything in it. This world tree connected the three realms of life: the underworld, the middle earth and the heavens above. It served as a mystical axis that kept things in place and it also provided nourishment for the gods, humans, and animals alike. This mythical, mystical tree also represented the threefold phases of existence that make up the ongoing creation of the world. Like the trees in a great forest, this world continually transits from birth to death and on to a renewal that begins things over again.

At the roots of the cosmic tree there was a well of white water, called Urth's Well, although we might call it Earth's Well. Three ancient sisters dwelt at the well, which was set at the center of the earth, and protected the living waters within it. Each day they poured the life-renewing waters from the depths of the well onto the roots of the great Tree of Life. The Sisters of Fate appeared at the end of the book of myths just as they had at the beginning. Now, they were described as being at the center of everything and at the roots of the cosmos. Here, they were called Urda, Verdandi, and Skuld; names that were said to mean past, present, and future. When taken together they were called the Norns and seen as personifications of the flow of time that arises from the ancient well of eternity and continually pours into the world.

The ancient sisters also gave the soul of each person about to be born its individual shape and style. They carved each soul from the living roots of the cosmic tree that was also called the Stem of Stories. Each soul was uniquely shaped and secretly rooted in stories that connected it to the Tree of Life. Each soul shared a common origin, yet each life grew around a unique shape and inner share of fate and destiny.

The story set within the soul of each person derives from the stem of all stories so that each carries a part of the eternal drama that continually regenerates from the inexhaustible springs of the holy water of life. Each individual is connected to the human family that enacts the great drama of creation over and over again. For life is an eternal story, a mythic drama that begins again each time a soul enters the world. In that sense, all souls were related to each other by virtue of being rooted in the same ever-branching, universal "family tree."

Our fate involves us in the great mysteries of being and sets us on the stage of life with a meaningful part to play, a role in life that can only be learned by living it out. For fate is more a story line than a completed script, more a pattern woven into the soul than a fixation of the mind, more a drama seeking to unfold from the center of our lives. Fate involves the core pattern and living story woven and set within us from before birth and seeking to unfold from itself.

What the ancients called fate is there at the beginning and there at the end and it appears in the midst of the defining events in each person's life as well. Fate holds us in life as much as it ties us to death. Fate which seems to speak deterministically of the end of life also refers to the essential moments of renewal each life must find if it would continue. Fate involves the accidents that are not accidental, the mistakes that turn out to be fortunate, and the curious twists that turn our lives around or upside down or back to where we started from.

Without a "sense of fate" we lose touch with the great dramas of life. We live outside the compelling myths and soulful literatures where fateful twists and fatal flaws bring the human heart and soul to the very center of life's incredible story. Without a felt sense of how we are fated to be, we can't find or draw upon the inner threads of our individual destinies.

Another name given for the world tree was the Tree Book of Fate; it was a tree, but also a living book. The Sisters of Fate represented the entire flow of time and the constant renewal of the universe. They had a hand in the beginning of each life and were present in the midst of each life change. And they were also at the root of existence where they protected the living flow and handled the renewing waters of life.

The book of myths concluded with some wise proverbs from the ancient Norse poems known as the "eddas." The last saying stuck with me as it seemed to tie together what the mind might know and what the heart might love. It stated that "the mind only knows what lies near the heart." It seemed to me that the threads of fate and destiny might be part of what lies closest to the heart and might provide the very heartstrings of one's life as well as the inner weaving that holds together our deepest thoughts and our greatest loves. What lies hidden within us and waits to be revealed in the heart of one's heart might be the inner text and living language, the life-thread of a story already woven within us; only waiting to be stirred and awakened in order to be followed all the way to the end of our lives.

CHAPTER 2

KNOW THYSELF

We must yield to the present, but we can choose our past.
Eavan Boland

"Coming of age" involves coming upon what is ageless in a person. Not just the predictable hormone changes and awkward experiments of youth, but the unique twists and turns through which the individual soul encounters the universal themes of life and death. In coming of age, we are all supposed to come in touch with that which is universal about life as well as that which is deeply human in ourselves. We are here to find our own way of being in the world and the onset of youth begins a great experiment.

People are fascinated with youth partially because youth become exposed to the eternal and open to the great drama of life. The touch of something eternal breaking through the ordinary makes youth both beautiful and vulnerable, both inspiring and dangerous, both purposeful at times, but also completely lost. More than a specific age period, the gift of youth involves an internal, eternal condition. What tries to awaken and become recognized during youth is the seed of the story sewn in the linings of the soul before birth.

When childhood comes to an end, life becomes more open-ended and a further identity is required as the inner seed tries to break through the earth of its origins in order to rise and stand on its own. The uniqueness within the individual soul is the essence of the seed waiting to be cracked open by the pressure of growth and the inevitable pains of life. The specific struggles and surprises of youth are the twists of fate through which the seeded story seeks to unfold and reveal itself. Such an awakening inside requires an outside drama that can match the intensity and innate style of the individual soul.

While many believe that young people take great risks because they feel immortal, youth is also the time when we first encounter our own sense of mortality. The advent of youth includes necessary encounters with fate that can serve to awaken the inner character and intended identity of each person. Often such fateful events have the feeling of life or death, as if the revelation of who we are at the level of our soul is itself a "matter of life and death." The defining events of our lives involve some sense of the mysterious and the weird touch of fate. As we begin to hunt for our fate in life, we are also being pursued by it.

During the same year that I received the book of myths, I began a practice of taking long walks through the city. Like many young people, then and now, I felt uninvited by and even alienated from the culture I was trying to grow up within. Somewhat disappointed with high school and increasingly feeling trapped at home, I felt on the edge of life, ready to step or fall into an unknown adventure. Instinctively, I searched for something as yet unseen; even in wandering aimlessly I felt closer to the place where real life might begin. Inspired by the old stories, I felt that any moment the young hero Jason might assemble the crew of the Argonauts again and begin the search for the missing Golden Fleece. Many of the old myths revolved around something golden and essential that was missing, some wondrous thing that needed to be found again in order for life to have nobility and meaning and purpose.

Meanwhile, the streets themselves were becoming more dangerous. At that time there were gangs sprouting up in poor and working-class neighborhoods all over the city. Amidst the increasing density of population and the lack of social cohesion, a gang would form every few blocks. Most were just local youth trying to feel that they belonged somewhere and had some "turf" to call their own. I saw a kind of parallel to the story of Jason and the Argonauts in the sense that he formed a crew and undertook a dangerous adventure in order to reclaim his rightful realm. Strangely, in the street language of the times, newly formed local gangs were called "crews."

The local crews were loosely organized with new sets always being formed. I decided to join a crew that hung out on a nearby corner and began to emulate the behavior of the older guys. I didn't fully resonate with the random, sometimes brutal gang fighting but I was intrigued with the bravado and rebelliousness of being a "hood." I wanted to belong somewhere, to be part of a crew and be "cool" like the older guys. I liked the edgy drama of the streets and at times I saw glimmers of genuine bravery and even hints of a little nobility. In some vague way I imagined that the recklessness and proximity to danger might somehow turn into a genuine quest.

I had barely become a member of the corner crew when we managed to get cornered ourselves. A group of us had gone to see a movie playing in a nearby neighborhood. It was just getting dark when we left the theater and headed back to our corner. We were walking along, talking about the movie, when we found ourselves surrounded by a gang of older guys. They had seen us inside the theater and wanted to send a message that the place was on their turf and no one from our neighborhood was welcome there.

There were more of them and they were bigger than us. Some of them brandished weapons and looked ready to use them. There was no visible way out, nowhere to turn. I was figuring out how best to protect myself and preparing to take a beating, when one of the older guys from our corner walked up. He stepped right into the middle of the circle where we were surrounded and stood with us. He was not very big either, but he was known as a fierce fighter and he had a certain way of walking and talking.

Without any preamble, he began to threaten them. It was not clear to me if he intended to fight them all or was warning them of retaliation if they attacked us. It all happened quickly. Despite all the odds being in their favor, they hesitated for a moment and he pushed right through them. Some energy rising in him just backed them down. You couldn't exactly see it, but you could distinctly feel it. He became bigger somehow and they couldn't seem to find any strength in the face of his fierce presence. It was as if his spirit overwhelmed them and the fight was settled on another level.

Just as suddenly as he appeared, he pivoted on his heel and said: "Let's go!" We turned and followed him, too scared and too mesmerized to do anything else. As we headed back to the safety of our neighborhood, our protector said: "Keep walking straight; don't look back and we might live through this." That was when I realized that he felt the same fear that we were feeling. The difference was that he knew something; he felt something else as well and he trusted that other feeling. It was not just bravado; he wasn't simply bluffing. He would have fought with us; surprisingly he would have fought *for* us. Yet something unseen had come over him. And whatever had altered him had changed the entire situation and saved us from certain harm.

The truth was that I did not even like that guy. None of the younger guys did. He never spoke to us; barely even acknowledged us. Yet he suddenly risked serious injury for us and seemed heroic in doing it. For a moment, he seemed like one of the Argonauts willing to risk himself for the crew and for something beyond us all that remained unnamed. He never said a word about what happened, didn't explain any of it; didn't even tell us why he happened to be at that theater. The only thing different after the incident was that when we saw him down at the corner, he would nod to us as if we all understood something that would not be spoken of.

Maybe it was something that could not be spoken of; maybe we no longer had the language for it. It seemed to me that often there were revelations at hand, but the language needed for describing them had become lost or was just out of reach. In the absence of that clarifying or defining something, everyone just pretended that the local turf and the local conflicts were the real issue at hand.

For me, the quest for the Golden Fleece also seemed real and was in many ways more compelling. Jason, the young hero, was a kind of orphan. He would have been the heir to a small kingdom, but a usurper had taken the throne just before he was born. As claimant to the throne, he represented a mortal threat to the new ruler. In order to protect his life, Jason's mother gathered all the women around him at his birth. She had them raise the cry of grief so that everyone would believe that the child had been stillborn. Jason was born of nobility and was the true heir to the realm;

but he grew up as an orphan and a refugee in his own land.

Meanwhile, the Golden Fleece had been stolen from the kingdom and taken to a distant, dangerous place. The mythical fleece represented both the spirit of the ancestral land and the unity of the people in the realm. Without this defining symbol and centering image, the local people felt diminished and disoriented. When he became a youth, Jason learned of the missing fleece and he heard the true story of his noble origins. Despite the threat of death, he went to the royal court to reclaim the heritage of his family. Surprisingly, the false king seemed willing to relinquish the throne to the young hero. There was only one condition.

In mythical stories there is always one fateful condition; typically, it involves great danger and at least a brush with death. All the aspiring youth had to do was find the Golden Fleece and return it to its rightful place; then he could claim the throne and become the new ruler. Of course, the king knew full well the great dangers that would be encountered on such an expedition and he never expected Jason to survive the adventure. Being full of youth and in need of a meaningful quest, Jason agreed to the deal, no questions asked. In fact, he seemed to prefer the quest itself to the power of the throne.

Word went out that a crew was needed for a great quest and soon enough all kinds of characters appeared. Hercules with his incredible strength came right away, but also Orpheus with his divine gift for music. Castor and Pollux, the twin brothers of the renowned beauty Helen came, as well as another pair of brothers said to be descendants of the North Wind. Having gathered the crew and christened their ship the "Argo," Jason and the Argonauts set sail. They set their course for a distant land where the fleece was said to hang on a certain oak tree in an ancient grove that was guarded by an unblinking dragon.

Of course, I identified with Jason and felt myself to be another outcast looking for a chance to correct the past and open the future wide. I liked the idea that the orphan was secretly noble and the true heir to an ancient realm. If you met him casually, you wouldn't know the real story; yet the truth of it was there, hidden just under the skin of life. I liked the sense that there was a missing inheritance and unifying symbol that could be sought for and might be reclaimed. I loved the idea that there was something golden that everyone longed for and that needed to be returned to its rightful place. And there was some subtle connection to the local gang and the sense of a crew of weirdly gifted, recklessly inclined and unpredictable characters.

Becoming a Storyteller

While I felt compelled by mythic tales, most people I knew found their stories at the movie theater. The closest theater to our neighborhood was just a few blocks from our corner, right under the elevated train. During quiet scenes in a movie you could hear and feel the trains rumble by on their determined routes to the center of the city. The location of the theater happened to be right between our corner and the turf of a gang from the next neighborhood. They had a reputation for violence; but mostly left us alone because we were younger and seemed puny to them. We kept our distance and only repeated stories we heard about how vicious they were.

An exception occurred when one of my friends had a run-in with them. He had a hot temper and would go off on anyone. He lived right on the borderline between the two neighborhoods and for some reason he had cursed and raged at them. When they came after him he escaped; but they were not finished with the incident, as I found out when they came after me to get at him.

A crew of us went to the theater for a Saturday matinee; that's when they usually showed the new movies that were aimed at teenagers. The place was packed with boys and girls with only a few harassed ushers trying to keep things in order. During the movie I had to go to the bathroom and began walking up the aisle while the film flickered against the dark innards of the theater. I noticed that two guys stepped right in front of me when I stood up. I did not realize that I was surrounded until I reached the popcorn stand at the back of the theater. By then, there were seven of them around me, all older and taller than me.

They motioned me over to the stairs that went up to the landing that held the projection room and the men's bathroom. I was scared, but didn't see a way out and any call for help would only be drowned out by the sound of the film. We all went up the stairs together. Once inside the door of the bathroom, I was thrown to the ground near the urinals. Looking up, I recognized some members of the crew from the next neighborhood. They had knives and wrenches in their hands as they glared down at me. They ranted about how my friend had insulted them and how I was going to pay for it.

I felt terrified that I might die right there, next to the dripping urinal while the latest teen film reeled on in the theater. Suddenly, I began to tell them a story. I didn't decide to do it, more like something clicked inside me and a voice began to speak both despite and because of my fear. Words welled up and flowed out as if to stop time and dull the edges of the blades before my face. Fully formed sentences poured out of me, paragraphs developed with a rhythm that didn't stop and a determined voice that barely paused for breath. I didn't know where the voice came from but knew that I had to trust that it would keep coming. It was as if something in me was thinking quickly and even responding to reactions in the faces of the surprised listeners. The gang bent on violence had become an audience held by silence. They kept listening as long as I kept telling the story as if we all had fallen under a spell.

What poured out of me was not an episode from Jason and the Argonauts or the tale of Seven Against Thebes. Classical stories would not have worked under the circumstances, being too foreign and complicated to alter the flow of events. Instead, I simply told the story of my friend and why he was so out of control. I rapidly described how his father drank every night and regularly beat the hell out of him. In addition, his older brother beat on him too. Maybe there was something else wrong with him or all the blows and beatings had made him kind of crazy.

You couldn't completely blame him, I argued. He wasn't really responsible for what he said or did. If he was sane at all he would never threaten them. He didn't understand who he was fighting with; he was just fighting with everyone.

It was as if something in me had silently been considering the story of my friend's life and trying to make sense of his reckless behavior. There was some primitive diagnosis involved and an attempt to make sense of the seemingly senseless behavior. Meanwhile, the shape and style of describing it was clearly storytelling. I added details that appeared out of thin air and embellished the tale without hesitation. Something keen and newly awakened in me could tell what affected them most and how to elaborate upon it. I saw their eyes soften as the tension in the air diminished and the weapons began to point down and drop to their sides.

Suddenly, the leader of the gang spoke. He looked at me with an odd sense of appreciation, the way you might look at someone giving you some interesting news. His eyes were steady and he spoke deliberately as if he wanted us to be clear with each other. He said that it made sense to call the kid crazy, otherwise why would he risk his life like that? Then, to my surprise, he said: "Alright, we're gonna let you go; but you tell your friend that if he even looks at us the wrong way, we're gonna cut him up. You got it?" Oh yeah, I got it and I got out of there as fast as I could. I hurried back to my seat and told my friends that we had to slip through the aisles and out the side doors… right now. Now! I was afraid the gang would change their mind and be waiting for us outside when the movie let out.

We snuck out of the theater and ran back to our corner. Excitedly, I told the story of what had just happened, how they threatened me with knives and wrenches, but let me go. Everyone became agitated, exclaiming how they couldn't do that to us. We were a crew too and we had older guys that would help us. That theater didn't belong to them. It was time to teach them a lesson. Once the word got out, everyone connected to the neighborhood would get involved.

I tried to explain that the issue wasn't a threat to our neighborhood, nothing had really happened, no harm had come to me. Besides, there was a bigger point. I was not recounting the story to provoke another gang fight. I was trying to wrap my mind around how it could be that telling a story was more powerful than wielding a weapon. To me, the point was that there *was* no fight, there was no damage when there should have been. To me, the story of what didn't happen mattered most.

No one listened to the rest of my tale; they had heard enough to be motivated for a battle. An invisible boundary had been crossed, the threat was in the air and the atmosphere was turning red. Most turf wars begin that way and many bigger wars as well. Meanwhile, I was in a different place. Part of me was still in the movie theater trying to understand what had happened, especially what had happened inside me. Where had the sudden speech come from; how did I know what to say and how to say it? Why would those guys listen to me and forget to do their damage and exact their revenge?

Telling the story about my friend's family clearly struck a chord of recognition within them. The tale of his wounds and burning rage mirrored stories that echoed through most of our houses in one form or another. The angry gang members were also being beaten and mistreated. Hearing the shared anguish as a narrative seemed to shift their blind rage to a kind of self-reflection. There was a deeper story behind the accepted tale of our lives. While a movie made for restless teens was projected in the theater behind us, we had slipped inside the actual drama of our lives. For a moment we were viewing our mutual pains and shared desperation. We were all caught in an old story that involved the loss of nobility and the absence of unifying, clarifying symbols.

In considering the fate of my friend we seemed to shift our own fates for a moment. Given the situation in that theater I should have been injured severely and they should have had more blood on their hands. And that should have led to reprisals and the payback should have provoked more revenge and things should have played out the way they do in neighborhoods everywhere and on battlefields all over. But something else happened that seemed to loosen fate, and at least for me, provoke some hint of destiny as well. In one sense, it was just another event in the neighborhood; yet seen another way it set the course for a much greater adventure.

In the oldest version of the search for the Golden Fleece, the Argonauts sailed on a ship that had the gift of prophecy crafted into it. When they became threatened with great danger or simply uncertain which way to go, something in the ship itself would know the right course to take. The hull of the ship contained a precious timber drawn from a sacred grove of oak trees that grew in the ancient sanctuary of Dodona. Something in the vessel of the deep self also knows which way the wind blows for us and which course in life our souls are naturally inclined to follow. Moments of awakening and occasions of oracular self-knowledge are part of youth; the only condition is that such inner gifts tend to appear when the pain of living can no longer be denied and often when life and death seem to hang in the balance.

Gifts of the Soul

I became a storyteller all of a sudden; the fact of it erupted from within me. When my thirteen-year-old ego recognized that it couldn't handle the danger I was in, it retreated and left the battlefield. In its place, something life-preserving and purposeful came forward. Something hidden inside me awakened and it knew exactly what to do. Not necessarily what someone else might do; not even what Jason or the Argonauts might do. Under great duress something deep within me knew exactly what *I* should do. In order to survive what felt like a life and death situation, I had to become more myself. Anything else would have had a false ring to it and might have made things more dangerous and damning. In the face of death something already seeded in my life responded fully and intelligently, somewhat defiantly, but also artfully.

Something had come over me and soon came over those who listened to me. It was not the same element that came over the older guy who stepped up to help us at the other theater. This was a different quality arising from a more central moment in the drama of my life. The back of the movie theater became a sudden stage on which a strange debut was required. Having no alternative and being at the last resort, an innate capacity in me suddenly took center stage. There was no conscious preparation, no introduction, and no time to consider the nature of it. The part of me that told the story did not want any rehearsal time and did not need it. The gifts of the soul, the natural talents and native abilities come to us fully made, just waiting for a meaningful time to appear.

The word *talent* has two root meanings; one has to do with natural aptitudes and abilities; the other concerns the weighing out of gold or silver. The core meaning of talent goes back to a sense of carrying or bearing something that has weight as well as inherent value. The shine of a talent is a reflection of the hidden gold of the individual soul. Although many now imagine that talents should be traded for as much money as possible, the older sense was that our innate talents are part of the inner gold that each person must find and learn to carry throughout life. When a talent is used improperly or taken for granted it can become a great weight on the soul regardless of outer success. If one's natural gifts are denied or refused, the inner gold can turn to lead.

There is always a significant story that goes with the revelation of the gifts we bring to life. Our innate gifts are set within a story trying to live its way out of us. The troubles and desperations of youth typically become the drama through which the inner gifts and hidden gold of the soul first surface and become known. Reflecting upon the strange stories of one's youth can help reveal the inner purpose and greater meaning of one's life as well as the deeper nature of one's god-given gifts.

Our inborn talents and natural gifts are woven within the greater threads of fate and destiny that are also set within us. The way that the gifts and natural abilities appear will include a story that foreshadows, prefigures and partially reveals the nature and style of one's soul. For me there was a threat of physical harm and a palpable feeling of life and death. Not every story has such dramatic elements, yet in many ways the question of each person's inner gifts and inherent gold is a matter of life and death to that person. However subtle or dramatic the story might be, we must revisit it, re-view it and inhabit it more fully in order for the shape and meaning to become known even to us. What is at stake at each critical turning point in life is the true nature of the story trying to come into life in the world through each of us.

The point of having natural talents and gifts is not to measure the size of them or compare them with those who have similar qualities. Everyone is gifted in some way and the point is to learn to give one's gifts and in doing so, learn the true nature of one's life. The inner gifts are divine seeds that can erupt at any time; they are intended to bring beauty and meaning to life. The talents and gifts set within us can be as a flame that burns a clear way through the confusions of life; but a bright talent can also burn with such incandescent heat that the one who bears it can be incinerated by it. The inner gifts are god-given, but the person who bears them must develop the character to live with them and learn how to deliver them.

The events at the back of the theater shape an inner drama that I continue to learn from; for the key stories of our lives remain present within us. Meaningful moments become life-defining, but also can continue to be life-revealing. Decades later, I began to work with young people in trouble. Needless to say, but I had an affinity for those caught up in gangs and violence. More importantly, I had a deep trust that all in trouble could suddenly find themselves closer to their inner gifts and strangely near the natural purpose of their lives. I found that I could help people find threads of meaning no matter how tragic or confused their life story might seem.

Each of us has our Golden Fleece moments when our innate nobility and natural gifts try to rise to the surface, when the shape and direction of our inner story tries to become known. For me, the moment of threat and danger in the theater brought the Golden Fleece near. When the inner gold suddenly became available it had to be given away in order to be valuable. For the true nature of the inner gifts only appears when they are given fully and given freely. It doesn't mean that people can't be compensated for their natural gifts; it does mean that they endanger themselves and others if that becomes the only reason for giving what has been freely given to them.

The Tablet of the Soul

The old myths seem to insist that each soul comes to life bearing gifts; that a person grows bigger and becomes deeper when the natural gifts are given in some meaningful way. Call it a universal myth, an open secret, an eternal truth; the human soul comes to life gifted and seeded and aimed. Call it a governing principle, a defining image, an inner code; the sense of each soul bearing a seed-story and carrying it to life appears in cultures throughout the world. After basic survival and continuance of the species, the search for the golden seed of the self can be seen as the primary purpose for each individual as well as the true responsibility of each culture.

Set within the seed of the soul is not just a fleeting image or a vague pattern but a lifelong story enfolded within, waiting to be cracked open and lived all the way out. Rather than the question of which kind of career to choose or the dilemma of what kind of person to become, the true issue is how to give birth to the life-seed that the soul already carries within.

Unfortunately, the modern world view favors an "accidental universe" inhabited by random people who must "make something" of themselves because they are born empty to begin with. To be modern means to live in an un-reconciled, uncertain world where the notion of random lives replaces the sense of having an inborn purpose. You may inherit certain genes and biological traits, but your soul is empty and your life has no inherent meaning. If there be any consideration of the soul at all it tends to take the form of a "blank slate" on which society writes its collective story. "Tabula rasa" is the old Latin term for the soul scraped clean at birth and ready to be filled and formed by family values, local rules, and cultural expectations.

According to this modern view, each newborn enters the world as a "blank tablet" unmarked by innate characteristics and lacking in any inborn knowledge. The soul is clean, if a little vacant, and any sense of character or meaning in one's life must be gained from experiences in the outer world. This sets up the common belief that our environment determines who we are and shapes what we might become. There is a seeming freedom in this blank slate or empty shell approach; yet there is also a great loss of meaning and a lack of soulful purpose in life. There is no sense of an innate purpose or intuition of an intended personality. Modern people may believe that they can "be all they want to be," yet may never know if they became who they were intended to be.

Under the rule of tabula rasa, all of us must "make something of ourselves" or run the risk of simply "being a nobody." On one hand, you might become just about anybody, for there is no limit or defining inner nature to discover. On the other hand, you might amount to nothing at all. On one hand, it's all up to you; on the other hand, your environment may have already damaged you and ruined any chance you had of being special or important. Either way, in this seemingly realistic world view, outside forces determine who you are and how you are valued and if you are rewarded.

If the soul is empty both of inherent character and specific purpose, then the knowledge and the resources needed to "become somebody" and "make something of your life" must be found outside oneself. In order to feel *fulfilled,* the original blank slate must be filled in; it must become in-formed by ideas, meanings, and purposes gathered from other people and from outer institutions. Lacking any genuine inner form, a person must learn to "conform" to whatever beliefs and systems happen to prevail. You must adapt to the circumstances that surround you and adopt an inner character that closely reflects societal "norms" and approved purposes.

Thus, personal success in life comes to depend upon an exaggerated adaptation to goals set by others that can be measured in terms of collective values. If the rules are followed or people are simply lucky, the outer goals are achieved, and they may retire from the struggle to "make something of themselves." Only in retirement might they recall some unlived longing or way of being that allows them to find some measure of individual fulfillment before they die. The sense of having inner meaning, genuine longings, and inherent aims becomes somewhat acknowledged, but only as an afterthought to a lifetime of adaptation to the collective "rat race."

Notions of genuine inner purpose and hints of a specific destiny were there all along, but were repressed in favor of adapting to a "normal life." Unfortunately, after lifelong adaptation to outer rules and collective goals the original shape and seeding in the soul may be hard to find and even harder to live up to. Searching outside oneself for what can only be found within can lead to a life lived in the wrong direction and sacrifices made for the wrong reasons. People can wind up alienated from themselves even if they achieve lofty goals set by others.

It's like the old story of the man who climbed a tall ladder that leaned against a high wall. He pulled himself up step by step and eventually reached the very top. When he finally stopped climbing and was able to see from above, he realized that the ladder was leaning against the wrong wall. He had learned to climb, but did not know what climbing was for. He had reached the top only to find that something essential and life-defining had been left far behind.

How a culture treats and answers the basic questions of human identity determines how it will be remembered. When young people are not encouraged and given a chance to awaken to the story seeded in their souls, something greater than careers and potentials becomes wasted. Something golden and noble becomes lost and more people begin to wander in confusion, seeking in the outside world what has been lost within themselves. As the inner character essential to human dignity and nobility becomes increasingly lost, one person seems to be exchangeable with another. Soon most believe that getting to the top of any heap will make life meaningful. Blind greed and rampant egotism begin to substitute for genuine vocations and for being called to find meaningful paths in life.

Clearly, myths of fate and destiny go the other way around. If people live out their inner aims and follow the living story seeded in the soul, they have a chance to arrive at a genuine destination in life. The individual soul has its own leanings and inner inclinations that would have us become deeply grounded in the terms of our own lives. When we follow how we are aimed from within, there is a growing down as well as a climbing up. A person becomes more fully incarnated and more truly rooted in life, able to handle power and contribute meaningfully to the life of others. The ladder of genuine success must be found where it begins in the inner grounding provided by one's innate way of being and instinctive way of becoming. All the ladders start in the depths of the human heart.

If the soul is secretly seeded before we are born there can be an instinctive orientation and inherent sense of direction and purpose in one's life. If the tablet of one's being already contains a core pattern and vital shape, then answers to life's burning questions can be sought and found within as well as encountered in the outer world. Answers to the age-old questions: "Who am I?" and "For what purpose was I born?" and "What should I do with my life?" can be found inside the questions themselves, inside the one asking, and inside the story already being lived.

Which One Am I?

The deeper questions of identity and life purpose may be exacerbated by the growth of mass cultures and the exaggerations of materialism, but they are not new problems. The fear that we may be hollow and empty inside has been with humanity all along. It is our human fate to question the very essence of life and struggle to learn how we might become meaningful and purposeful. There has always been a tension between the inner life and the outer world and a struggle between the unique individual and the collective way of being.

There's an old story of a simple country fellow who had to go to the big market town for the first time. All his life he had managed to remain in the little village where everyone knew him, where he knew most everyone, where he had little reason to question himself or his familiar world. Now, something else was demanded of him and he had to step into the wider world and face the unknown. He had heard travelers tell of the hordes of people and the rush of activities in the market city. He feared that in going there he would become lost in the confusion and lose himself amidst the crowd of unknown people.

So he went to seek advice from a friend who was more experienced than himself. He blurted out his fears along with his questions. "When I go to the big city I will have to stay in one of those inns where all the workers and travelers stay in the same room. I will have to sleep in a room full of strangers. I have never done that before and I am afraid that I will become lost and confused. I will know myself when I lie down to sleep; but amongst all those people, how will I know which one I am when I wake up?"

His friend saw a chance to play a trick on him, as people often do when someone indulges in their innocence too long or in their foolishness too much. The friend advised him to first go to the market and buy a large and colorful watermelon. He instructed him that before going to sleep he must tie the watermelon to his ankle. After that he should take his rest and not worry. The friend went on to explain that in the morning when he woke in a room full of strangers, he would be the one with the watermelon tied to his foot.

The foolish fellow thought for a while, then asked: "What if during the dark of night someone unties the watermelon from my foot and ties it onto theirs? How will I know which one I truly am if the watermelon has been switched?" At that point, his friend was wise enough to become silent and say no more on the subject of individual identity.

It is a simple story of a simple-minded fellow, yet in the modern world more and more people seem to depend on a watermelon, or a degree, on a certain home address or prestigious title for proof that they are in fact an individual and someone of worth and value. The massing of people into age groups and social categories, the insistence upon measurable goals, and the modern obsession with appearances make the dilemma of the country fellow an increasingly common experience. Ironically, more and more people fear becoming victims of "identity theft;" as if one's identity is some kind of external attachment. The watermelon approach seems to take precedence over the sense of a genuine identity that is seeded in the soul and waiting to grow from within.

If our identity can be determined by other people and shaped by forces outside ourselves, then our sense of self will be like a colorful item that we purchase in the marketplace of life and simply tie onto our bodies. If our identity in this world can become nothing but an appendage, we can easily be manipulated and are in increasing danger of becoming empty inside. In forgetting how the soul is seeded to begin with we can be in danger of becoming wildly disoriented and completely lost in this world. Without a genuine feeling for an inner life we become increasingly hollow and subject to exaggerated fears. Lacking a true identity, we become subject to those who cleverly manipulate the marketplace as well as the political process.

Being more interested in nurturing adaptable citizens and lifelong consumers, modern cultures have a vested interest in people believing that they are but blank slates waiting for society to write upon them and empty shells needing to be filled with one product or another. Most advertising is based upon the notion that people do not know who they are inside and secretly doubt that they are anything at all. Most ideologies depend on the "watermelon theory" where people attach themselves to abstract ideas in order to feel that they belong somewhere and mean something. In a world where "everything has its price" and all is for sale the human soul can seem empty of value and individual human life worth less and less.

Life is rarely neutral and genuine humanity is a value that must be sought and struggled for. When people fail to face their fate in life and find the identity seeded within, they tend to invent a virtual life or adapt to outer values unsuited to their soul. When a majority of people seek to cheat the hand that fate has dealt them, mere cleverness and raw power become the dominant cultural values. The loss of inner values and individual meaning becomes a depression within the soul and a collective blindness within the culture. The underlying problem is that in refusing fate, we lose our destiny and we fail to find coherence in ourselves and in the world.

A Modern Tragedy

A great tragedy occurs in the modern world where mass cultures overwhelm the importance of the individual soul and the notion of a life lived in accord with it. The growing tendency to treat people as statistical segments and voting blocks, as interest groups and age categories serves to diminish the psychic fact that each is also a unique individual. In the blind rush to the future some things of primary importance and common to most traditional cultures have been left behind. No notion of collective freedom and no amount of good intentions can substitute for the felt sense that one's life has inner meaning, that one's soul is uniquely shaped, and that the inner spirit of one's life is aimed at something beyond mere adaptation and survival.

Besides the job of instructing and socializing its youth, a genuine culture has a responsibility to assist all young people to find and develop the unique qualities already existing within themselves. When childhood comes to an end, life becomes more open-ended and a further identity is required as the inner seed of the soul tries to break through the earth of its origins in order to rise and stand on its own. The advent of youth includes necessary encounters with fate that can serve to awaken the inner character and intended identity of each person.

Despite growing pressures to blend with the collective will and submit to the leveling required by mass cultures, genuine culture and community can only develop through the essential character and natural potentials of its individual members. A society that fails to water the life-seeds of its members may be capable of instructing its citizens, but will be incapable of truly educating its children or wholly embracing its youth.

When it comes to issues of the human soul there is no normal condition; rather, each soul carries its own norms and seeks to manifest its own inherent style. In the long run, the freedom that all seek and need most is the freedom to become who they already are at their core. For life is supposed to be a revelatory drama and it is the uniqueness of the individual soul that can never be predicted, that cannot be completely repressed or be fully accounted for. A community best serves itself when it truly serves the awakening of the unique story trying to come to life through each person born.

What makes us each unique and therefore genuinely human is more vital than any dogma or doctrine and more creative than any system of belief. For the ideas seeded in our souls from the beginning confound all the ideologies and trump all the abstract systems. It is the spark of spirit within the individual soul that makes religion possible and that makes culture meaningful. It is the uniqueness imbedded in the soul that makes each life valuable, that makes love a possibility, and that makes each moment susceptible to an awakening and vulnerable to the eternal.

The true individual is not the increasingly isolated self, fostered by modern mass societies, but a more awakened self in the lifelong process of learning to express its original nature. Genuine character cannot be gathered from outside sources, but can only be grown from within and ripened from the seeds of self sown before we were born. Only such inner growth can provide a true orientation to life. Turning our attention to the life seeded within and nourishing it leads to the development of a true identity that cannot be simply lost or become misplaced. Such a soulful presence and genuine sense of self has inner value and cannot be purchased at any price.

Most of the cynicism, violence, apathy, and depression that young people suffer can be attributed to not being recognized and welcomed as the unique individuals they already are inside. Much of the trouble that youth get into secretly seeks to reveal the inner character and natural genius within them. Too often, those dealing with the problems of youth try to apply general rules and abstract systems of morality to situations that are unique. It is the inner character of each young person that is trying to awaken; that can be the source of the person's greatest problems, but can become the natural cure as well.

Young people are bound to encounter their fate in order to learn who they already are inside. Fate appears as the trouble we cannot avoid and as the shell of the inner seed of life that must be cracked open in order to reveal the destiny hidden within it. A certain amount of trouble is needed to provide the heat for the inner seeds to generate and sprout. Young people quickly acquire the habit of getting in trouble, as if the soul knows something about the drama needed in order to uncover and discover the inner story.

The issue here on earth is not to avoid trouble, for trouble eventually comes to everyone's door. The issue in this life is to get into the "right trouble" and learn from it who we already are inside, how we are seeded and aimed and what gifts we have to give. What may be an overwhelming threat or unbearable pressure for one person will be just the right turmoil and exacting challenge for another. What may be an overwhelming threat or unbearable pressure for one person will be just the right turmoil and exacting challenge for another.

Coming of age means coming to know something of one's true self and awakening to the way we are each already seeded and aimed at life. What happens during youth marks each of us in some way that remains indelibly tattooed on the walls of our soul. The life and death circumstances that attend the dramas of youth remain in the soul and wait to be re-viewed and opened again. The seeds of our innermost stories surface repeatedly and especially when a life change is required or when life itself is threatened or challenged in fateful ways.

In reflecting back on the fateful events in the theater of my youth, I realize that I had gotten myself into the "right trouble." The book of mythic stories that fell into my lap at the onset of youth became the basis for becoming a storyteller. In the sudden grip of fate, when both life and death were at hand, I had to tell a story, I had to become what was seeded within me. In doing that I began the process of coming to know myself.

"Know thyself" was the advice carved in stone above the threshold of the famous oracle at Delphi in ancient Greece. Know thyself before trying to simply fit in somewhere. Know thyself by noticing what tries to surface in the midst of pain or trouble. Know thyself from the inside out, for what is deep inside is trying to become known and be delivered to the world. Know thyself, and the tangled limits of fate turn into the golden threads of destiny. Know the oracular speech and natural ways of expression of the inner self that holds the seed of the exact story trying to unfold from within.

During youth a blossoming and budding forth of the deeper self tries to happen as young people encounter what is seeded in them and gifted in their soul. The inner garden of the soul sends forth shoots of imagination intended to take root in the world and become an anchor for the soul throughout life. The beauty of youth exists in those blossoming moments when the inner gifts become revealed and the young person becomes able to bring more life to life.

After a sudden blossoming, however, the land may become silent; the seeds of the soul may become obscured by outer responsibilities and the expectations of others. Then the hidden beauty and seeded story must wait for another season to return to awareness and awaken further. For what is native and indigenous to one's soul will keep trying to manifest itself throughout one's life. Yet as in any compelling drama, specific limitations and lapses are needed to shape the plot and give it tension and intrigue. The dynamic tension for each living script grows from the limits of fate and the longings for destiny that first awaken in youth. What becomes revealed at the end of a life fully lived is the story that was trying to surface all along.

CHAPTER 3

LIFE SENTENCES

Liberation happens each time we become
conscious of the contents of the soul.

The long journey home from war that forms the books of *The Odyssey* has often been seen as a defining metaphor for the Western World. Odysseus, or Ulysses as he later became known, spent ten troubled years trying to find a way home after being victorious in the Trojan War. Often enough those who lose a war are left to bury the dead, while those who win find themselves far from home in some way. A poet once said that every war has two losers; for war is kind to no one and brutal to most. Those who know war best also know that the effects of battle continue to burn within the soul after the fires have been put out and long after the bodies have been buried.

Ulysses was considered to be both clever and wise. He was called "double-minded" or "many-minded," meaning one who could see more than one side of a given issue; one who had "second sight" and deeper insights than most. Being double-minded also meant being "wily;" both able to see the tricky ways of others and capable of devising tricks himself. It was Ulysses who invented the famous strategy of the Trojan Horse that hid danger inside a shining gift and led to the downfall of Troy and the success of the Greek forces.

Not all of Ulysses' tricks worked as well as the Trojan Horse. When first summoned, Ulysses tried to avoid going and declined the invitation to "the great war." He tried to trick his way out of the war before he ever agreed to go to it. He must have seen beforehand something of the great troubles that the battles and their aftermath would cause.

Eventually, Greek officers were sent to his island kingdom to invite him personally and learn why he had not responded to the original request. When Ulysses saw the war lords coming, he began to act so strangely that it appeared as if he had lost his mind. The officers found him in his fields plowing away behind a team of oxen. Looking closer they could see that he was sowing salt instead of planting seeds in the earth. Being on a mission, the officers determined to test the apparent insanity of the young ruler of Ithaca. One of them found the infant son of Ulysses and placed him in the furrows right before the oxen and the oncoming plow. When the father quickly drew the oxen back and stopped plowing in order to avoid crushing his son, they knew that he was sane enough to go to war.

Clever as he was, Ulysses could not manage to escape what would come to be known as one of the greatest odysseys of the world. You could say that it was the fate of Ulysses to serve in a battle that he did not choose and to survive a war that claimed the lives of most of the heroes of his time. It was also his fate to suffer great dangers and come near death many times while trying to return from that war. He could not find a trick to get out of the war and after going to it, he could not find an easy or direct way to return home from it.

Perhaps the real Trojan Horse is war itself which can appear so noble and shining and even glorious, but which also can eat away at a person's soul and gnaw at an entire culture from the inside for many years after the battles are over. The case made for undertaking wars and the grand causes that seem to justify them tend to fade in importance over time, while the traumatic effects of a war linger and malinger inside those who survive it and inside their offspring as well. To this day it remains easier to undertake a war than to recover from it. To this day soldiers and warriors can survive a war only to succumb to the battle that ensues when trying to find a way back home.

I thought of old Ulysses when I received my own summons to war. Like many others at the time, I was drafted into the army during the ill-fated war in Vietnam. I received the draft notice when I was twenty years old and at first declined the invitation. Having followed news reports, I had concluded that the war made little sense. In fact, it was not a declared war, more of a "military action." I sent a letter to the draft board arguing that the reasons for fighting were not clear, nor were the goals properly defined. I declined the invitation, but offered to consider future requests. In short order, I received a summons to appear before the local draft board for a hearing.

After listening to my arguments the members of the board insisted that I was either an objector on religious grounds or a draft resister who could be sent to prison. They sent me to a minister who explained the rules for applying as a "conscientious objector." I found myself unable to sign the document that could lead to a deferral. Receiving objector status required that I claim to never have been involved in violence and swear that my appeal was based in my religious training and practice. Since neither was the case for me, it seemed too devious and overly clever to make those claims. My objection was deeply personal and looking back upon it, was wildly subjective.

My objection came from my own judgment and individual conscience. So, I drew up my own document of "conscious objection" only to find that summarily rejected. Soon I received a letter ordering me to appear for induction into military service or else be subject to arrest and a prison sentence. I found myself in the greatest dilemma of my young life. My objections were clear, yet they were subjective and personal, not religious and doctrinal. I objected to the war that was not actually a war; yet I felt both cultural and familial pressure to conform to the collective expectations and appear for duty.

The antiwar movement was just getting started and I had no immediate connection to it. Almost everyone in my family and in my neighborhood stood in favor of the war. To my surprise and regret, they were uniformly in favor of me joining it. My father and many uncles had answered the call during previous wars and my mother seemed to say that our sons always answered when they were called. Yet I did not feel called to it at all. I was waiting for a different call, waiting for a more specific "calling." For some, military life and battle can become a true calling. I knew that wasn't the case for me; yet I didn't see an honorable way out of it.

For weeks I wandered the streets of the city turning the issue over and over in my mind. The pressure to accept what seemed to be the demand of the culture, of my immediate community, and my family was clear and quite palpable. Yet something in me, an instinct or intuition, a foreboding or oracle pulled me in the opposite direction. It wasn't simply that I would not fight, but that I needed to know more truly what the fight was for. It wasn't simply that I was afraid to die, I certainly was; but I was equally afraid to die for the wrong reasons.

The truth was that I did not see any Golden Fleece in the adventure; for me true nobility was not involved. At the same time, I did not want to go to prison and could find no clever way out of the dilemma. So, partially out of fear of being considered a coward, partially out of fear of going to prison, and partially out of family and fate, I went into the army. I decided to show up for my induction appointment and let the chips fall where they might. It was clearly not the appointment with a greater life that I had harbored since my thirteenth birthday; it was far from that. Yet, in the strange and twisted way of fate and destiny, it did lead to unexpected experiences and a further awakening of the deeper self within me.

Selective Service

Suffice it to say that I was not a good soldier, although that did not become evident until some months in the army had passed. Initially, I liked the activities and exercise in basic training and enjoyed meeting guys from different backgrounds and ethnicities. I found some good companions and hoped for the best. However, there was a basic problem that I had not anticipated: I did not take orders well. I had always been headstrong and willful and inclined to go my own way. Now people were ordering me all over the place. At a certain point, I just could not go along with it; I just wouldn't do it, and couldn't be made to do it.

I began to be selective about which orders I would comply with. If an order made sense, I would likely accept it. However, if I was given an order that seemed foolish, mean-spirited or clearly ignorant, I would simply refuse to follow it. Such personal discretion did not sit well with my superiors. I found myself facing a new dilemma. Despite threats of severe punishment, I could not simply follow orders; despite increasing pressures, I would not back down.

Inside, I realized that I had made a crucial mistake and it would be better for me to leave military service. Of course, my military superiors took a contrary view to that and simply gave me more orders and greater punishments. When endless stretches of KP duty and constant threats didn't change my mind, I received the first of many company courts-martial actions.

Several officers became curious about my actions and even interviewed me about my reasons for refusing orders. I tried to explain the dilemma of wanting to be responsible to others, but needing to be true to myself. In a kind of reverse psychology strategy, they offered me an immediate placement in officer's training school. I explained that I could hardly give orders to others that I was reluctant to follow myself. But they seemed to think that I would change my mind once I had a chance to command rather than follow orders. Being young and idealistic, I was outraged by this kind of reasoning and by the notion that it would be better for me to give orders that might cause others to die than to follow such commands myself.

Arguments with various officers about justifying the war and reasons to "do my duty" seemed to boil things down to two things. One was the redlined idea that the enemy was the embodiment of evil. If the Communists were not stopped over there, they would soon overrun the world and destroy all the freedom in it. I argued with many officers about this reasoning, including several colonels and one general, and felt that none could make clear the connection between the general fear of evil and the seeming civil war in Vietnam.

The other reason intended to convince me to risk my life and moreover my soul came down to the necessity of doing exactly what you are ordered to do. When I challenged the legitimacy of following all commands and the sanity of simply killing on demand, I was informed that I had signed a paper accepting induction into the army. At that point, I had given up certain rights and had agreed to follow orders no matter what they entailed. To me that seemed to argue that in order to save freedom from the evils of Communism, I had to give up my own freedom to choose. Either way, freedom was being lost.

Before showing up for the draft I felt terribly confused and conflicted within myself. Now I could feel the battle lines being clearly drawn between my inner sense of self and the outer claim of duty. Although my situation in the military was becoming more difficult and conflicted, I was becoming clear within myself. I realized that I did owe some kind of service to life, but what I owed involved being true to my self, not abandoning what I felt to be true.

Eventually a special court-martial was planned where I would appear before a panel of officers. A military lawyer was assigned to defend me. He was barely older than me and a recent college graduate like myself. I found him intelligent and likeable. He explained the rules for a military trial and took notes on my reasons for disobeying orders. He also arranged for me to use the little library on the base to prepare my own defense. I enjoyed the sense that a line was now being drawn in a court of justice and took advantage of the opportunity to research the reasons for the war and to clarify my own thoughts and feelings.

I took the preparations seriously and wrote a kind of personal treatise. However, the court-martial proceedings never addressed any of the issues that caused me to question the war and defy military authority. In fact, the night before the court convened, the lieutenant assigned to my defense informed me that everything had already been decided. He revealed that he had just come from the officers' club where my case had been discussed. Over drinks, the verdict had been decided as well as the sentence that would follow it. With so many draftees questioning the war, they wanted to make an example of my disobedience. He seemed a little stunned himself when he told me that the next morning I would be found guilty and sentenced to a term in military prison.

I made my defense anyway and read my entire treatise. The officers asked a few questions, but seemed to be grading the quality of the paper rather than considering any substance or meaning it might have. As had been predicted, I received a sentence of six months in the stockade. That was the longest sentence such a court could decree at the time. The officers assured me that they would have given me a longer sentence had it been in their power.

Unremitting Circumstances

From the moment of being convicted I began a long descent. It wasn't simply that I felt betrayed by a system that claimed to be based upon honor. It was not only the diminished feeling of being placed behind bars. A line had been crossed inside myself and there would be no turning back. I had chosen to enter the army rather than go to prison; yet I wound up in prison anyway. The choices had narrowed down until something like fate took over and I could not escape it. Of course, I was singled out for special attention by the guards in the prison and subject to an endless series of orders and threats. When I continued to refuse orders, I wound up in solitary confinement and stayed there for many months. I felt alone in a way I had never felt before.

As the situation deteriorated and greater punishments loomed, I suddenly decided to fast. My idea was to demonstrate that I was not present in any normal sense. To further make the point, I threw out my uniform and bedding and began to live naked, unnourished, and solitary in my cell. If I did not eat or wear a uniform I could not be considered to be participating in any way.

In the little cell of concrete and metal I had little contact with anyone except the prison guards. They would bring trays of food several times a day and leave them in the cell in order to tempt me to eat. The only other visitors were officers who would suddenly appear at my cell door and give me orders. It was as if my disobedience threatened the very structure of their lives and everything they believed in. Each officer seemed to think he had the magic power or unique authority that would cause me to obey. When I refused they would often sit down and talk as if they also had a great need to converse with someone outside the chain of command.

It was strange behavior to be sure, but not completely out of context or out of character as I learned later when I read about Irish political prisoners fasting. When faced with overwhelming British power Irish prisoners fasted and even died rather than forsake their vision of freedom and justice. As it turns out, there is something ancestral in Irish blood that can not only boil hot with a temper, but that also can respond to injustice by fasting against it. From ancient times the Irish would fast rather than submit to what seemed injustice at the hands of a superior power.

Fate tends to place people in unremitting circumstances and will force hidden aspects of character and surprising qualities to the surface. There I was, barely over twenty, isolated and alone, caught up in a cause that gripped me and would not let me go, and hard fasting against those in charge. The fellow in the cell next to me went another way entirely. Whereas I refused to ingest anything, he swallowed strange objects including some nuts and bolts under the theory that eating hardware would prove him too disturbed to remain in the military. Although his scheme had some of the cleverness of Ulysses in it, it didn't get him out of trouble. After he wailed with pain for days, the guards did take him to the hospital for x-rays. But after the doctors surgically removed all the nuts and bolts, they sent him back to his platoon. Later, he was not only sent off to the battlefield, but they charged him for the surgery to boot.

Meanwhile, I held to my plan of refusing to eat until I received a discharge and could return home. Day after day, night after night, I remained alone in my cell, only leaving for a shower every other day. Once in the shower I would drink as much water as I could. I found that I could go a long time without food, but after two days without water I would be on fire. At night I would listen for the sound of trains in the distance and long for home. At times I thought I heard a boat sounding a horn. I would dream of clear water and see myself diving in and swimming away.

Eventually, doctors who specialized in the effects of starvation were brought from Washington, D.C. They solemnly informed me that my organs could fail and I could die at any time. Still, I would not eat; somehow I could not eat. Something had been triggered deep inside me, as if I had found *my* battle. Despite losing well over a third of my body weight and being warned repeatedly that my organs were failing, I would only agree to eat when I received discharge papers. In a strange way I had found an adventure that took all my energy and all my will and that almost cost my life. Once again, I found myself in life and death circumstances and also in the hands of fate.

Many things happened during those months in solitary, but certain things became indelibly emblazoned on my mind. Except for periodic checks by the guards and occasional visits from officers, I was alone with myself for long periods. I was not allowed any reading materials and my pen and papers had been confiscated. In the depths of solitude I found myself recalling myths and stories and imagining the characters in them. On one level I was simply returning to my old love of stories; but the characters seemed to be more alive and even seemed to have things to say to me.

At first, it was shocking and I feared that I was falling apart, coming unglued because of the isolation and starvation. Yet, the presence of mythic figures also felt reassuring and seemed to settle something in me. It occurred to me that I was either losing my mind or I was just finding it. Either I was going "round the bend" or I was actually coming around to my own way of seeing the world. I had been struggling to find something; clearly anything I might find now would have to come from inside me. Accepting the presence of mythic characters seemed better than simply succumbing to despair, so I began to welcome them and tried to learn what they wanted me to understand. That shift of attention brought the mythic world closer; it opened something inside me and helped to settle and focus my mind. It also seemed to provoke an even stranger series of events.

By then, everyone connected to the military knew the story of the strange kid who had been in solitary for months, had stopped eating food, and refused to wear a uniform. I was in a unique position and everyone seemed to figure that out. Although I was told that I was not allowed visitors, a veritable parade of officers appeared at the door of my cell at night. As before, they would begin by formally calling me to attention. When I failed to respond, they would sit down and begin to talk. Inevitably, they would confess something that weighed heavily on their heart or soul.

Some spoke of their fear of dying in battle and never seeing their loved ones again or never learning what their life might have been without the war. Some wanted to explain how they also questioned the war, but felt they had a duty to perform. Most wanted to unburden themselves of something deeply personal; as if they just needed a place to confess. Having been raised Catholic I understood something of the ritual of confession and I reluctantly played the role of confessor. I did not give them absolution for their sins or assign penances, but I did listen with all the attention I could muster and even offered guidance when it seemed appropriate.

In the quiet of my cell, I learned how some beat their wives out of blind frustration and felt terrible for doing it. I heard how others frequented the prostitutes always waiting outside the base only to feel anguished about betraying wives and sweethearts back home. Some wanted to tell of an old offense that involved a friend or a family member. Mostly, they did not want to die without stating how sorry they felt for some past transgression or painful omission. The captain in charge of the prison came frequently, usually with a long list of complaints and worries. Strangely, he also felt imprisoned. He feared he would wind up in prison for his whole career. I could sympathize with that and had similar concerns.

Stealing Life

I withdrew from life in order to save my sense of life. I refused to eat in order to demonstrate that I was not part of the military, not a combatant, not even a member. After weeks of fasting I became quite thin and felt increasingly fragile. It turns out that no one can predict how long a particular person can live without food; it varies greatly depending upon genetics, health history, psychological factors. The authorities became concerned that I would die suddenly and create a scandal. They decided to move me to a small cell block at the back of a hospital that had been built during the construction of the Panama Canal. Hardly anyone knew about those cells; I was told that no one had been in them for decades.

I was examined regularly by doctors who would often wake me in the middle of the night to tell me that they could not find my pulse. They would ask if I really wanted to die. I would say that I did not; that dying was not the point as much as making clear what I was living for. They had great trouble understanding me and I had trouble understanding myself. I refused the collective fate of going to war only to enter my own personal battle. I became literally caught between life and death and surprisingly found that in order to learn my own meaning I had to face death in my own way. Somewhere in those long, empty nights I made my peace with death. After that, it came as a big surprise that I had to make my peace with life as well.

Because of some technical rule I now had to be guarded by soldiers drawn from my original company. Despite my frail condition, an armed guard had to sit at the door of my cell twenty-four hours a day. They were mostly draftees and most turned out to be sympathetic to my situation if not exactly to my cause. They also felt caught in the hands of fate and seeing my desperate condition made our shared mortality all the more evident. A strange turning point developed when one of the soldiers suddenly slipped me a chocolate bar.

I was on the verge of dying from intentional starvation and now unintentionally had chocolate in my hand. I felt a new dilemma taking shape within me. On one hand the chocolate clearly represented the sweetness of life. On the other hand, eating it would violate my earnest code of not being present and not participating. Technically, it was not military food and it was being offered out of genuine concern for my well-being. Yet eating anything at that point seemed to be giving in and could be seen as a sign of giving up. I had been on a mission for months; I feared that even one bite of chocolate could change everything and compromise the clarity and purity of my position. Then again, not accepting this helping hand could represent a final turn away from life.

The little bar of chocolate was clearly a gift and some risk had been taken in offering it. So, I held the chocolate in its colorful wrapper and told myself that I would decide later whether to eat it or not. Later came sooner than I expected as I found myself thinking of the concealed sweet continually. I had little else to consider except the basic issues of life and death and the subtle exchange between one breath and the next. Being under constant guard, the only time I had any privacy was when I went to the toilet. One day, I took the chocolate bar with me.

Without further consideration and driven by what I now realize was an instinct for self-preservation, I unwrapped the chocolate and quickly ate it. I found it moderately enjoyable and decidedly strange. Having been so long without food it did not register as a sensual treat. The fact that it was semi-sweet chocolate seemed to capture the feeling of the situation. As soon as I ate the contraband chocolate I knew that something had changed within me. I knew from a deep place inside that I wanted to live and that I would even break my own rules to do so. At the door of death I received a bittersweet reprieve from the extremes of my own excesses.

In a strange way, I owe my life to a fellow soldier and a piece of chocolate. My fight against the military and the idea of blind obedience could easily have ended in my death had not a fellow soldier taken a risk for my benefit. Obedience may make a good soldier, but taking risks for another is the essential glue in the deep bond between warriors. His willingness to disobey the order not to assist me in any way somehow freed me from my own severe regimen. It wasn't that a little bar of chocolate could suddenly make me healthy or even offset the effects of starvation. Rather, it was like a trick in which a little move towards life seemed to cause life to move towards me.

Shortly after I ate the chocolate, military intelligence decided it would be counter-productive to have a young draftee die of starvation while in military prison. Experts who had treated survivors of the Nazi holocaust camps were brought in and they quickly decided to force-feed me. I soon found myself facing an archaic-looking device used to force food into the mouths of the unwilling. The medieval-looking instrument would pry my teeth apart and allow food to be forced into me with a plunger. Accepting the little bit of sweetness seemed to produce a greater, if less pleasant, flow of nourishment. Strange to say, the ice cold mixture of liquid nutrients often came with a chocolate flavor. I was nourished back to life by food that was literally forced into me; each feeding was a chilling assault of nourishment often administered with sadistic force.

Having chosen death repeatedly, I was now being forced to accept life. I was being saved from starvation against my will. Except for one thing: I had already chosen life when I accepted the bit of chocolate before food was forced upon me. If I had not already decided to eat on my own, I think I would have fought to the death against any attempt to force me to live. Accepting the chocolate gift and eating it made the force-feeding redundant and allowed me to accept it as well. Although part of me felt I had broken my own code and cheated, I also realized that I had stolen my life back from death. By accepting a gift from someone ordered to guard me, I stole my life back from my own will. On one hand I was forced back into life; on the other hand, I stole my way there. Seen yet another way, I accepted the gift of life all over again.

Years later, I took up the study of tribal initiation rites in order to understand what could motivate a young person to act the way I did while in prison. I came across the idea that initiates in tribal Africa could be required to steal food. Under the norms of the tribe you would never steal; especially never take the food of other people. Yet during initiation, all normal rules would be suspended. In order to become fully initiated into life young initiates had to violate the rules and steal what they needed for survival. In some tribes, the penalty for stealing could be death, as if to further demonstrate that each person must risk death in order to become fully committed and invested in the value of their own life.

The act of stealing was literal, but it was also symbolic. Tribal groups would often act out what for modern people would be the psychological situation or inner condition. For example, an elaborate mock battle might be staged to depict an actual conflict, but also might be used to actually avoid a war. As soon as someone drew blood the battle came to an end. The depth of the conflict had been made more evident, while the use of force became mostly symbolic. A little loss of blood attested that the issue has been brought into reality. A "little death" had occurred and life could move on.

Initiation involves seeing beyond the obvious and being able to hold contrary ideas at the same time. Stealth was the old tactic that stood in opposition to the idea of using force. Normally, it would be wrong and irresponsible to steal. Yet at certain times, for survival or growth or change a deeper meaning had to be found, a deeper ethic had to be served. To *steal* means "to take without permission, to carry away surreptitiously or artfully." In ritualizing stealing common morality is turned upside down as well as inside out. At critical times a person has to be willing to take without permission and become wily enough to circumvent the social norms and moral rules.

Life is a gift; yet each person must also steal their life, steal it from their own family, from their society, even from their own willful attitudes and certainty of beliefs. There is a greater will, a greater need and purpose hidden within each life; there is an inner law that knows best how each soul can best live in this uncertain world. Awakening to the inner value and exact longings in one's own life is a goal worth stealing for; it can be worth dying for, and must become worth living for as well.

Whether a given culture admits it or not, youth present society with a dilemma. Young people must learn the collective rules and social norms of their society; yet they must also learn how they themselves are distinct and unique and most valuable in the world. Thus, initiation rites most often occurred in nature and outside the daily life of the village. At issue is the true nature of each young person and the normal rules of behavior can only limit the potential for self revelation. In the great drama of this world a young person is an initiate trying to learn the meaning and true direction of their life.

Initiation rites offered an opportunity for a rebirth, an inner labor and essential struggle through which a second birth occurs. In this sense, to be "born again" means becoming conscious of innate qualities as well as more aware of the life-purpose trying to grow from within. This second birth makes a person more psychological, more "double minded" like Ulysses and thus more able to see levels of meaning where others see only social norms and simple rules. Common rules must be broken and penalties must be risked in order that being fully alive becomes a truly conscious act.

Rites of initiation have virtually disappeared from the modern world. Yet, the human psyche understands that the inevitable crises of youth become the dramatic conditions through which the natural way and inner law of one's soul try to surface and become known. When the natural law of the soul becomes contradicted a "fate worse than death" can occur. Eventually, we must learn to live within the life sentence we received at birth, within the plot line that both limits us with fate and challenges us to a greater life. In accepting that unique arrangement, a thread of destiny can unwind and open the way before us.

Under certain conditions it becomes necessary to violate all the rules, even violate one's own professed beliefs in order to feel the deeper pulse of one's being. After contradicting the beliefs of my family and the rules of the society, I still had to go against my own rules in order to encounter something greater than my little-self. Something within me desired to live and would not allow me to throw away the life I had been given.

Fateful Interventions

The whole adventure might still have ended badly had it not been for a mysterious twist of fate and a surprising intervention. I had assumed that I was moved to the cell at the back of the hospital in order to be closer to medical care. The guards informed me that there were other factors. Reporters for magazines like *Time* and *Life* were poking around trying to get the story of the young soldier who was starving to death. I never learned how reporters discovered what was happening to me. Since I only spoke with guards assigned from my company and the doctors who monitored me, one of them must have leaked the story.

One day an officer appeared and simply offered me discharge papers. All I had to do was sign on the bottom line and I would be on my way home. The idea of being released came as a shock; it was hard for me to believe the offer. I had been threatened many times and had been mistreated in many ways. Several times I had been offered an immediate commission as an officer if I would just sign some papers and agree to salute the flag each day. I did not trust the authorities or even the military doctors to be acting honestly or in my best interest. I knew that my health was deteriorating despite the forced feedings; yet I suspected some kind of Trojan Horse intended to cause me to give up my fast and then lose my resolve when a discharge failed to materialize.

When I refused to sign or even read the papers, an entire group of officers gathered to convince me that the discharge was legitimate. They insisted that there was precious little time; we had to act now. I thought that they feared I could die at any moment, but soon learned the real cause for their mounting concern. It turned out that a U.S. senator had sworn to come and see the situation first-hand if I were not released from prison and returned to the States. And, it was not just any senator, but Robert Kennedy himself. Someone had gotten a message to his office telling him of my struggle and my precarious condition. Apparently, he had called the commanding officer and insisted that I be released or he would come in person within forty-eight hours.

No one involved wanted Bobby Kennedy poking around in the back rooms and hidden cells of the army. The authorities did not want the situation to become public and turn into a media event. Back home the protest movement was becoming more public and questions about the legitimacy of the war were intensifying. Nearby, there were many soldiers interested in how my strange protest might turn out. Suddenly, there was a big rush to give me my discharge papers and get me out of Panama as soon as humanly possible.

I had to be persuaded that the deal was for real and we also had to find a description in the military code that satisfied my interests as well as those of the army. Eventually, I signed the discharge papers and began to eat hospital food. In short order, I found myself being escorted to a military transport plane by two young sergeants returning from the battlefields of Vietnam. They had each earned his stripes in brutal combat and were returning home at the completion of their tour. They were under orders to keep me handcuffed between them and I was to be under armed guard on the flight back to the States.

Once on the plane, they asked what caused me to be so emaciated and decidedly strange looking. I had grown a beard, had long hair, and was wearing very loose fitting civilian clothes. Everyone else on the plane was in uniform. Although I feared it would make me seem like the enemy to them, I told them how I had refused orders and been given many courts martial punishments. I briefly described how I wound up starving myself while in solitary confinement. To my surprise, they both declared that I had been in my own war. An even greater surprise came when they assured me that I had won.

Where I expected them to attack me for standing against a war that they had barely survived, they felt we had each entered our own battles and received our own wounds. Where I felt confused and still caught in a struggle to survive, they felt newly released from the hell of war and wanted me to feel that sense of freedom. It is strange to consider and contrary to most expectations, but those warriors barely out of battle took me to be a brother in arms, or at least someone who had fought for freedom in his own way.

Although their orders only required them to deliver me to the base, they stayed with me throughout my contentious discharge process. They could see how fragile my health had become and witnessed how I continued to be threatened by hard-line military types. After their official guard duties ended, they volunteered to continue as my protectors. They went wherever I went and even gave up some off-duty passes when I they feared I would be attacked by other soldiers. After my release I never saw them again. Due to the altered state I was in at the time I failed to remember their names. However, I have never forgotten their instinctive integrity, their depth of understanding, and their care and kindness towards me.

They never questioned my integrity or explained their own feelings about the war, but they exhibited for all to see the difference between a soldier and a warrior. There are deep places in the human soul where all the conflicts at the surface of life become mute. There are currents of empathy that surpass even the most intense conflicts and disagreements. There are depths of understanding that become available when people survive a brush with death and touch what is most universal and common to the human soul. I received a lesson in love and compassion from those battle-weary warriors and hope in my heart that they found a way home from the war. They gave me a way to view my own battle and renewed my faith in the human spirit.

In less than a week I was back in New York City. I was home again, but was not really home at all. I had gained my freedom yet had little understanding of what had happened. The stroke of fate that caused my release remained a mystery to me and I struggled to describe, much less understand, what had caused me to act in such an extreme way. The whole thing seemed a tangle of threads that I could not untangle and a pile of issues I could not unpack at the time. Only later did I begin to see the elements of fate and the threads of destiny that placed me in circumstances where I had to fight for my life and steal it back or else lose my sense of self.

Shortly after my military experiences the government established a lottery to decide who would have to go to the war. Of course, the idea of a *lottery* begins with the stories of the Sisters of Fate. *Lachesis* was the fateful sister whose name means "disposer by lot or dispenser of lots." The sense of a lottery to decide who was drafted seemed an unconscious way of putting everything back in the hands of fate. The time of birth became a literal moment of fate for many young men and for their families. Despite all the modern arguments for free will and the heavily gilded ideas of fighting for freedom, individual lives would be publicly placed at risk on the basis of fate.

Some received the dark fate of dying in distant lands; others survived the battles only to leave parts of themselves on the battlefield. Even those who avoided the draft or protested against it carry the war with them as part of a shared fate as well as an individual lot in life. A slender thread of destiny would seem to be the fine filament that pulls a soul in one direction or another. Certain events mark a person indelibly and continue to live inside the soul where they can become a deep source of meaning or remain a profound and suppurating wound.

Many years later, I learned a compelling detail that amplifies the mysterious ways of fate and destiny. After the tragic assassination of his brother, Bobby Kennedy fell into a place of darkness, sorrow and loss. His Catholic faith in a providential god was shaken and he was unable to find a way out of the depths of his despair. He hardly ate any food and his clothes no longer fit. He became wasted and gaunt as if being devoured by grief.

Jackie Kennedy, the widow of the fallen president, suggested that he read the ancient writings on tragedy. She gave him copies of Edith Hamilton's works on Greek myths and the tragic plays. The idea was that the ancient ideas on tragedy and the wisdom of the ancients might provide guidance during his dark night of the soul. Bobby began to study the material, apparently annotating certain parts and memorizing many passages. The ancient philosophy and tales provided him solace amidst the great devastation in his heart. He would carry the texts everywhere and wore out their covers. Biographers say that he discovered the ancient notions of fate and hubris and that he studied and quoted them frequently.

It seems that he was reading Hamilton's writings on the ancient myths and philosophies of life at the same time that I was recalling them from memory in my solitary cell. A weirdly winding thread of fate caused him to have immediate sympathy for a young man he knew nothing of except that he was wasting in prison and was likely to die of starvation unless someone intervened. It was as if the hand of fate that caused the Greek myths to fall into my hands when I was but thirteen influenced him when he called for my release from prison years later. Some might call such strange events accidental, just the result of an odd coincidence. I was already learning to see the weird workings of the hand of fate and also learning to perceive how a thread of destiny can unwind from a precise twist of fate.

The Old Thief

One thing a person can learn while in a prison is that all of us are "doing time," each having our own life sentence to deal with. We do time when we are grieving a loss or when we have lost our way. School can often feel like a prison to young people and many jobs have an incarcerating effect. Marriage, which can be such a delight, can also come to feel like a life sentence and even a spiritual path can lead to an isolated condition. An illness can entrap one's soul as well as wreck the body and the loss of a loved one can leave a person enshrouded for a long time. Anything that restricts the story trying to live out of one's soul can feel like a prison.

Most people wind up doing "hard time" at some time as they encounter their own dilemmas and become caught somewhere in the intricate web of life. Everyone gets trapped and everyone gets caught, eventually. The holy man is caught making love to the wrong person. The caring mother mistreats animals and the peaceful saint secretly slaughters thousands in his mind. No one in this life can exist without some kind of shadow and some fateful dilemma. Eventually, the question becomes whether or not we find some element of destiny inside the fateful situations that entrap and imprison us.

There's an old tale of a thief whose fate caused him to be imprisoned in a dark cell that seemed to offer no way of escape. He had been a thief for most of his life; yet he knew the tricks of the trade well enough that he had never been caught or charged with a crime. Having spent so much time sifting through the possessions of others he knew a great deal about hidden things. I'm not recommending stealing as an occupation as much as considering the secrecy and solitary skills involved in doing it and the capacity for observation required in order to do it well.

Besides, stealing goes back to the beginnings of human culture. Didn't Prometheus steal fire in order for humankind to be able to cook food? Didn't Eve take some forbidden fruit just to get things going? Wasn't Ulysses using stealth when giving the gift of the Trojan horse? Didn't Jesus hang with thieves in the end? He made a distinction between two kinds of thief. One was but a common crook who took from others to satisfy personal greed; the other was capable of a great awakening and wound up stealing his way into heaven.

Most of those who handle power also learn to take things for themselves. But counselors and therapists are also thieves in the sense that they steal into the minds and hearts of others. They sort through the memories and feelings of those who trust them seeking to find motives and reveal secrets. Academics of course can be compulsive thieves; most only make their way by taking ideas from those more original than themselves. Typically, they disguise the stolen thought as their own and use it to attack those who think another way. Some even steal the unripe thoughts of their students in order to ripen them in their own garden and trade them for recognition in the marketplace of ideas.

Artists, they say, are the greatest thieves of all; for all art involves stealing and borrowing from the unseen sources of inspiration. Great artists re-create whatever they touch and are often the first to admit that creativity and theft often appear together; while lesser artists try to disguise what they have stolen and borrowed. Call it imitation or inspiration, a willingness to steal is required for many an occupation.

The old thief was an artist in his own way, having elevated stealth to the level of art. While some thought him a common thief, others considered him something of an artist because he gave to the poor and had never been caught red-handed. At least, not until the day he was in the local marketplace and decided to steal some herbs in bright daylight. Perhaps someone was ill and needed a potion; perhaps he was simply taken by the smell of flowers or the shape of roots. Perhaps it was simply an accident, a moment of weakness or else it was a moment of fate. At any rate, the thief was spotted taking the herbs and caught in the act.

The authorities lost no time in taking him before the most severe judge in the realm. The judge promptly found him guilty and demanded a heavy fine that the old thief could never pay. The only alternative to the fine was a lengthy jail sentence and the old thief was led away without recourse. Under heavy guard he was taken to an old prison and led down to the deepest dungeons in the realm. Throughout the descent, he observed everything, carefully looking for any means of escape. However, he could find no crack in the defenses of the place. By the time he was thrown into a dark cell, he had begun to give up any hope of an escape.

Since there was no way out, the old thief turned within and spent his time in deep reflection, recalling all that he had seen and learned of life. After some time had passed, he called out to the guard and insisted that he be brought before the king of the realm. When the guard laughed and called him a lunatic, the old thief explained that he had a gift of extraordinary value that was only fit for a king to receive. The guard was impressed with the seriousness of the demand, but had no idea what to do about it. Eventually, he told the warden about the gift the old thief claimed to have. That ignoble character quickly imagined how he might be rewarded for bringing such a valuable gift to the king.

Soon enough the warden brought the old thief up from the depths of the prison to make an appearance at the royal court. The king and the queen sat on large thrones in the center while all around them sat the members of the cabinet and the elite of the realm. The king was used to receiving gifts and had come to expect valuable things to be delivered to him. He wondered aloud what treasure a lowly thief might have that could be fit for a king. Whatever it might be, he insisted that it be handed over quickly as he had important affairs of state to attend to.

The old thief announced that he came to present a rare and valuable gift. He slipped his hand into his old cloak, carefully withdrew a small box, and handed it to the king. The ruler opened the box and peered inside, then suddenly flushed with rage. He yelled at the thief and demanded an explanation for why after expecting a great gift he found himself holding nothing but an ordinary plum pit.

The thief readily agreed that it was a plum pit, but suggested that it was by no means an ordinary seed. He explained that whoever planted the seed would reap a golden reward. For once planted the pit had the wondrous ability to instantly become a sapling that would rapidly rise in the form of a tree. The tree would then branch before their eyes and blossom in no time. From those blossoms golden fruit would ripen before their very eyes. That was the remarkable nature and hidden value of the little seed that he feely offered as a gift to the king.

The king thought for a moment, then asked why, if the seed was so magical, had he not planted it himself and avoided the life of a thief? The prisoner explained that whoever planted the pit had to have a clear conscience and a soul unblemished by common theft or the misuse of power and abuse of authority. If someone who had stolen from others or misused power planted the seed it would not sprout at all, but would simply be inert. Since he was widely known to be a thief, the magical seed would not sprout for him. However, he was certain that if the king, being so noble, having a clear conscience and an honest soul, would plant the seed he would immediately receive the golden reward.

The king became quiet again. After thinking over various shady dealings and some downright cruel events, the king realized that he would be exposed before all as a thief and a scoundrel if he attempted to plant the magical seed. So, stating out loud that he had never possessed a green thumb, he passed the pit to the queen. After a brief reflection, the queen passed the thing to the secretary of state who passed it along to the secretary of defense, who gave it to the leading general, who sent it on to the treasurer, who offered it to the head of the prisons, who simply stood in a deep confused silence. Other leaders politely and promptly declined any need to handle the seed and a number of wealthy patrons simply shook their heads and turned away.

The old thief spoke again, this time saying that it was clear that all of them were guilty of treacheries and violations that they did not wish to have revealed. He searched their faces as he spoke and declared that he had been sentenced to years of isolation and dark confinement simply for stealing some herbs; while they committed grand thefts and held themselves above the laws they claimed to enforce. He pointed out that all the people knew that they misused their power and authority, yet they never went to jail or paid for their crimes.

At that point the king felt that things had gone far enough. He called all the officials together for a consultation. After discussing the situation, the king announced that all of the present company would contribute to paying the fine placed upon the thief and that he would be completely absolved and immediately released. He announced that everyone had been educated on that day, further promising that they would remember the lesson and be more just and more forgiving in the future. Then the king handed the box with the little seed back to the thief and quietly asked if it was true that the plum pit could produce golden fruit. The old thief simply slipped the seed back into his cloak as he turned and walked off, a free man again.

In surrendering to the period of descent and dwelling in the depths, the old thief had found the roots of imagination that alone can undo the locks of self-imprisonment and that can surprisingly restore the deeper foundations of fairness and justice in the world. Once he accepted the fate that had befallen him, he found himself near the source of his release. The key needed to unlock the prison he was in turned out to be hidden in the darkness within him. Once he realized the nature of his own divine seed, he had the key to unlocking many doors. In finding the inner seed and essential core of his own life, the thief became able to at least momentarily open the minds and even the hearts of those in power.

The trick employed by the old thief involved more than simple trickery or sleight of hand. It was genuine magic, in the sense that *magic* means to change one thing into another. The thief turned everything upside down as those who held themselves above the law had to bow their heads in acknowledgment of their own crimes. He managed to be released from his sentence while putting all the authorities in a prison of their own thought. Each wanted to receive the shining reward; yet they had to recognize the darkness within them that could be so readily revealed.

The story does not offer psychological information or specific details of what the old thief found when he looked deeply within. Rather, it offers a symbol of the deep self that is both a common pit that can be easily overlooked and a golden seed of great value. In the ancient alchemy of the soul what appears to be a common pit can become a magical seed when one's inner condition becomes conscious. The alchemy that changes an individual life from the inside out can also affect an entire realm or a whole culture. For history begins in the darkness and depths of the individual soul, and greed and injustice can give way to a deeper understanding that on occasion can open the doors of a unifying imagination and the need for forgiveness.

The plum pit is not an accidental image of release and renewal. Plum trees often blossom before the warm breezes of spring appear. The courageous plum represents a flowering from darkness and a surprising blossoming from a deep source of life. In Asia, plum blossoms carry the sense of eternal youth and the capacity of life to renew itself from old roots that survive winter's dark retreat. The humble plum pit can symbolize the radical root of new life ever ready to arise from unseen depths and produce a surprising flowering of beauty and truth.

Inner Authority

The old thief turns the common world upside-down, but also inside out. He brings to light a great secret about this world where most people believe that real power resides in outer wealth and collective dominance. People are continually surprised that those who rise to power tend to abuse it rather than learn how it can be used to enhance justice or produce genuine beauty. Yet outer power that is not rooted in the genuine nobility of the soul will always lead to cheating and manipulating in order to retain a false order in the world.

It is most common in this world for people to rise to the top who have not done the work of inner transformation. This causes those who become subject to the abuses of power to believe that all power is abusive and all authority must be unjust. *Authority* is a big word that troubles most people, especially in the form of "the authorities." Yet, the roots of authority go back to words like "author, augment and authentic." There can be forms of "genuine authority" that develop from authoring things and being truly creative when faced with the inevitable inequities of life.

In order to shift the typically unjust situation in the outer world, the old thief must become an authority unto himself. He must draw upon a greater source of authority than common law or elitist rules. He must be connected to an authentic authority that transcends common institutions as well as common law. Authentic authority is rooted, not in the common world, but in something deeper that is both more creative and original.

When people draw from the root of their deeper self, they become authentic and able to act with true originality; for the deep self is secretly connected to the origins of life. *Authenticity* involves acting from one's deepest essence, so that the "uniqueness" of one's soul awakens and can be "brought to life." Such an inner awakening is the deeper purpose of initiation; a self-revelation that allows a person to be truly authentic and act with first-hand knowledge and inherent creative force. When in touch with the authentic essence of the soul, a person can draw on the threads of being that can alter the darker aspects of fate.

As fate would have it that which is truly authentic and original in a person exists deep within; it remains hidden, buried like gold that must be mined in the dark depths of the earth. In order to reach the gold seeded in the soul some descent into the depths of life is required. Since such descents are always painful and forbidding, most people avoid them at any cost. Because such descents are necessary for true growth, life provides them in the form of fateful events that pull each of us deeper into life than we would choose to go on our own.

We all harbor a golden seed in the depths of our souls; that is the true gift of life. Yet, in order to find the key and unlock the hidden brilliance, we must come to know the darkness within us. We must enter the darkest places in order to find and steal our own golden inheritance. A person must become double-minded like old Ulysses and able to see more than one level of life and more than one meaning in each life-changing or life-threatening situation. That is the nature of life here on earth where gold must be mined in darkness and in the depths of one's heart and soul.

CHAPTER 4

WHAT NOT TO FORGET

Life can only be understood backwards; but it must be lived forwards.
Soren Kierkegaard

One of the great problems found throughout the modern world is a lack of meaningful leadership exactly when both culture and nature seem about to unravel. Amidst an endless flood of information and a seeming increase of practical knowledge, there is a tragic lack of the wisdom needed to make sense of a rapidly changing world. In many traditional cultures the search for wisdom would be part of the quests that youth undertake, but would also be a primary practice of the elders. Although they stand at the opposite ends of adult life, youth and elders naturally share a common interest in finding wisdom and sustaining the core imagination of a culture.

In many traditional cultures, young people would be taken aside from daily life in order to be introduced to their inner selves through rites and rituals. Initiatory rites would serve as occasions for self-revelation as well as opportunities for the youth to absorb wisdom from the elders. The true elders were those wise enough to know themselves. Having experienced the world and learned who they were at their own core, the elders were in a position to recognize the unique character and natural gifts of the young, all of whom were trying to grow and become themselves.

Often, the exchange between youth and elders included a conversation about death. After all, a kind of death was required if the young people were to end the period of childhood and begin the next stage of their lives. At the same time, the elders were approaching the last stage of life and facing a more literal form of death. The youth had to leave the ways of childhood behind in order to grow bigger lives and the elders had a need to grow deeper and wiser as the end of their lives approached. Issues of life and death as well as the authentic core of the soul are the ancient and natural themes of the age-old conversation between youth and elders.

Unfortunately, modern mass cultures tend to overlook the uniqueness at the center of each individual while also avoiding the presence and meaning of death in the midst of life. Whereas traditional cultures would introduce the presence of mortality at the onset of adult life, modern societies put off questions of death until the very end. Even then, many refuse to even admit the inevitability of death or the possibility that their death might be meaningful for others.

Something of great meaning has been lost as modern cultures seem to forget the unique nature of each person and deny the role of death in the meaning of life. It is not just that people go to great extremes to prolong life at any cost, but also that most have an extreme fear of death and a wish to deny it altogether. Death is only admitted when the bodily functions fail and there is finally no alternative left but to give up on life. Unfortunately, when death is diminished, life loses some of its natural dignity and sense of inner purpose. Many people die without dignity because something essential about life has been forgotten and death has lost its dignified place in life's mortal drama.

Having lost its natural connection to fate and its secret ties to destiny, death has become nothing but a failure of life. Yet, death is not the simple opposite and mortal enemy of life; rather it is the opposite of birth, and a full life includes more than one brush with death. All who receive the wondrous gift of life must also bear the burden of mortality. Since life includes death, an exaggerated fear of death can only lead to a growing fear of life. Those who avoid death at any cost will also fail to live life fully. In the end, the issue isn't that life fails us and death claims us, the more common tragedy involves a failure to face up to one's fate in life and live the life seeded in one's soul.

Wisdom involves knowledge of both life and death. Life and death are the two great teachers in this world where revelation can happen at any time. As an old proverb suggests: "You don't know who a person is until their last breath has gone out." In that sense, the last breath can be a revelation about life as much as a failure of it, a meaningful statement rather than a simple dead end. Each life is a specific question being asked of the world and the answer is not complete until the story comes to an end. The end of the story brings around the original question of the meaning of one's life on earth.

It's like the story of the old rabbi who lay upon his deathbed as the final hour drew near. His name was Zushya and he had lived a long and meaningful life. He was a holy man who had studied scholarly texts and been a teacher for many years. He was widely known and greatly respected; more than that, he was revered and loved by his students for his honesty and for his wit.

Now that his time had come, many of his faithful students gathered to share in his final moments. When they asked how it felt to be at the door of death, the old teacher told his students the truth of his situation. He explained that with the hour of death approaching he feared having to face God. "I am afraid," he said, "of God's final justice. I fear that I will be punished in the world to come."

The students were shocked; how could such a thing be possible? Their teacher was an exceptional religious leader who had taught them generously and guided them wisely. Now, it was the students who began to reassure the teacher: "Rabbi, you are a pure and righteous man. You have shown the leadership of Abraham, the courage of Jacob, the vision of Moses, and the moral fortitude of the greatest prophets. What do you have to fear in facing God?"

With diminishing breath Zushya replied to his students, "I am not afraid that God will ask me, 'Zushya, why were you not more like Abraham? Why were you not more like Moses?' I can answer honestly that I did not have the god-given abilities of Abraham or the talents of Moses. But, if God asks me, 'Zushya, why were you not more like Zushya?' for that I have no answer at all!" In so saying, the good rabbi passed into the world that waits beyond this one.

Death, they used to say, is a great teacher and sometimes great teachers will use their own death as a final lesson on life. The old teacher continued to teach and offer wisdom about life even at the very end. When people's lives become meaningful to them their death can have genuine meaning for others. The old teacher made his death both meaningful and memorable by stating the question that the divine asks at the end of each life. In facing the end honestly, it became clear to the old teacher what the divine was interested in all along. While you had the chance to live, did you become your true self? Having received the gift of life, did you learn the nature of your gifts and the purpose of them? Have you lived the life that was given to you or substituted some other model or abstract ideal?

The last lesson of the good rabbi made the case for the uniqueness and meaning of each life. The final exam comes down to a single question that involves the specifics of the individual life rather than the generalities of religion or the abstractions of philosophy. People go about asking: "What is the meaning of life?" In believing there is some general answer they miss the fine point. Since each life is specific and cannot help but be so, a better question would be: "What is the meaning in my life?" If each has but the one life to live, then there will be but one thing in question when the time for living comes to an end.

Although the same question fits everyone, it also distinguishes amongst them. All may meet a common fate, saint or sinner, rabbi or banker, rich or poor. Yet each can only answer with the life they have lived. Those who believe that all the answers are "out there somewhere" are in for a shock when the final question asks who they are within themselves. It turns out that the answer to the question of life was hidden inside the questioner all along.

There are important points in this final teaching regardless of one's religious training or philosophical orientation. Rather than religious dogmas or general moralities, the divine has something specific in mind when considering the meaning and value of individual lives. When it comes to the question of whether or not you have become yourself, there is no fixed morality or doctrinal authority to call upon. The qualifications for entering the afterlife do not derive from following rules and obeying commandments as much as learning the natural laws and inner ways of one's soul. We qualify for recognition in the next world by living uniquely and creatively in this one.

The Uniqueness of Life

Certainly, the saints and prophets, the great philosophers and wise teachers may be proper models for finding the paths of discovery, but in the end each life must become a revelation of itself. Simply imitating a Moses or a Jesus, an Abraham or a Mohammed does not satisfy the question that the divine has placed in each soul. Living by religious rules and precepts may open a path of learning, but in the end no outer model can lead us all the way to becoming who we are intended to be at the core of ourselves.

The point seems all the more profound as the rabbi had lived a religious life. The students may have expected a display of piety or the reassurance of a man of faith meeting his maker; but the holy man proved to be a genuine teacher right to the end. He turned the attention of the students not to some divinity outside themselves, but towards the seeds of the divine already seeded within them.

When the time comes for those created to meet the creator something specific must be considered. If each soul is unique something particular must be examined. In the end, as at the beginning, the divine turns out to be most interested in the unique life of the individual soul. That's what was meant by the old idea that "inside people is where god learns." This is not a religious notion, but more of a spiritual insight. For this conversation *god* is simply the shortest way to refer to the divine. When a unique life becomes fully lived everyone involved learns something and it becomes clear that god was involved all along.

The final judgment will not pivot upon doctrines or dogmas; for there is no theory or system that can substitute for a life unlived, for a story undeveloped, for a fate not faced, for a destiny not embraced. That is the final lesson, the last word, and the essential wisdom that the good rabbi was honest enough to communicate with his final breath.

Human life is full of questions and beset with all kinds of problems; but in the end each soul is faced with the "Zushya problem." Each must answer for the life actually lived; better then to begin the consideration of the question sooner rather than later. That was part of the wisdom found in the "wisdom traditions" and the ancient initiatory practices. Better to enter the question of one's life while still alive rather than be in fear of a final judgment. If there is a unique seed hidden in one's soul, it would be best to uncover it while there is still time to learn its wisdom and live by its guidance.

One of the open secrets of life on earth is that the answer to life's burning question has been inscribed in one's soul all along. The soul is a kind of ancient vessel that holds the exact knowledge we seek and need to find our way in life. Each life is a pilgrimage intended to arrive at the center of the pilgrim's soul. From that vantage point, the issue is not whether we managed to choose the right god or the only way to live righteously; such notions fail to recognize the inborn intimacy each soul already has with the divine.

Moses did not become Moses when he received tablets on the top of a mountain. Moses began being Moses when at birth he was placed in a basket and given to the river of life. The way in which he was abandoned introduced him to the waters that would save him from persecution. Later, he knew how to part the waters and lead others from bondage to safety. The waters held both his fate and his destiny; the knowledge he needed most was within him even as he was being abandoned. Didn't Noah become awash with dreams before he could receive divine instructions on how to fashion ships and survive floods? Each became a prophet in his own way and each is remembered for the way he listened within and followed unseen guidance.

When viewed from the end of life, great dramas and meaningful biographies reveal what was trying to rise to the surface all along. The great religions help to outline ways to serve the divine, yet what truly serves is specific in each person. Buddha had to find a way to go between the two great religions of his time because he could not go along with either of them. In following the thread of his own life he passed through the eye of the needle and a "third way" was found between extreme negation and blind acceptance. Those who are remembered and revered had to first remember the divine seed already planted in them and learn to water and nourish it until it blossomed from within.

The wise rabbi honored the old prophets best not by trying to be like them, but by becoming more like himself. Those who learn to paint like Da Vinci certainly imitate a master; yet as long as their own inner mastery remains unknown, they remain impostors creating forgeries. They may grow by following the brushstrokes of an original, yet only become themselves by grasping their own originality. Great teachers and artists can indicate genuine paths to follow, yet following them can only take us so far. We may enter paths where others have found revelations; but in order to answer the question of our own lives we must risk taking our own steps. In the end, the only genuine safety in this world comes from risking oneself completely in order to become oneself more fully.

The figures most revered in the many traditions found throughout the world became memorable because they became uniquely themselves. They may have become commonly revered, but their actual behavior was markedly uncommon and exceptional, even radical in some way. Whether a spiritual teacher or an artist, a healer or a leader, they are remembered because they managed to manifest something transcendent and express something unique within them. They had to awaken to an inner vision and find a destiny already set within them in order that the tale of their life could become instructive to others.

Rabbi Zushya may be remembered for many valuable qualities, yet the tale of revealing god's final question has carried his name throughout the world. Being a true teacher, he revealed an essential truth about life at the moment of his death. His death became a gift of life for others. It is especially a gift for those who take hold of the lesson that the divine is most interested in the self revelation of each soul. Because the question at the end of life is universal, because the divine is involved, and because the rabbi pointed to the uniqueness of each life, the tale speaks to everyone.

Those who claim a great interest in godly things often forget that the divine is most interested in the spark of the eternal already burning in the depths of each living creature. Meanwhile, a person doesn't have to believe in god or subscribe to a particular creed in order to intuit the question waiting at the end of life's road.

Some view the final encounter as a meeting with the deep self that was dwelling within us all along. Call it the inner spirit or the great soul within, what is hidden at the core has many names. Some call it the wise old woman or wise old man or the inner sage that already knows the way our lives are seeded and styled and inclined to go. Wisdom, like love, like life, depends upon the specifics of the person and the situation that person is in.

Meanwhile, the older, wiser parts of the soul try to catch up to us throughout our lives. Each critical turning point in life has a little death in it and a chance to deepen and become wiser about the path we have been given. Whether the occasion involves a little death or a great awakening, the wisest thing is to become oneself. The great moments of life and each brush with death conspire to uncover the core meaning and inner essence of the living soul.

An old idea suggests that wise people will find in the depths of themselves a pattern into which everything they know can fit and into which all that they don't know might fit. Thus, the inner pattern in one's soul provides a genuine world view, a core imagination that is somehow equal to the world. This inner image holds the "uniqueness" of one's soul and contains the exact knowledge needed for that life as well as a potential for enriching the lives of others. Thus, human wisdom begins in radical and revelatory forms of self-knowledge before it can become wise enough to be helpful to others.

Weird and Wise

In living fully and dying meaningfully, Zushya played the role of a genuine elder. His final breath and last words served to open wider the hearts and minds of his students. Teaching was his bright gift, a part of his fate and part of his destiny as well. As an aspect of fate, our inner gifts incline us in certain directions and shape us in distinct ways. As an aspect of destiny, our gifts can carry us beyond normal limits and to higher levels of awareness.

At the end, the living spirit of one's life is supposed to shine through the tatters of the body's mortal cloak. The gold of the self is supposed to become more visible despite and because the body begins to fall apart. The flame of inner knowledge can shine through the garment of life and become more available as the elder becomes a kind of "living library." As a bridge between this world and the next the elder can become a valuable resource and depository of knowledge who can provoke wisdom in others.

Elders can be wiser about life because they have spent some quality time considering death. Knowing something about death tends to deepen one's understanding of and appreciation for the gift of life. Zushya was at the end of his life, yet he was teaching at a high level. Perhaps he was fearful at the end; perhaps he was using the fears of his students to point to the importance of being fully alive before the end comes. They may have come to mourn his human fate, but he turned their attention to their own destinies.

Becoming older can only lead to being wiser when it involves growing deeper and incarnating further into the unique story being lived out. Just as the devil is in the details, wisdom is in the specifics. What is most wise on one occasion can be decidedly foolish on another. Just as there can be no general wisdom, there are no "normal" elders. Normal follows the "norms" and fits into the collective patterns that society uses to regulate people. Eventually, normal becomes the problem and can become the prison that locks down the sage trying to awaken from within and locks out the dreams trying to arrive from the other world.

The awakened soul will find creative ways to express its inner pattern and will find its own weird way of being in the world. An old idea suggests that those seeking for an elder should look for someone just weird enough to be wise. More than simply feeling or seeming odd, *weird* relates to the supernatural aspects of the world and the presence of the unseen amidst the obvious. In Norse mythology, as in Shakespeare, the Fates appear as the Weird Sisters who hold time and the timeless together. *Weird* is an old word that refers to fate and destiny and the strange way that each person is woven into life's mysterious web.

Weird refers to all the uncanny aspects of life and all that is "unearthly" here on earth. Those who would become truly wise must become weird enough to be in touch with timeless things and abnormal enough to follow the guidance of the unseen. *Weird* can also mean to "have a foot in each world." In old traditions those who acted as elders were considered to have one foot in daily life and the other foot in the otherworld. Elders acted as a bridge between the visible world and the unseen realms of spirit and soul. Those who are in touch with the otherworld stand out because something normally invisible can be glimpsed or felt through them.

Elders are supposed to become weird, not simply "weirdos," but unusual in meaningful ways. The weirdness of the elders involves roots that reach back to the origins of life and branches that stretch towards a vision of the future. This double-minded stance serves to help the living community and even helps the species survive. Elders are supposed to be more in touch with the otherworld, but not out of touch with the struggles in this world. Elders have one foot firmly in the ground of survival and another in the realm of great imagination.

A genuine elder stands at least partially outside the social order and beyond the lines of civil authority. The elders are not the keepers of law and order, for they serve a higher purpose as well as a deeper order. The authority of a true elder is of this deeper order. Elders have inner authority developed by becoming the authors of their own lives and the bearers of a living destiny. Elders learn to dwell where they are most deeply connected to the vitality of life; for the deepest places of connection here become avenues to the divine.

The elders lead by remembering farther back than others as well as by seeing more clearly ahead. Thus, they are less likely to be strictly political leaders and more likely to be cultural and spiritual guides. The elders serve as "seers" who can see behind and beyond the politics of the day and perceive the needs of the future. They become natural healers because they have seen the wounds of life. Having survived their own troubles, the elders are not shocked or overwhelmed by the mistakes and dilemmas of others. Having seen how things can fall apart, they also know the uncanny ways that life renews and comes together again.

Traditional elders often become dream interpreters and keepers of life-enhancing visions. Elders become "agents of the weird." Thereby, they are able to bring the wisdom of the eternal to both the need for survival and the necessity to sustain the great imagination that allows culture to continually renew and revitalize itself. The wisdom of the elders connects survival with creation so that sustainability depends upon true creativity. If more people become weird enough to become wise, it becomes more likely that solutions for the great dilemmas that plague both nature and culture might be envisioned.

Olders not Elders

Elders fall into the category of things that are made, not born. An infant becomes a child simply by aging, but a person cannot become an elder by simply becoming older. Old age alone cannot make the elder, for the qualities most needed involve something more than physical change. Becoming an elder is not a "natural occurrence;" there is something metaphysical involved, something philosophical and spiritual that is required.

The passing of time makes everyone older, but not necessarily wiser. People either wise up to who they are at their core of their soul or else tend to slip into narrow, egocentric patterns. Either they develop a greater vision of life as they mature or they simply lose sight of who they were intended to be and what they came to give to this world. Many actually become more childish in old age. An extended old age can easily lead to a return of infantile attitudes and exaggerations of basic neediness.

In traditional societies the old people became the guardians of the mysteries and keepers of the higher laws of life. Having grown both older and wiser, they knew best what needed to be preserved and remembered in order for human life to be noble and meaningful and in tune with nature. Those "old enough to know better" would become living depositories of wisdom for the next generation to draw upon; if not, everyone would suffer a loss of knowledge and greater disorientation in the world.

At this point in the current collective drama of the world something strange has developed as modern societies become populated with older folks who become more disoriented as time goes on. Although many people live longer, fewer seem to be the wiser for it. Due to better diets, medical advances, and technological improvements many people live to a ripe old age. Yet few seem to ripen into elders able to harvest knowledge from life experience and pass it along as genuine wisdom.

Simplistic ideas of progress and material comforts seem to diminish the true value of older people even while adding years to their lives. Instead of helping to answer essential questions about life and death, those who live longer often seem to become more disoriented about both. The end of life becomes less revelatory and less meaningful while death becomes more and more meaningless. There seems to be a loss of memory and a lack of wisdom exactly when you might expect to find older people passing on meaningful knowledge. There seems to be a great forgetting where you might hope for a deep recollection of what is most important.

It is not just that people try to appear younger than their years and seem willing to trade the possibilities of wisdom for the appearance of youth. It is not only that people exploit the present moment in ways that damage the future for others, but also that those expected to remember what life is all about increasingly forget who they are and have been. Modern societies seem to produce "olders" who forget instead of elders who remember what is most important about life and about death.

Some great confusion has fallen like a shadow across the world, a mass forgetting in which the sense of meaning waiting to be discovered right under the surface of events has been obscured in favor of a compiling of information and a recitation of facts that only become forgotten. Something has happened that makes the end of life full of forgetting instead of a place where the essentials of existence are recollected and preserved. An increasing number of people arrive at life's final hours having forgotten who they are.

Instead of elders sustaining imagination and wisdom in the world, there are hordes of "olders" who might just forget who they are and where they came from at any moment. Instead of having answers to the essential questions of life, the olders become a growing question mark themselves. It isn't simply a matter of disorientation, but a collective vacating of the later stages of life. The olders are elders "in absentia;" not just absent minded, but increasingly lost on the roads of life.

When there is no genuine growth in growing older, aging becomes all about loss. The longer people live the more of life they seem to lose. Some mutual forgetting is going on in which those who should help recall what is most important about life now tend to forget the meaning of their own lives.

People retire as if there were no later stage of life to bring their full attention to. Many wander golf courses while keeping track of their handicaps, as if willing to exchange a common handicap for a genuine purpose. Others can recount a lengthy list of their growing ailments and complicated drug treatments, while forgetting what meaning their life might entail. Some go on "permanent vacation" as if to vacate all premises before disappearing altogether. Modern culture seems to encourage older folks to remain in the cocoon of egotism with notions of simple retirement or fantasies of being forever entertained.

What is the point of living longer if it doesn't mean becoming wiser and being more able to serve something beyond one's little self? Youth may often be "wasted on the young," but now old age seems to be increasingly wasted on the elders. When those old enough to know better forget what it is all about, then older is not wiser and aging is being wasted on the aged.

A Great Forgetting, a Loss of Wisdom

"Knowledge makes a person older," they used to say and the opposite was implied, so that growing older should make a person more knowledgeable. Yet it has become more common now to associate aging with forgetting. Some forgetfulness is natural, just as eyesight begins to weaken over time. There is a difference between simply dropping some details and becoming lost altogether. Losing all sense of who and what we are involves a different order of forgetting.

The first kind of forgetting involves short-term memory loss that causes us to misplace things in the moment. We can't recall a name and more frequently misplace common things. This loss of short-term memory causes short-term losses. Things come and go; we lose things and find them again. The deeper kind of forgetting has long-term effects. People lose touch with themselves and become lost in the shuffle of common things. There are tragic results for individuals and great suffering for their families; but there is also a collective symptom involved. When those expected to remember what is most important forget almost everything, then everyone loses something. If the end of life becomes less meaningful, the rest of life becomes more meaningless.

Certainly, there are medical questions and biological mysteries involved; but there is also a mythological ailment, a sense that more and more people are falling out of the story of life even before the end is in sight. The shared story of human life seems to be fraying at the end. The increasing disorientation in modern culture makes it more difficult for individuals to find a genuine orientation in the course of their lives. Amidst notions of an "accidental universe," people come to feel that they are also accidental and lacking in genuine purpose.

The problem is not just a loss of some details of the story, but a great forgetting of the meaning and purpose of individual human lives. A collective forgetting in the later ages of life drains something from all the stages of life. When those old enough to know better fail to become wise and forget who they are, there is a collective loss of wisdom. There is an increasing lack of wisdom in public affairs and a loss of knowing elders who can recall essential things in midst of the great crises troubling both nature and culture. This great forgetting creates an absence that leaves holes in reality; it causes a loss of continuity and leaves too many stories unfinished.

The meaning of human life depends upon the originality and uniqueness of the individual soul. Only there do we find history being made and real facts in the making. The loss of memory that increasingly characterizes the end of life may begin with a failure to awaken to the purpose and meaning of individual life to begin with. Under common notions of the soul as a blank slate, more and more people may be losing touch with the genuine threads of fate and destiny that make it possible to become who they are actually meant to be. In believing that "I can be anything I want to be" people may more readily forget who they were intended to be to begin with.

Does the problem of memory loss begin with many people forgetting that they have come to life with an inner story already seeded within them? Can the increasing loss of memory be a collective symptom trying to call attention back to deeper issues and greater meaning than the simple length of people's lives? Is it possible that life itself is trying to provoke an effort to recall the deep memories and imagination that form the true inheritance of humankind?

An old idea has it that symptoms are purpose seen from the other end of life. The symptoms of forgetfulness can be seen as attempts of the psyche to call attention to the importance of remembering, especially remembering what is most important in the life of each person. The disease of forgetting that plagues modern people may be related to the lack of finding a conscious purpose early in life and failing to recognize oneself as a true individual.

The massing of mass cultures may so undervalue the uniqueness of the individual soul that people can more readily forget not just why they are here, but also who they truly are. Amidst the flood of changes, the mass confusions, and the great forgetting already underway, the awakening of the innate character and purpose of the soul becomes increasingly important for both the individual and society. The lack of coherence and orientation on the outside makes the inborn seeds of self and inherent sense of direction more critical than ever.

The ancient Greek word for truth was *aleithia* which translates as "not to forget." Being true to oneself means not to forget the nature of the life-seed planted in one's soul to begin with. Truly becoming oneself means to bring to fruition the life already seeded within. The inner truth of one's life tries to surface during youth and again at each critical turn along the path. In the second half of life, inner awareness and reflection are intended to replace simple reaction. The evening of one's life offers a second adventure as the soul tries to slow down and deepen and return to its original dream of life.

The later stages of life are not intended to be an appendage or an afterthought, but a chance to reveal more of life's inherent meaning before entering the afterlife. Unless this second and inward adventure develops, the outer arc of life expansion can continue long after it has meaning. Later in life our eyes begin to fail and the details of the world around us become more difficult to see. The loss of common sight signals a natural in which developing one's vision is more important than simply being able to see.

The wisdom of nature seems to invest in the creation of elders by dimming simple sight in favor of greater, more enduring visions of life. After a while we have seen enough and developing genuine vision serves life better. Old Native American teachings suggest that the elders learn to make the most critical decisions for the tribe based upon results that will not appear until seven generations down the line. The elders were seen as those with the longest vision and most able to remember things of great importance. For no one can see very far ahead who is not well anchored in the deep past.

Memory is a river that flows in both directions at once; seeing what lies ahead requires remembering what went before. If we lose the deep memories we lose the future as well as the past and lose our footing in the present to boot. Amidst the collapse of their bodies the elders stand for all that is enduring and weird and eternal in life. The loss of common sight makes inner reflection and deeper insights more possible. In order to see generations down the line a person must be somewhat free of the ego's typical entrapment in immediate needs and self-serving designs. Aging may lead to "coming apart at the seams;" yet falling apart can also lead to revelations of what held us together all along.

In order to see far into the future we must stand firmly in our own lives. True insights develop from finding the deeper currents that run within one's own story. At the end of life our own soul must question and consider what we did with the thread of destiny we were given at the beginning. At the end of our life the gods who spoke the inspired words of fate into us review and judge what we did with that divine breath of life. At the end we become responsible for how close we came to intuiting and living out the life breathed into us at the beginning.

The Well of Memory

The old myths and wisdom traditions try to help us remember what is important about life and how to perceive in depth where many go blind. Remember old Odin, who gave up an eye in order to better see into things hidden below the surface of life. From the beginning Odin had a great desire for wisdom; he had a dream of becoming wise and knowing more than what meets the eye. When he learned that the giant Mimir kept a deep well where all wisdom originated, he went in search of the waters of ancient knowledge.

It may be helpful to know that *Mimir* means "memory" and that the deep well of knowledge was also known as the Well of Remembrance. Mimir's Well was said to contain the living waters of life wherein the ever-flowing ancient memories continually rise to the surface. The well was said to be situated at the roots of the World Tree that stands at the very center of life. So Odin followed his dream; he went searching for wisdom and eventually found himself approaching the center of life. It could also be said as well that reaching the center of one's life places a person at the well of wisdom.

When Odin reached the well he encountered the old giant guarding the sacred waters. It may be helpful to know that *Mimir* can also mean prophecy. The secret of prophecy is that it involves the capacity to remember all the way back to the origins as well as to see all the way into the future. In order to see both ways, however, a person must enter the present more fully and that usually requires some kind of sacrifice.

When Odin asked the old giant for a little draught of the mead of wisdom, Mimir was quite willing to give it. After all, the seeker had made his way all the way to the center of life. However, it turned out that there was one condition, a price to pay for a sip of the waters of life. No free lunch in this world and no wisdom for free either. In this case the price for a taste of wisdom was the sacrifice of an eye. In order to see more deeply into life the seeker had to give up the normal way of seeing the world. And that is exactly what Odin did; he sacrificed an eye and learned to see another way. Ever after he had one eye that gazed upon the world of incarnated things and another that you could not see, but that looked inward and gazed upon eternity.

Becoming wise means seeing things differently; it means not seeing in the usual ways that others see. Whoever would become a true seer must also become a little blind. Gaining such great vision and insight requires a sacrifice at the ordinary level of life. Odin had to sacrifice common sight in order to gain uncommon wisdom and he did so at the well of memory. Thus, deep memory can be seen to be essentially related to wisdom. Wisdom runs deep and the ancient sources of life can be tapped; but those who would become wise in this world must sacrifice something to the otherworld.

Old age can be seen as a sacrifice that nature makes in order that wisdom and otherworldly vision might become possible while a person is still alive. Failing eyesight is bound to dim the outer world with all its passing glories. Yet in losing sight of common things the vision of an uncommon knowledge might grow more fully. Many immediate things may fade in order that enduring things might clarify. True learning involves a great act of remembering and short-term memory loss may be a little sacrifice intended to open the mind to a recollection of what is most important about both life and death. The elders are supposed to forget some things in order that they might better remember the most important things.

The last stages of life either move towards a cloud of forgetting or towards a dusky light in which people come to see the reflections of meaning and purpose in their own lives. The later stages of life are supposed to revolve around the resilient tree at the center and the deep well of memory where life ever renews as ancient memories become the source of life's future dream. Those who would be wise in that way must seek and find the center of their lives and once there learn to drink from the deep well of imagination and memory.

Those who would become elder and wiser learn to extract living knowledge from the specific dramas and struggles, the tragedies and comedies they experience in life. This shifts a person from holding a closed ego to a having a greater circumference that can connect the troubles of this world with the wisdom of the otherworld. Experience alone cannot add up to genuine wisdom. Wisdom combines life experience with insight into oneself and into the world.

The elders carried a greater vision of life because they developed insight into their own lives. They faced up to whatever fate had in store for them and found threads of destiny amidst the illusions and delusions of life. In turning consciously within, people may more readily find what they were longing for and looking for all along. The point of aging is not simply slowing down, but growing downwards; specifically descending further into the life intended by the soul. In consciously "slowing downwards" something ancient and meaningful becomes available.

The elders are not supposed to be simply "out of it" or be out of touch with the difficulties that younger people and future generations must face. Being in touch with ancient things means being both old and young at the same time. The ancient and knowing part of the soul is the seat of the "beginner's mind" as well as the dwelling of the wise old soul within us. Those who become truly old also become young again as the dream of life continually returns to them. In becoming wise old souls, the elders more firmly know and more clearly hold the inner sense of meaning and purpose that first surfaced during their youth.

At the same time, the presence of deep thought and attention in an aged person attests to something eternal amidst the time-bound, something enduring within the temporary conditions. Sustained attention, generous intention and wit in an elder are perhaps the greatest evidence of something eternal seeded in human life. The continuity of consciousness amidst a collapsing body speaks of an invisible, underlying continuity in all of life. Thus, the elder becomes the physical embodiment of the eternal, both a dying life and a living shrine.

The genuine elder becomes a complex living symbol: on one side evidence of the inevitable decay of life; on the other side an example of the inner gold of the deep self shining through the tatters of one's life. When people learn to become who they already are at their core they leave footprints that others can follow at least part of the way. They mark the road of life with signs that remind everyone that there are ways the soul would follow no matter the condition of the world.

Thus, the issue at the end of life is not so much the horror of death as the tragedy of not having lived the life one was given. Insofar as we become ourselves, we can be said to have lived meaningfully. Only if we live meaningfully can our death also be meaningful in some way. In the end, it becomes clear that the primary task we have is to find and fulfill the shape seeded in the soul before birth broke the spell of eternity and dropped us onto the road of life and death. To conform to that shape which can only be found by shedding all other shapes, that is the "natural law," the higher law and inner dharma of our own nature which requires that we at times go against nature and against the narrowness of culture.

The idea is not simply to age well, but to become ancient in ways that can draw upon the archetypal knowledge that sustained the ancestors and that can guide the future. If those growing older become more like elders, the roots of deep imagination that nourish the ongoing story of life may be found again. If life becomes more attuned to the promptings and yearnings of the inner patterns of life, culture may become less random and accidental and become again more purposeful and meaningful, less filled with fear and more imbued with beauty. Living wisdom requires a sense of story, a narrative intelligence that recognizes what is important and enduring and weird enough to survive.

CHAPTER 5

OUR LOT IN LIFE

*Success and failure both become more acceptable
within a right orientation to the world.*

There's an ancient tale that tells of a great earthen jar with bits of wood in
it. The pieces of wood are taken from the Tree of Life and each bit has an
essential word written upon it. Before a child is born the jar is shaken and
the first chip that falls out becomes the "lot in life" for that soul. *Lot* is an
old word meaning a "chip of wood." In a sense, we are each a chip off the
same old universal block and each a living word taken from the Tree of Life
that stands at the center of the cosmos. Our fate falls to us by virtue of a
mythic lottery and our lot in life secretly connects us back to the tree at the
center of the world which is also called the Tree of Destiny.

"In the beginning was the word." Each birth repeats the original act
of creation, each soul becoming a further pronouncement of life's endless
song. Our individual allotment is but a small share in the great game of
life; yet it is also our human lot to be inscribed with a divine word. At
some essential level we are each a word in the great alphabet and intricate
language of eternity; yet our life potential is inextricably woven to our
exact limitations. So begins the great mystery of human existence and the
paradox that makes each human life temporary and limited; yet seeded
with the divine at the same time.

We are human by lot and divine by origin; limited by fate, yet driven
by destiny, each person a living puzzle as well as a divine experiment. The

divine word shapes a living pattern within us and gives us our essential chance at life. It provides the specific inner language and poetic nature of our soul. In the midst of the confusion and uncertainty of the world around us, the divine pattern is the underlying source of unity within us.

Yet again, finding the inner unity of the soul requires that we first accept our strange lot and the necessary limitations of our life. No one can "have it all," so all of us must begin with our specific share in the grand lottery of life. For whatever comes to life must pass through the womb of necessity where eternity becomes wounded by time. Our fate includes the bit and bite of necessity that places us in time as well as the timeless song in the soul that keeps us longing for the eternal.

If we learn to express the divine word within us, our destiny becomes expressed and we become agents of the ongoing creation of the world. If we fail to live out the portion of eternity given to us, no one will ever live it. For each soul is unique, each life a project conceived by the divine, and each a chance that life itself is taking. Life is the original game of chance and our fate is the hand we were dealt when we first entered the game. Our weird, inner woven complex of fate and destiny is what we enter this world with and truly "what we bring to the table."

Coming to life is always a big gamble, one our souls have an essential stake in. For there are risks our souls would take, even where others might play it safe. In the end, when all the "chips are down," our true safety in life involves risking the life story already set within the soul. We either play the hand dealt to us at the beginning or run the risk of not really living the life we were given. If we refuse our fate and deny how we are threaded, we lose our genuine sense of destiny. Yet as long as we follow the threads of fate and destiny woven into our soul, we always have a chance. The divine word that gives us our first chance at life can also provide us with a surprising number of second chances.

Some say that the great earthen jar that holds the endless supply of individual lots in life was held by the goddess Fortuna. We draw our sense of good fortune and bad luck from her. Others say that it is the three Sisters of Fate who handle our initial allotment of fate and destiny. Of necessity, there are many stories, but all the tales of fate involve a strong feminine presence when it comes to the mysteries that tie each soul to the origins of life and the Soul of the World.

When considered as a group the Fates have the title *Moira* meaning "allotment or share;" for they share out the elements that make each life specific and limited and uniquely woven within. *Moira* refers to the lot given at the beginning, but it also shares roots with *mors*, an old word for death that gives us our sense of mortality. In that sense, the Fates are the arbiters of our chance at life and they are the harbingers of death as well; they are part of the immortal realm, yet they also represent the presence of mortality in this world.

The Sisters of Fate represent the essential mystery of life and the ceremonies of birth and death that surround it. They are primordial members of the universal mythic family who layer the world with secrets and set each thing in its place and lace it through with light and dark filaments. They spin the subtle threads of existence and weave the lasting patterns of life and set the endless web in motion. They are the "wyrrd" behind the web of life, the eternal feminine spirit and life-quickening touch that weave the subtle designs and intricate patterns set within each soul.

In Greek myth the Fates were considered to be first-born, the primal daughters of life birthed from the eternal darkness of Night and the elemental presence of Necessity. Of necessity, they sit at the intersection where the threads of the eternal become woven with the limitations of time. They touch each thing created and incarnated into this world where necessity rules and even the gods must at times obey. In mythic terms, the presence of fate is as necessary as the night for the world to exist.

Being first-born, the Fates must themselves attend each subsequent birth and give each newborn its particular share of life. The gods may pronounce their words upon us, but the Fates do the handiwork of connecting the divine threads to the earthly fabric of life. They handle the fine filaments of fate and destiny and weave the warp and weft that together set each living soul into the web of the world.

Being weavers extraordinaire as well as divine storytellers, they set the plotline of each life and dress our souls in the threads of fate and destiny.

They spin the inner stories that tie us to the web and pull us onto the stage of life in order that we may take a part and play a role in the divine drama. As master spinners they know how to weave a good tale, how to imbue it with secrets waiting to be discovered and mark it with fateful events that cannot be avoided.

Lachesis is the sister who presides over the process of dispensing the lots. She is also the one who sets the divine word within the soul and pulls from it the subtle and surprising thread of one's destiny. Clotho is the sister who sets the soul's pattern within us and fashions the inner text and defining texture within each soul. We derive the word *cloth* from her name as well as *clothes* and a wide patchwork of words related to spinning and weaving. It is Clotho who gives the unique twist of fate that makes each person an original, never to be repeated no matter how many souls are born.

Of the three sisters, Atropos was considered to be the oldest. Being oldest also makes her the first one born, yet much of her work has to do with how things end. Atropos is the hard sister in life who fixes the pattern in the depths of each soul, but who also cuts the life thread when the time has come. *Atropos* means "inflexible," it also means "she who cannot be turned." She represents all that is irreversible in life and "hard wired" in us, the inescapable qualities and inevitable characteristics that cannot be denied.

Atropos was also called "the inevitable." From her name we derive "atrophe," the sense that things diminish and wear down and wither away. The third sister stands at the end of life's road, but she is also present whenever we encounter the specific limitations and dramatic twists of fate that move us toward our soul's intended destination. Being mostly involved with endings, Atropos specializes in "hindsight." Often the inevitability of fate appears only in review, as looking back we begin to see what was bound to happen all along.

Midwives of the Soul

The Sisters of Fate are the original midwives for they touch each soul when it is midway between the divine realm and the manifest world. They hold the soul again when its earthly tale has reached an end and the time has come for it to return to the place of origins. The old practices of human midwives derived from the original sisters of the soul, for midwives used to attend to wakes and funerals as well as tend to births. They would wash each newborn and wrap it in swaddling cloth and they would also anoint the newly deceased with oil and wrap them in mournful shrouds. You can sense the presence of the original midwives in the cloths that cover the newborn as well as the dearly departed.

As handmaidens of the critical moments of birth and death, ancient midwives worked intimately with the mysteries of life and were considered to have the sense of "second sight." Modern people may have x-rays that expose aspects of the fetus before it is born, but midwives were keen observers and subtle seers who could often perceive qualities that elude even the finest instruments. They were natural diviners, able to catch glimpses of divine elements that appear more clearly at the critical moments of life.

Midwives were the earthly representatives of the Sisters of Fate and were often the first to notice the inner nature of the children coming into life with their allotted patterns, their innate gifts and their woven destinies. When assisting at births they would watch for the signs and symbols that indicate the inner nature of the soul being born and the way it was aimed at the world. For each birth is a literal event that can be measured and recorded, but also a symbolic occurrence that can be interpreted on other levels.

An old Mayan tale tells of a time when midwives could see with second sight and recognize the gifts being carried from the other world to this one. That was before the flood of disasters that made it so difficult for contemporary people to perceive the natural gifts and spiritual aspects that are born which each child. They say the trouble began in a simple village where a certain woman entered her time of labor and called for the midwife to come. Shortly after the midwife arrived the crowning moment occurred, and the newborn could be seen for the first time. The midwife observed that it was a boy, but she could also see that the child came bearing gifts.

The little fellow had a green cloak on his back and he held a in his little hand a small bowl filled with water. In the intensity of the labor and excitement of the birth no one else noticed the child's gifts. The mother was too exhausted from the labor and the infant was too new and helpless to know anything of the gifts he carried to this world. The midwife took the green cloak and the clay bowl from the infant and hid them away.

After seven days, the midwife arranged the traditional ceremony for welcoming the newborn and giving thanks that both the mother and child were healthy. Everyone in the village came to celebrate the birth and make a proper welcome for the new one in the world. The infant was washed and cleansed and prepared for a naming ceremony. He was given the name Poder. It was as much a title as a name, for it carried many meanings. Poder meant gift, for every child is a gift to this world. Poder also meant power and ability; it meant fate and fortune as well. Some said it also meant luck and they repeated the name at the ceremony as if to instill good fortune in the child.

After completing the welcoming ritual, the midwife took the child's gifts and carried them up into the mountains that stood silently beyond the village. She gave the gifts to certain people out in those hills and they in turn hid them away carefully. No one told the family of the gifts the child brought with him and nothing of those talents was mentioned to the child Poder.

After being welcomed into this world and being nursed by his mother the boy took to life and grew rapidly. He did all the things that a child is expected to do and had his share of the good and bad experiences that shape childhood. Eventually, Poder reached the period when childhood must come to a close and something else must begin. Upon becoming a youth Poder began to ask the questions that young people often ask. He wondered why he was here, if he had a purpose, and whether he had something to give to this world. Being unable to reach a meaningful conclusion on his own, Poder sought out the midwife who attended his birth and whom everyone considered to be a wise person.

When he found the wise woman he asked her if there was a purpose for his life. He asked if he had a gift to give to this world and if the world had something to give to him. Being wise in the ways of this world, the midwife answered the direct question indirectly. She said that everyone comes to this world with gifts and that all gifts are intended to be given. She explained that each child was welcomed by everyone because most understood that they would be the beneficiaries when the children became able to give the gifts they brought to this world. In the meantime, she suggested that the time had come for him to leave his childhood behind. If he wished to learn the nature of life he would have to make a journey to the holy hills and seek answers for himself. Poder wasted no time. He went to his parents and told them that he would be leaving in order to search for knowledge. His mother gave him food for the journey and a blessing for the road and Poder prepared to leave the village and leave behind everything he knew. With nothing but a little food and some water he began to wander into the holy hills. After a time the food from home had been consumed and all he carried were the questions he had about himself and about the nature of this world.

While wandering high in the hills Poder came upon some people keeping vigils and doing ceremonies. They welcomed him warmly and asked why he walked the hills alone. Poder explained how he carried certain questions and came searching for answers. He told them that he desired to know if he had something to give to the world and if the world had something to give to him. The people listened to him and answered that both things were true, for each person was intended to be part of the vital exchange that sustains the world.

After sharing food with the youth, the people in the hills fetched the green cloak and the earthen bowl full of water that formed his birthright. They handed the items to Poder and explained that he had been born with those exact gifts and that the time had come for him to learn the meaning and the purpose of them.

Poder was introduced to a person who had similar gifts and abilities in order to receive training in how to handle and protect his god-given talents. The youth was surprised to learn that those born with a green cloak and bowl of water were intended to become rainmakers. Since that area was hot most of the time and dry most of the year a talent for bringing rain was important and could be life-saving for everyone.

Poder began his training and paid close attention to his teachers and the lessons for understanding and using his gifts. Soon he became able to roll up into the clouds and loosen the waters that they held in the sky. He learned how to handle his gifts and how to protect them. He learned when to use his talents and how to be ready to participate in life and give something to this world.

When the time came for Poder to return to his village, he took his leave and thanked the people who had welcomed him and had given him back his gifts. With his natural gifts and the knowledge of how to use them, Poder began to serve the people of the village. He watched the weather and learned to read the clouds and sense when making rain was possible. He helped bring rain down to earth so the people could grow corn and beans and enough squash to sustain life. When he was not using his gifts, Poder kept them hidden. Somehow, people recognized that he used his talents to the benefit of everyone and Poder became a favorite son of the village.

Then it happened that there was a youth in the village who had no idea of his god-given gifts. He had no knowledge of whether he had something to give to this world. No one else seemed to know the nature of that boy's inner inheritance either. As a result, he felt that he had no power in his life, no purpose, and no luck that he could draw upon. No one seemed able to help him find his own way; so he became interested in Poder who everyone else had an interest in. He began to follow Poder around in order to learn where he kept his gifts and to observe how he was able to accomplish the rainmaking.

One day, when Poder was occupied elsewhere, that fellow went to where the cloak and earthen bowl were kept. He took them from their hiding place and began to imitate the motions Poder used to roll up into the clouds. He found himself rolling up and landing in some dark clouds. Up there in the land of clouds the fellow began to experiment with the little clay bowl. Soon enough, the clouds began to rumble and rain started falling from the sky onto the earth below.

People were glad to see the rain. However, the one who stole the gifts had no real knowledge of how to use them. What began as a shower soon became a great downpour. The imitator had no notion of how to stop the rain once it started and in no time the downpour swelled into a great storm.

Great winds gathered and torrential rains pounded down on the village and pelted the crops in the fields. It became clear to those being rained upon that all their plantings were being washed away and that soon the entire village might be lost in the ensuing flood.

No one knew what to do; no one had the power to stop the flood that been let loose on the world. People say the flood would have encompassed the entire world had god not become angry at the misuse of the god-given powers. They say it was god who finally stopped the rain and knocked the false rainmaker back down to earth.

After the deluge ended, Poder was able to reclaim his gifts. The people eventually restored the village and planted new crops when the land dried out. Nothing more is told of the fellow who took the gifts that were not his own birthright. However, after those dramatic events people say that no one, not even the midwives, had the ability to perceive the gifts that children bring to this world when they are born. Furthermore, they say that we are the descendants of those people and that explains why most people now do not know what their natural gifts and powers might be.

Everyone remains gifted in some way; for that is a necessity in human life and even the anger of god can't take that away. Meanwhile, the god-given gifts of most people remain hidden and fewer people know what they are intended to give to this world. Many live their entire lives without finding their inner power and learning the nature of their gifts. They say that is why so many people imitate what others do and become envious of those who find their gifts and learn how to give them. They say that is why so many people rise to the top without really knowing how or what they are intended to serve in this world, which can become flooded with troubles of all kinds.

Second Birth, Second Sight

The story of Poder is an old cautionary tale, the kind of folklore the ancient folks used to explain how the world can fall into chaos. It is also an initiation story intended to remind everyone that coming of age involves a search for self-knowledge and that the results can affect the lives of everyone. What was given to each before birth tries to be found again when childhood comes to an end. Since life is rarely neutral, those who fail to find and use their natural gifts run the risk of darkening the fate of the world and adding to the storms of life. The fate of the world repeatedly turns according to the way such inner qualities are used or become neglected and wasted.

The story of Poder is a birth story, but also a second birth or re-birth story. It is a basic human story of losing and finding one's natural gifts and learning one's genuine orientation to the world. It is a rites-of-passage tale about the necessity of awakening the individual as well as a myth about human community. For each society grows greater or else suffers more deeply depending upon the recognition and use of the natural gifts of its members.

Each person is "star-crossed" at birth, marked by the web of stars, touched by the eternal milk of the Milky Way. Yet amidst the modern exaggerations and delusions of objectivity, the subtle signs go unseen and the markings on the soul are missed as birth become more mechanical than miracle. In the attempt to see everything through the narrow spectrum of rationality we become blinded by the factual and actual. The life of the soul is reduced and we become increasingly uneasy with the presence of the eternal just beyond the veil of the evident.

In the world of myth, meaning is a fact and each fact carries hidden meanings. In the current world, literal facts and figures dominate and radically limit the flow of living ideas and meaningful images. Birth is viewed as a biological, medical event and a similar attitude is brought to the mysteries of death. Seen mythically, the birth of each infant is also a rebirth of meaning in the world. We are born within a meaning that we live an entire life to learn. We are each a version of Poder, continually grasping and losing the signs and symbols that make our lives meaningful. Only at death can we say what it all meant; but at any point along the way we can open the hands with which we cling to life and see some of the "natural stigmata" with which we incarnated.

Signs and symbols, auguries and fates attend every birth and are part of each birth-rite. For symbols are the original speech of all who ever speak and the necessary speech of the gifted soul. We give gifts to the newborn who can neither see them clearly nor understand them. We do so because we intuit that the new arrival is itself a gift to everyone. Gifts are given because life is a gift and birth is the arrival of unseen values and meanings that attend each newborn child.

Once upon a time, midwives and others studied the moment of birth looking for signs not just of physical health, but also seeking for indications of where that child might go in life. That was before the floodtide of facts and figures obscured the second sight needed to see the more subtle aspects of this world. Now, the mystery of new life with its inherent threads of fate and hints of destiny becomes reduced to statistical measurements. The vital signs are reported, but rarely include glimpses of the vital symbols that are the inner inheritance of each child. Birth has become more literal, just as life has become more linear, and death has become simply a dead end.

Meanwhile, each child still arrives as a little epiphany accompanied by symbols and imbued with hidden gifts and unseen potentials. The word *infant* comes from the Latin "non-fans," meaning "not speaking." The infant cannot speak for itself or of itself, but can only cry out with the sound of life caught between the teeth of time and the song of eternity. Midwives used to take a position midway between the mother giving birth to life and the child being born; but also between the immediate family and the larger community. For each child is a gift to the community as well as a descendant of their family.

Poder represents each child born, each a descendant of the Unseen, each arriving already marked and gifted; each fated to lose touch with the original gifts through the labors and pains of becoming human. *Poder* stands for the luck and power, the fate and fortune that all people carry whether they know it or not. For no child comes to this world empty-handed or with a completely clean slate. All have their own "poder complex," their inner mixture of talents and gifts and inner woven story that needs to materialize in order for their soul to fully become incarnate.

At birth we are not completely born; subtle parts remain stillborn, waiting to be delivered when the inner life awakens and the inner speech is invoked. In youth the hidden signs and defining symbols try to appear again. The inevitable troubles of youth are part of a second birth that tries to reveal the second nature and inner gifts of the child. During youth the infant that was unable to speak for itself becomes a young person trying to learn and fathom the inner language and speech of its own soul.

Not recognizing that the gifts are there from the beginning makes it harder to see the inner qualities and core meanings trying to be discovered through youthful adventure. Each child is a gift to its people, but can be a troublesome burden until the true gifts are found and given. Of course, understanding that each child is gifted by nature is important; yet general acceptance or simple recognition do not solve the problems of identity and self-worth that develop in youth.

In many ways, recognizing that each child carries inner gifts creates a bigger problem as it shifts the welcoming of youth to a deeper level of engagement. Youth need an education of the spirit, not simply the kind of general instruction given to children still unable to speak for themselves. A second birth is required as the hidden signs try to appear again as part of a psychological birth intended to reveal the distinct inner pattern of the individual soul. The second birth of youth creates a second chance as well as a more conscious responsibility for a community to welcome fully and properly bless the child who came to them bearing gifts.

Like Poder, the soul of each person expects to have a revelatory appointment with its own gifted nature as well as meaningful encounters that confirm and anoint its purpose in the world. The inevitable troubles of youth are a kind of second labor of life intended to birth a revelation of the inner nature and innate gifts of the soul. Young people need hints of their inner value and confirmation of their purpose or they can be rebellious in the wrong direction or simply become passive consumers at the table of life. Each child may be a gift to its people, but children can become a burden to the community until their inner abilities are found and their life orientation becomes conscious.

The original potentials present at the birth of the newborn return again and try to surface at the crossroads between childhood and adult life. The basic human questions echo in the soul of each young person: Do I have something to give to this world? Does the world have something to give to me? Each person is such a question being asked of the world. Each is marked from birth, not necessarily with an original sin, more likely with original gifts and an imbedded sense of meaning and purpose. Some kind of offense or sin against nature does occur when people are not welcomed as gift-givers and not assisted in the necessary search to reclaim their own birthright.

That which is ours most naturally must become consciously known to us; otherwise we are but uneasy guests on the dark face of the earth. If the soul's critical appointments remain unfulfilled we can become ill-fated and deeply disappointed with life itself. Instead of feeling invited into the great dance of life we can find ourselves lost in a wasteland of accidental hills, trapped in the valleys of forgetfulness or simply passing the time while wasting away in the village of the unawakened.

In Poder's story, the great flood of destruction was precipitated by someone who lacked a proper welcome and a meaningful orientation to this world. When people fail to find and use their innate gifts and life-enhancing powers those who have no idea how to handle power will rise to the top. It happens all the time as those who do not know their inner value or true purpose become hungry for power of any kind. At the same time, others who lack purpose and self-knowledge willingly give their power to those who can't help but misuse it. When power is in the wrong hands, all kinds of exploitation results and even the basic elements and rhythms of life become endangered.

Culture means to cultivate, both to grow crops that sustain life and to nurture the inner resources and natural talents of each person. Life is not tame and each person has the ability to become a boon or a bane to the rest of the human village. The difference turns on whether people feel truly welcome in this world, on whether they find their inner gifts and learn to make a meaningful way in life. When a culture forgets this kind of spiritual cultivation it will fail to welcome the newborns, it will neglect to bless and guide its own youth, and eventually its old people will live in fear and cling to lives not fully lived.

At each critical turn and at each new stage of life the essential questions and fateful issues of the soul try to arrest our attention and return us to the search for our inner inheritance. Meanwhile, the paths to discovering the inner gifts become more difficult to find. Wide roads and broad highways run in all directions while the pathways for inner awakening become more obscure. In the rush to "get somewhere in life" more and more people wind up disoriented and unwelcome in the world. From the view of natural talents and inner purpose, from the angle of fate and destiny, the world seems to be turned backwards and upside down.

Despite the ancient instinct to become one who gives as well as receives from life, most people now identify as consumers. The trouble with consuming is that in the end people can't get enough of what they don't really want. The trouble with a "consumer society" is that it eventually consumes itself. Deficient in signs and symbols, lacking portents of purpose and destiny, humans are reduced to becoming vagrant consumers in a world in which they have nothing essential to give or to learn. Within the concept of tabula rasa, the blank slate approach to life, can be found the roots of blind materialism and blatant consumerism; from there the table can be set for nihilism. Loss of the sense of meaning within each life gives birth to a meaningless world.

With the loss of inherent meaning the sense of a life-purpose also wanes and everything seems less meaningful. The expectation of a vocation speaking from an awakened soul diminishes to an anxiety over choice of career. Instead of the village waiting to receive the innate gifts of its children, youth become a fearsome burden, an increasing cost in a world where everything has a price. Society becomes a disoriented aggregation of insatiable consumers. We become meaningless creations rather than creatures of meaning participating in an ongoing creation.

In becoming aware of one's natural gifts the need to give something to the world becomes stronger than the hunger to consume it. Giving from the inherent gifts leads to receiving a blessing from the world. Such a genuine exchange nourishes both the individual and the community at the same time as it employs others to become proper mentors and elders.

The Holy Hills

The tale of Poder is a "teaching story," a story about teaching and learning because it points to the nature of genuine education. Life-defining gifts are present in the student, waiting to be recognized and blessed. However, specific gifts also require specific learning or they will be poorly given, or not given at all. Something within us already knows how we are intended to live, but needs to remember carefully. General learning cannot touch the core imagination of a person, although it can easily obscure it.

A general education, whether it be in the finest schools or the school of hard knocks, only prepares a person for getting along in life. It usually reflects local customs and one's social status; it often involves us in plans made by others, intended to serve the needs of others. Genuine education involves a remembering of essential things, a reclaiming of lost knowledge. Until modern times, when it became mostly a civic issue, education was considered a sacred task. Education was sacred because it touched the spirit in the student and because it depended upon an awakened spirit in the teacher. Spirit to spirit, genius to genius, soul to soul go the deeper lessons and greater learning of genuine education.

The story of Poder illustrates the idea that someone has to give us anew what was given to us at birth. All people have a potential appointment with their own potentials. For that which is most "naturally" ours must be found again and become consciously our own. In the lost and found of life our innermost gifts become lost and must be found again. Our souls enter the world with expectations of awakening to a genuine life. The desire is placed deep enough to be pre-verbal, therefore hard to bring simply to words and reason. A true passage from childhood to adult life requires that we become lost enough to find our way back to the original symbols and meanings that attended our birth.

In order to find genuine answers to essential questions, Poder had to leave the village of daily life and wander into the holy hills. The hills are holy because lost gifts can be reclaimed there, because the people dwelling there understand the nature and purpose of god-given talents and can give training in how to use them. The holy hills are the true ground of "higher education" that can appear wherever people recall the deeper purpose of learning and the wisdom of self-revelation. Before walking the paths of responsibility, youth need a "walkabout" that gives them the lay of the land as seen from their inner eye.

This is an essential issue of education. Omitting this step toward self-awareness in favor of general instruction creates a loss in both the individual and the community. We each have our in-born gifts, but they must also be given back to us; we carry them from birth, but must find others to help us reclaim our true birthright. Traditionally, midwives able to perceive the god-given gifts of the children became the "god-parents." Typically, someone other than the natural parents must protect and nurture the hidden nature and genuine core of the child's soul.

Midwives are the predecessors of the mentors and teachers who later nurture the life projects of youth. The genuine projects of the soul require spiritual parenting and those who assist at the second birth become the metaphysical parents of the individual trying to awaken. The true teachers and genuine guides in our lives are those who can see the gifts we bring and help us learn how to handle them and give them. Whoever does that, man or woman, younger or older, becomes a midwife to the birth of meaning and purpose in our souls.

The inner gifts and natural inclinations are trying to become conscious to us; when someone takes an interest and offers a helping hand, even mistakes can help us awaken. At a critical time in youth my aunt acted as a midwife for the hidden spirit in me. She asked what I was most interested in at school at the time I was just beginning to ask the Poder question: What do I have to give to the world and what does the world have to give to me? I could not have phrased it that way, but I was certainly questioning what life was all about and whether I had a meaningful place in it. For a moment, my aunt and I met in the holy hills as the hand of fate turned a seeming mistake into a gift that spoke to the signs and symbols trying to awaken and become conscious in me.

The holy hills can suddenly appear wherever fate and destiny conspire to bring us closer to who we already are and what we contain at our core. It is a human birthright that everyone must have at least one occasion in which their inner gifts and natural inheritance can be seen and felt. The occasions when we stand near the complex of our birthright mark us in some way that cannot be erased, but can be seen in reviewing our life and in reflecting upon our youth.

People complain that young people think that "the world owes them something" and actually, it does. Those who remain unclear or unsure of their own gifted nature tend to resent the natural desperation of young people who need blessing and confirmation. The world owes young people genuine opportunities to find what gifts and abilities they carry within and what story they came here to live out. Feeling existentially unwelcome and unblessed, young people can easily become overwhelmed and lost in the floods of change and in the storms of life. When the second birth expected by the soul doesn't occur or else happens in a haphazard manner people can be disoriented throughout their lives.

The "generation gap" is not supposed to be chasm that alienates youth and elders. Rather, the cultural gap between youth and adults exists so that genuine education might develop and creatively connect everyone to the deeper meanings of life. Mentors and elders are those who have awakened to their own inner gifts and become aware of their purposes and callings in life. In learning to live with genuine purpose they develop second sight and become able to perceive the gifted nature and natural inclinations of other people. In assisting young women and men to grasp their natural gifts, older folks retouch their own potentials and reactivate their own gifts and purposes in life.

Ultimately, each person holds the key to the story trying to be lived from within, but first someone else must help unlock the mystery of one's life. Genuine teachers represent the inner qualities of the soul lived out and made visible in the world. Mentors become guides insofar as some of their true potentials have been actualized and the purpose set in their soul has been truly embodied.

Remember old rabbi Zushya teaching from his deathbed? He was trying to remind everyone that the question asked at the end of life develops from the questions that form in the soul during youth. In seeking to learn what we have to give to the world we move closer to finding a genuine way to live the unique life we have been given. Since each person is unique, each needs to find an exact blessing and a specific welcome in this world. Lacking a genuine welcome and meaningful guidance, young people can be inclined to throw their lives away or waste them on distractions. Lacking an inner orientation, a person can drown in the common details of life.

Feeling unwelcome and disappointed in their lives, young people can turn to self-destruction or even wreck the lives of others. The young thief in the tale of Poder had not been recognized by anyone in his community. He had no sense of his true nature and no knowledge of his inner name. He had no wise midwife or caring guide to turn to and no blessing to take on the roads of life. Feeling empty of purpose and meaning he tried to steal from others what he could not find within. Unlike the old thief in the tale of the golden plum pit, he had no sense of what he carried inside the cloak of his life. When he grew old enough to have an effect on the world he caused a furious storm by trying to handle powers not tuned to his own nature.

The misguided and abandoned youth stands as a prime example of what has been lost in the modern world. Amidst the deep turbulence and flood of changes common to modern life we arrive at a place where most adults, lacking a meaningful welcome and blessing for their own inner lives, become powerless to bless the lives of the next generation. Instead of a village waiting to receive the innate gifts of its children, youth become a burden, an increasing cost in a world where everything has a price.

Feeling fundamentally empty and bereft of genuine life purpose, people settle for a received life. Fearing the hungers of their own progeny, the space between generations grows and distance from life becomes the cultural legacy. Unable to imagine a meaningful role in the drama of life, people accept the role of simply consuming the world, as if the hunger of infancy is extended to the entire course of life.

The overblown importance of choice in consumer societies is a weak sister when compared to the old idea of having a genuine calling in life.

The exaggeration of choice helps sustain the blindness of the consumer mentality. But in the long run, the important point is to be chosen, rather than to simply learn to choose from a menu of options. In being chosen and in responding to a genuine vocation a person becomes more capable of meaningful choices. Youth become lost in order to find themselves. Youth need to be needed and once awakened to their inner value and inherent self-worth young people prove to be naturally altruistic.

Once they feel welcomed into the world on a meaningful level, youth more readily seek to study and learn and naturally give of themselves. A culture that takes the time to welcome its youth in meaningful ways becomes the immediate beneficiary of their natural talents and creative abilities. The generation gap exists so that genuine education will occur and creatively connect the generations through the streams of living knowledge and imagination.

The Second Hand of Fate

It may be our shared fate to live at a time of great storms and sea changes that affect both nature and culture. The ocean of facts and figures and the speed of mass communications may seem to drown out the importance of individual life. The holy hills of learning and the paths of genuine discovery may be obscured by the flood of changes that threaten to overwhelm everyone. It may be our mutual lot in life to be born at a difficult time and in an era when many essential things are forgotten. The powers and abilities that enter the world with each child may be increasingly hidden from the eyes of people, but even god cannot remove the natural gifts altogether. Forgotten knowledge does not simply disappear and the gifts of life can never be completely lost.

What people forget falls back into stories, waiting there to be found again. And the stories always turn upon the awakening of the individual soul that alone is the carrier of the true gifts of life. It is only in the deep recesses of the individual soul that the true meanings and genuine purposes of life continue to be born. The old stories suggest that those born into a certain era bring to life the quality of "poder" that is needed at that time, the powers and gifts, the luck and the fortune necessary for surviving that age.

The world always hangs by a thread and seems about to end; yet fate always has another hand to play. Destiny is the second hand of fate that tends to be found when the trouble is all around us and all seems lost. When we accept that which limits and restricts our lives from within, we become more open to finding fate's second hand and touch the hidden threads of purpose and meaning imprinted at the core of our lives.

Both our fate and our destiny travel with us throughout life. They are the "familiars" of our lives that limit us with one hand and open us to great possibilities with the other. We are each in the "hands of fate" before we are received into the world and our own hands bear a unique imprint that will never be repeated exactly. Fate is inscribed upon our hands with compelling lines and distinct fingerprints that mark us as already scripted in mysterious ways. We are touched by fate and leave our own imprints on everything we touch.

Fate becomes the specific tangle of life issues to which we must surrender if we wish to find a pathway to our intended destination. Fate inscribes a territory that we are bound to enter and the threads of destiny mark the only way out of the area we are fated to experience. We must begin life with the hand that fate has dealt to us; yet our fate is more an oracle set within us than an outcome determined for us. Acceptance of fate does not mean resignation to a cynical or blind force.

The acceptance of fate is not fatalism; for it only happens in the moment as when young Poder accepts that something essential for his life is missing and must be found. A similar shift from a restricting fate to awakening destiny happens when the old thief stops trying to find cracks in the dungeon walls and begins to look for the key to liberation inside his own soul. In surrendering to the circumstances of his fate he finds the golden seed that opens the prison gates for him and even opens the minds of those who callously shut the gates of opportunity to those less fortunate.

The gift being sought and the seed needed for growth are inside us all along. They try to awaken during youth but can appear at any time of life. Our fate restricts us so that our destiny can find us, so that we can find again the gifts we came to give to the world and receive the blessing the world would give to us. Destiny hides within the unique twist of fate that makes each soul original and capable of contributing to the ongoing drama of creation and the imagination needed to transform a world of fear into a world of beauty.

Myths remind us of the symbolic presence within all the lost-and-found adventures that alone can give life meaning. Losing touch with the world of myth means losing the sense that life is deeply meaningful, full of meanings trying to be revealed at each twist and turn in the ongoing drama. Truly participating requires that we find and learn to give what we have already been gifted with. A second birth and greater awakening are required in order for us to awaken to the divine word hidden within our lot -in life.

II

The Dream of Life

*We are wrapped around a mystery to which we
were drawn before we were born.*

CHAPTER 6

THE TWO AGREEMENTS

To be purposeful is not to be goal oriented,
but to seek to reconnect to the source of one's life.

Soul is everywhere, but hard to see. The soul is an indwelling, animating, and connecting force without which we cannot live. Yet it cannot be seen directly or be proven to exist. By its nature the soul is "there-not-there;" we can feel its subtle presence and we can languish in its absence, but we cannot pin it down or hold it firm. Soul is an essential part of each living thing, but has no evident substance of its own. The soul can grow and more soul can be made; but it cannot be hoarded, measured or fixed in a certain place.

The soul is a betwixt-and-between thing: neither simply physical nor strictly spiritual, but something that participates in both realms. The soul is there before life begins and it continues on after we lay our body down. The soul is another kind of body, a subtle body that partakes of both spirituality and physicality. As the third element in the trinity of existence, soul fills the subtle space between spirit and matter. It grounds the spirit even as it animates the body, and helps to refine the senses. Soul keeps spirit and matter related by sustaining an in-between realm of imagination, emotion, and deep reflection.

Soul is the essential intermediary and subtle go-between that connects unlike things; it holds the physical in touch with the divine and keeps the immediate contemporary with the eternal. Soul is the connecting principle of life, the "both-and" factor, the unifying third between any opposing forces. As natural intermediary and go-between, the soul is the magical third; it is the narrative force that keeps the story going; it knows how things are secretly connected and that the third time is a charm.

Soul is the glue of the world and the connecting agent of existence. By its nature soul is the mutable, multiple, changeable aspect of both the world and individual life. As the animating force of natural life, soul was termed "anima mundi," the living, breathing Soul of the World. Aboriginal people in Australia called it "Yorro, Yorro," everything in the world having soul, standing up and speaking to you.

When we lose our way in this world it is the soul's way of being in touch with the pulse of life that has been lost. For we are most lost and truly abandoned when we have lost touch with our own soul, with our own inward style and way of being in the world. Soul is the missing ingredient when things fall apart, just as it was the animating force that first brought us to life.

The intimacy and subtlety of the soul secretly hold subject and object, mind and body, spirit and matter in touch with each other. Yet modern world views prefer to define human life in terms of hard separation and enduring opposition between subject and object. Older and wiser ways of viewing life involve a unity of three instead of a paralyzing polarity of two. When the old imagination and threefold way of seeing collapses into a bifurcated world view, we are left with the famous mind-body split and the blinding limitations of either-or thinking.

The soulless split between mind and body helps generate the widening gap between culture and nature. As culture becomes more abstract and ideological, nature becomes mere matter, there to be manipulated and exploited. When life becomes more polarized than it need be and things become more divided than they should be, it is the way of the soul that is missing and desperately needed in order to heal the divisions and make things whole again. For the soul is all-embracing, not seduced by either-or thinking, by us-and-them divisions, or by the pretensions of subject-object dichotomies. In contrast to the tendency to unify under a single idea or abstract symbol, the soul thrives on diversity and multiplicity.

Soul involves the genuine cultivation of ideas and the living imagination that produce art and culture; but soul also relates to the essence of nature and to natural ways of changing and growing. Soul is the secret way to the unity of the world. Soul is the secret breathing within the heart of nature and the dream hidden within the heart of culture. Wherever nature and culture meet, soul is present just as it is the missing element when culture and nature collide.

Soul is the arbiter of our incarnation and the source of our deep connection with certain places. Any intrigue with place is also an intrigue with soul. For our soul instinctively knows where and how we should sink our feet into the mud of creation and grow our roots down. Spirit may seek peak experiences and the heavenly heights; but soul would have us become fully incarnate and would help us to grow deep roots that allow the spirit of our life to settle down and branch out.

Soul knows which "walk of life" the soles of our feet are attuned to, just as it knows which rhythms and tunes can keep our hearts beating and singing and remaining open to the world. As the "missing third," soul represents the mysterious, hidden aspect of any situation. Soul is the erotic factor between people, and the blessed intimacy of all things. It is the inner quintessence that holds things together within us and holds us within the world. Soul adds "psychic reality" to common experience; without our soul and the inner pattern that animates it, we are no one in particular and therefore no one at all.

Insofar as we are truly individual from others, insofar as we come to know ourselves and live uniquely, we are "en-souled." When soul becomes diminished in us we become as an empty shell regardless of our physical attributes or lofty station in life. The soul keeps body and mind, blood and spirit connected and we are most connected, body and soul, when we live close to the innate pattern set within our souls to begin with.

Soul is the light hidden inside the dark as well as the shading that gives beauty its shape. Soul has hidden gold, inner vision and a light that continually rises from the deep. The inner light of the soul is not a reflection of the outer world; for the soul flickers with an inner flame, a candle that burns with emotional heat and also knows ecstatic brilliance. Ancient philosophers imagined the soul to be a butterfly or "night moth" undergoing continuous transformations, or else a beautiful and mysterious woman.

Origins of the Soul

The old Greek word for butterfly was *psyche*. That was also the name of the soulful woman in the myth of Eros and Psyche. As the psychological factor in life, soul can be called *psyche*, as the inner animating life force it is called *anima*. As a deeply related and essentially connected aspect of life soul has a feminine quality that keeps us in touch with our deepest feelings and would have us longing and ready for continuous transformations.

In many ancient traditions a person was considered to have more than one soul. In addition to the immediacy of the personal "body soul," there could be a second soul that maintains a secret relationship with particular aspects of nature. Then, a specific bird or type of tree would become a living symbol of the individual soul and could provide an indelible connection to the soul of nature. This "second soul" could also be imagined as a flame on a candle capable of illuminating the darkness and lighting the way for the one who both carries it and is carried by it.

Tribal philosophies often connected the living soul to the breath in the body. Thus, fainting could be imagined as a momentary loss of soul, a slipping out of soul's palpable connections to this world. Dreaming could also be seen as the nightly adventures that the second soul undertakes while the body soul sleeps its sleep. Seen that way, our souls cannot help but be mysterious and mythic, multiple and mystical as well, for we are threaded through with dreams each night just as certainly as we exchange each breath we take with the breathing trees of nature.

We are double beings with eyes that see what is immediately and measurably before us and inner vision that can perceive all that remains undetected by the ordinary eye. Our dreams see with the other eyes, the mythical, mystical eyes of inner vision. Ancient myths in South America describe the dreaming soul as journeying to the center of the cosmos. When the body falls into sleep each night, the soul is said to travel all the way to its place of origin. As cosmic go-between the soul keeps each person secretly connected to the origins of life. Having arrived at the center, the soul receives a dream message to carry back to the dreamer sleeping back on earth.

Thus, the soul carries intimate messages between the center of the cosmos and the center of each person's life. Since each soul is uniquely shaped, the dreams must use images and language that the dreamer might recognize and learn to decipher. By attending to the steady flow of dream messages we can learn the inner lexicon and native language of our souls. At one level our dream life draws upon daily events in order to reveal subtleties of our current psychic condition. But the core of our dreaming seeks to reveal the driving myth and essential narrative that our soul brings to life. As inner cosmic connection the soul is the carrier of the living dream of one's life, the keeper of one's innermost imagination and the renewing force of one's being.

In imagining cosmological origins and cosmic connections of the soul, Siberian tribes describe a central, mystical tree of life with roots that descend deep into the underworld and great branches that stretch across the upper regions of the heavens. This mythic tree forms the unseen axis that connects heaven and earth. Human souls were said to rest upon this origin tree, perching upon its sky branches before descending to the earth to be born.

As yet unborn souls wait in silence, watching like birds until something in the world below intrigues them enough to cause a sudden descent. Pulled by a certain image down to the earthly realm, the bird-soul seeks to become incarnate and enters a womb where human life is about to be born. Some say that the descending soul chooses its parents as if intrigued with a specific drama already underway or set of issues entwined between those entwining souls. Some say it is the spirit of an ancestor seeking to be reborn in the family line. Others imagine the returning soul as having unfinished business or karmic residues that compel a return to earth.

However the cause for incarnation may be depicted, the soul brings to life a core pattern and essential imagination, a life-dream around which the body grows. The fact that the heart can suddenly flutter, that a person can be deeply and inexplicably moved, and the sense that each one born longs for something greater all serve as evidence of the bird-soul that remains within us, watching for opportunities to incarnate itself further and spread its wings on earth.

The First Agreement

A West African story relates what happens to the soul just before it enters the world of bodies moving in time and space. According to that old tale, the soul encounters a divine spirit as soon as it begins to move towards earthly life. This "divine twin" or "spirit familiar" clarifies the image that first moved the soul and describes the terms through which this particular life adventure will be shaped. That spirit becomes the inner companion that accompanies the soul on its journey through the realm of incarnate beings.

Compelled by the vision that first drew it to earth, informed by the knowledge just received, the soul enters into a lifelong agreement with its spirit companion. At the same time, the divine twin commits to travelling the road of life with the soul in order to protect the understanding they share together. Spirit and soul are on their way to join the body for the unique adventure of a lifetime.

At this point, the soul has not yet been born, but has agreed to live a certain kind of life once it arrives on earth. It has made its original agreement for coming to life and its first deal with the world. This first agreement becomes a kind of divine contract that binds each soul to a core imagination before it can enter the body and begin to live on earth. This original agreement and divine arrangement keeps each soul secretly connected to the eternal realm throughout its life on earth.

The original agreement with life affects an inner union of both worlds as it is the nature of the human soul to know both realms and feel the longing between them. The most genuinely human moments are moments in which the soul awakens to its original dream of life. In those moments of true awakening time, breaks apart and eternity seems near and the breath of the divine can be felt. In such moments the soul grows deeper and takes further root in this life, even as it may feel anew its secret connection to the tree of all life.

The human connection to the divine realm exists in the soul as a mystery that seeks its own unfolding. Any originality a person might display derives from the original agreement that the soul makes, and any enduring satisfaction a person might find will involve a reflection of the soul's first agreement with life.

No sooner has the first agreement been made than the soul is in motion again. In the close company of its companion and guide, the soul moves towards the womb of life. Before arriving there it comes upon a garden and finds itself standing before a radiant tree. Having recently departed from the world tree, the soul cannot help but embrace the tree that stands before it. The branches seem inviting and the soul feels moved to touch the tree the way people instinctively touch certain things as a charm or knock on wood for good luck. As soon as the soul touches the radiant tree it forgets the core image that first moved it towards life on earth and the essential agreement it has just made with the divine twin.

The mysterious tree of life has appeared again; this time it stands at the junction where the two worlds meet, but also diverge. The soul is about to leave the garden of eternity and cross over to the earthbound realm where time rules. By its cosmic and universal nature, the Tree of Life is connected to everything and that includes its own shadow and opposite side. As the Tree of Unity it is the unifying stem of all life; however, at the point of departure from the eternal realm, the Tree of Unity becomes the Tree of Forgetfulness.

Only after touching the other side of the Tree of Life can the soul be born into the incarnate world. Entering the common world means leaving the divine realm behind and forgetting the very thing that first moved it towards life as well as the original agreement just made with the divine twin. There is a central image and primary orientation towards life, but it has been forgotten in order that life on earth might begin. The rest of life will be a drama through which the soul attempts to remember why it came to life and what it agreed to do with its allotment of time on earth.

The act of forgetting what brought one to life is the original irony and enduring enigma of human existence. It is the unwritten rule and the original rite of passage for each soul that makes its way across the threshold that separates the timeless and the time-bound, the unified and the divided, the eternal and the temporal. Being born on this earth is both a begetting and a forgetting and what becomes forgotten is the very reason why each soul agreed to become embodied in the first place. The soul must depart from the place of primal unity in order to be born into a specific life story and the essence of that story involves the search for the lost unity.

After birth on earth, the divine realm becomes a deep memory; something that seems left behind, but also remains buried deep within us. Human experience begins when we enter this world, but human memory extends back before time and well beyond earthly limits. Were that not the case people would be more tame and less full of longings; they would be more easily satisfied and less likely to risk everything on a hope or a dream.

It is our human fate to become separated from the eternal and it is our individual destiny to search for the divine connection in the rampant confusions and strange delights of this world. We are never far from our original agreement and divine connection although it often seems the farthest thing from us. Regardless of outer appearances and contrary notions, each soul has its inner imagination that tries to return to full awareness through dreams and visions, through sudden insights and strange revelations. Inside each soul the core imagination and original intention wait to be found again and the life-dream waits to awaken fully.

Throughout the course of life the soul will create impossible dramas and persistent dilemmas in order to crack open the shell of the time-bound, little-self and reveal the living seed and the original agreement it carries within it. The soul needs an outer drama that can help awaken the inner myth that it carries and the first agreement it made with the divine realm. Although limited by time and shaped by its earthly allotment, the soul instinctively longs for a reunion with the eternal. It will seek to find and feel again the divine connection in religions and philosophies, in visions and in ecstasies, and in the person of parents and teachers, in lovers and in soul companions.

Original Agreement vs. Original Sin

Each loss in life can provoke an unearthly feeling of overwhelming separation from something essential and necessary. For the sense of separation from an earlier divine state is part of the collective, archetypal human story. The "loss of paradise" appears in many myths and finding it again has often been the driving force of human history and religion. The primal sense of separation from the divine realm has been seen as mankind's fall from grace and even as our original sin. The earthly realm has been termed a fallen world by many who see it as devoid of the presence of the divine.

By contrast, the ancient tale of the soul and its divine companion presents the "fall" as a necessary forgetting rather than a moral transgression or primal violation. Where some see the commission of a sin of disobedience, others perceive an omission that is necessary for life on earth to continue. Rather than a punishment for some original misdeed, the primary purpose of suffering in this world then becomes the labor pains needed to break open the divine seed set within the soul and recover the primary agreement that unites one world with the other.

The notion of a forgotten agreement places the divine connection as a living potential, ever present inside one's own life. Rather than giving us hope for redemption at the end of our lives, the underlying unity of life becomes a revelation waiting to be found in the soul at any moment. The essential struggle of the soul then revolves around a desire to awaken to one's inner nature rather than a moral struggle against it. That which is "second nature" to us will be our natural, instinctive, and intuitive connection to our first agreement in life.

In the soul, back and down, behind and within are the same thing, so that what seems lost in the distant past can be found in one's present depths. Finding the divine reconnection depends upon learning who we already are and have secretly agreed to be. Redemption becomes the step-by-step process through which people become who they already are within. Saving the fallen world depends less upon heroic causes and more upon awakening from within.

An old idea suggests that all knowledge comes from remembering, that true learning occurs when we recall what we formerly knew, but somehow forgot. This notion of knowledge as remembering is helpful when considering compelling images like the Tree of the Knowledge of Good and Evil in bible stories. Trees are potent archetypal images for the human soul and are often determining factors in spiritual thought. Didn't human struggles begin at that fateful apple tree; didn't the Buddha first struggle with darkness and awaken under a tree; don't Native Americans pierce themselves and hang from a symbolic tree to make things sacred again?

Another name for the tree said to be involved in the great fall was the Tree of Division, as if to say that the knowledge gained from the fruit of that tree involved awareness of all that was divided in this world. What is often forgotten is that the tree representing good and evil, like the Tree of Forgetfulness, was depicted as being at the edge of the divine garden. What is most often forgotten is that the tree of divisions and oppositions itself stood in direct contrast to the Tree of Life that grew at the center of the garden called Paradise.

Human life may begin at the place of troubling divisions and painful separations, but the goal of each life was to find a way past all the oppositions in order to touch the unifying Tree of Life again. Being born at the Tree of Division means separating from the original unity of life; being born again means beginning to awaken to the inner unity that the soul secretly knows. Life on earth begins with separation from the divine, but the divine connection is not lost altogether. Reaching the divine goal doesn't require departing from life on earth as much as awakening to the garden within the soul and remembering the unifying Tree of Life at the center of each life and all of life.

Seen this way, eating the forbidden fruit becomes a necessary evil, as awakening to the pain of separation is necessary to the process of remembering the primal unity and one's original connection to it. Recalling the soul's first agreement with the divine provides at least a temporary return to a sense of the underlying unity of life. Thus, life can suddenly seem like a dream and can become "heaven on earth." In awakening to the inner dream of life a person becomes a living, consciously witnessing bridge between the two worlds. Each moment of unity is a kind of redemption for both the individual and the world that is so often torn apart by conflicts and oppositions.

There is no objective proof of this; in fact, subjective and objective are aspects of the common state of division. Being born on earth means entering the world of separate things and divided energies, right and left as much as right and wrong. In many ways, people make a leap of faith every time they open their eyes. Those who require absolute proofs have not yet awakened to the unique story and inner truth seeded within their soul. Until some hint of the divine appears within, no outer proof can ever be found satisfactory or conclusive.

Second Agreements

Seen mythically, the moment of birth is both a beginning and a separation, both the start of life on earth and the end of the feeling of otherworldly unity experienced in the womb. The newborn arrives wailing, perhaps longing already for the otherworld, but certainly calling for help in this one. The struggle for nourishment and shelter, care and love begins immediately and a language must be found to express one's basic needs. In order to have essential needs met, a newborn must communicate and the only language it has is "body language." Body language and bodily needs take priority over all else as adaptation to the immediate situation takes precedence over all other considerations.

At the same time, the mystery of life causes the human infant to remain in secret sublime contact with the otherworld through the open center at the top of the head. The original agreement of the soul is there, but daily life and common concerns soon close around it. The newborn must become a child of time, a member of a family, a witness to history, and a recipient of a cultural inheritance before the time comes for the first agreement to be recalled. In order for the infant to survive, to grow and become a viable person, the first agreement of the soul must become a secondary issue of life.

In order to participate in the flow of life each person must make a series of agreements that include family and friends as well as society and its institutions. This complex array of "second agreements" is necessary for individual life and for the human species to continue. The process of making second agreements begins with the subtle negotiations with one's mother. Finding ways to relate to one's father is also necessary as each child seeks to secure a place in the family arrangement.

For some, adapting to life means agreeing to be quiet and undemanding, while others are expected to speak up and demand exactly what they want, even cry for it. Some receive special treatment for being first-born, while others are resented for coming at the wrong time or in the wrong way. Some will have to steal whatever they need, while others will be given more than they can ever use. Each will negotiate in necessary ways and each will make a variety of deals in order to simply fit in, in order to receive some attention, and in order to play a part in the drama of existence.

When childhood comes to an end, new agreements must be made with parents and with the community or else the young person will always be treated as a child. Separation must occur exactly where union was once so desperately sought. The parents also have a need to renegotiate agreements with their grown children; both have an increasing need to be on their own. At the confusing and necessary threshold of youth, all the agreements between parents and child must be renegotiated or both will suffer unnecessarily and each will feel diminished.

Second agreements are the necessary negotiations made between one's soul and the "facts of life," between one's deepest desires and the reality of one's circumstances. Since second agreements originate in the realm of time, they tend to be "time sensitive." Each new stage of life and each critical turning point involves new agreements and additional negotiations with the forces of life. Genuine growth requires renegotiation of all the second agreements or else meaningful change will not occur and life becomes stuck. Change and the negotiations that it requires are a fact that underlies all the facts of life.

Intimacy with family and friends is essential and can be a great solace amidst life's slings and arrows, but even the closest relationships must be renegotiated at times. One cannot remain as a child and still be true to oneself. No one can be a true friend who fails to recognize how friendship changes and grows and requires different loyalties over time. All human relations need occasional adjustments and need essential renegotiation when life calls for critical changes.

Genuine changes involve the secret pull of one's original agreement. Truly stepping up to the challenge of life requires renegotiation of prior arrangements and agreements. Whether it be a great opportunity knocking or a blow that lays one low, critical junctures and meaningful changes in life become the crucible through which the first agreement of the soul tries to awaken within and return to our awareness. Since the original agreement was made before we were born, it antedates and supersedes all other agreements in our lives. In the long run, and it is the long run that our eternal souls are concerned with, all second agreements become negotiable and "all contracts are made to be broken."

Non-Negotiable, Indelible, Unchanging

The one exception to the rule is the first agreement of one's life; the original agreement that our souls made before our first breath was taken is non-negotiable. The first agreement is indelible in the soul; it is the source of our deepest capacity to change, but it does not change. The original agreement of the soul is life shaping and life defining. Without it we can be like anyone else; when in touch with it we can't help but be who we were originally intended to be.

Despite meaningful responsibilities to others, the first agreement remains the primary obligation and deepest responsibility of the soul. The first agreement is the inner dream of our soul, the pattern that brought us to life in the first place, and the core imagination waiting to awaken and blossom from within. Because it involves the divine source of our lives as well as the aim of our individual existence, the first agreement cannot be dismissed or replaced. It may be neglected, but it cannot be substituted for; it cannot be traded in for another dream or exchanged for a better deal. It is the original deal we made with life and presents our only chance at having a truly meaningful life. For us, it is the real deal, the only deal. If we try to bargain our way out of it or try to compromise with what it requires of us, we simply double-cross ourselves.

The original agreement with the creative force of life is what drives the soul's greatest longings. It feeds ambitions and drives heroic fantasies; it inspires acts of love as well as occasions of nobility. Although it is forgotten at birth, remains mostly invisible in childhood, and may be denied throughout one's life, the first agreement cannot be erased from the soul. It is the agreement that must be kept and all other agreements must be renegotiated in order that we keep it.

The first agreement is a living echo in the soul that calls us to a greater life than we might otherwise seek. As the essential inner text of the soul, it becomes the context through which each person's talents can best be delivered. As divine contract it is the basis for one's true vocation and source of one's essential calling in life. Each person arrives in this life with a calling; what calls to us is also a re-calling of the divine agreement made before earthly life began. Unfortunately, what the first agreement calls us to become is frequently at odds with what our second agreements seem to require.

In the sleight of hand enacted by the hand of fate, the first and second agreements are typically at odds with each other. The tension between the first agreement of the soul and the second agreements that life requires places each person in a double bind. Both involve matters of necessity as each person is bound to the eternal as well as subject to the immediate pressures of time and place and social conditions. The two agreements make each person a "double being." Each person is a citizen of both worlds; each a descendant of eternity and each a child of time. Being fully human means being double-minded and often means being at odds within oneself.

Each soul lives on the verge of remembering the forgotten agreement and original dream that it carries; yet each moment can be another point when the dream of life becomes lost again. Each meaningful step we take on the path of life involves some tension between the needs of the common world and the dreams of the soul. This inherent tension can stop us in our tracks, yet can also be the source of vital energy needed for the soul to grow. Each time we remember a piece of why we came to life we pull the seeds of eternity farther into the world of time. The inner seed keeps trying to sprout, but often our fate must place us in a crossroads or nail us to a cross before we pay proper attention to it.

The Divine Twin

In the tale of the origin of the soul the divine twin also enters a primary agreement when it commits to accompanying the soul on its life adventure. As guardian angel and natural voice of one's innermost conscience, the divine twin remembers the pattern etched in our souls and continually recalls us to its essential message and aim. The old Latin name for the inner spirit that can guide one's life was the *genius*; the Greek term for the same divine presence was the *daimon*.

Since the ancient Greek word for happiness was *eudaimonia*, it could be deduced that something deeper than simple pleasure was being considered. True happiness could be found by satisfying the *daimon*, the living spirit in one's soul. Being truly happy depends upon living close to the pattern woven in the soul. For that satisfies the genius in us and makes some level of spiritual fulfillment possible here on earth.

The genius or daimon appears as an "intermediary," a betwixt–and–between figure that occupies the space between the human soul and the divine source of life. As divine twin it is responsible to the original agreement, as "spirit familiar" it is most familiar with our core pattern and more familiar with our purpose in life than we are. As an inner resident of the soul and keeper of one's life-dream, the daimon knows best which way we should turn when we find ourselves at a crossroads in life. Being close to the essential dream of our life, the daimon can be seen as another aspect of the complex arrangement of one's fate and destiny.

If we allow for a nearby realm of indeterminate things, we leave room for the guiding spirit that knows the true nature of our inner nature. We participate in such a "daimonic relationship" when we respond to intuitions and hunches, for the inner spirit can act like a resident oracle speaking from within at crucial moments. Whether we term it a guardian angel or a "little bird that told me," the inner guide tends to move with the subtlety of wings. An idea or image suddenly appears, seemingly arisen from nowhere. Should we hesitate before the unseen, doubt too much or require definitive proof, the inner oracle goes quiet. Like a dream, the subtle sense of inner guidance can disappear and slip back into the unconscious, only returning when a greater crisis brings it near again.

This inner guiding spirit is commonly dismissed in the modern world where hard facts and exact measurements determine reality. The sense of a subtle space between one thing and another gave ancient people a greater sense of the continuity of all of life. Nature could be experienced as the realm of spirit and mystery, a natural screen through which the unseen might become manifest at any moment. People lived closer to the mystery of life and side by side with the "invisibles." What most now define as nature was then seen as the closest thing to the supernatural as well.

Whenever things become too far divided and too firmly separated, some of the essential in-between, either-or aspects that give the world continuity are being lost. In losing a felt sense for the mystery that is always nearby, we lose some of the connecting tissue of life and feel more isolated in the world. In dividing the world into stark opposites and endless defining categories, the subtle realm of those things that are neither one thing nor another has been lost. In losing such subtleties we also lose touch with our own souls which are part of the there-not-there realm.

The insistence on the division of the world into an opposition of subject and object reduces the subtleties and complexities of life just as it falsely divides literature into fact or fiction. Neither life nor literature can be divided so simply; the separation of fact and fiction is itself as much a fiction as it is a fact. Much of what people fervently believe to be the absolute truth one day turns out to be patently false. Much of what might be dismissed as fictional with no actual basis in fact turns out to be true. Subject and object are only two parts of a greater mystery that cannot in the end be reduced to simple opposites or be solved with a single-minded point of view.

When the in-between things and intermediary factors are dismissed simply because they defy categorization, then the parts fail to add up to the whole. Wholeness includes all the parts, even the invisible aspects and the mysterious elements that defy definition but refuse to be dismissed. The intermediaries hold the continuity between nature and culture just as they form the connections between the human and the divine. Without the living sense of the betwixt-and-between we not only lose touch with our inner sense of fate and destiny, but the human community becomes isolated from the soul of the world.

The Genius of the Soul

Whether it be called a guardian angel or an inner muse, a divine twin or the genius within us, the resident spirit of the soul gives each person a unique way of perceiving life. Genius and its older form *genii* refer to the "spirit that is already there;" an exact shape and often exacting quality that is native to them. The inner genius marks not simply the exceptional person within the norm, but more importantly the style through which each person can escape the dull trap of normality. For each person has genius and each genius presents its own "norm" and unique inner ethic.

As indigenous inner spirit, the genius is the source of our true identity; however, should it fail to be recognized, it will create great identity problems. Through the presence of the inner genius we are called and recalled to the first agreement of our souls; we are pulled and stretched and driven until we enter and accept the grip of our destiny. The genius within can inspire a person to reach great heights or, being rejected, can distort whatever the person might touch in life. Fulfilling an individual destiny involves the revelation of one's genius as well as the development of the character needed to carry it to the world.

As resident spirit in the soul the genius combines the inherent gifts and talents with inner inclinations and a style of being that together shape one's character from within. Genius appears as an original arrangement of subjective qualities, an inner pattern that holds the keys to understanding the meanings and purpose inherent in each life. At critical moments, people must follow the rule that reflects the inner constellation of their soul or they will "miss their star" and "follow the wrong gods home."

The resident spirit of one's life acts as the guardian of one's true destiny. It is the inner tutor and intuitive guide that can be cultivated by paying attention to the little voice inside oneself. In crucial moments the inner spirit or muse of the soul will offer its guidance, but we must first learn to hear its language. Although the genius is a natural inhabitant of our lives, general education and social training can make us deaf to its speech.

In tribal lore, the helping spirits can often be hostile when first encountered. The individual must undergo initiatory experiences that open the inner eyes and ears of the soul. Although native to a person, the genius must often be won over and a psychological container must be shaped in order for it to become useful. Remember the old fairy tale of the Spirit in the Bottle? It was a great *genie* that was trapped in a bottle caught in the roots of an ancient tree. It could become the source of amazing gifts, but it caused great trouble once it was first released.

As the tale goes, a young student went into an ancient forest looking for signs of rare birds. He came upon a great and compelling tree, so large that it could have been the tree at the center of the world. The youth thought he heard a tiny voice that seemed to come from the roots of the ancient oak. Looking amongst the roots he found a strange bottle; holding it up to the light he could see a little being inside it. Out of curiosity he opened the bottle and released a huge and powerful spirit that loomed above him.

Instead of thanking the youth for its release, the genie from the bottle roared angrily and threatened him, expressing great rage for having been bottled up too long. In order to save his life the youth had to devise a way to trick the powerful spirit back into the little vessel. Only after the genie became contained again did it agree to be of service to the young seeker. In order to be released again, the spirit offered to reward him with magical gifts. Once in possession of the gifts the student found the true path of his life and eventually became a great healer.

He was but wandering through life until he encountered the hidden genie. Of course, *genie* is another word for genius and it was the rare bird of the spirit that the young student instinctively went searching for. It was his own bottled-up genius that needed to be released in order to begin the great adventure of his life. Like young Poder, he had to learn how to hold and use the gifts that were waiting to be found. If the inner spirit could simply be commanded, it would not be much of a genius. In this case, he had to trick the spirit back into the bottle and learn how to handle its power before he could derive any benefit from its presence.

There it is in a nutshell, maybe more accurately in an acorn, for the tree where the gifts became revealed was an old oak. Oaks were sacred trees in ancient Europe and the acorn was considered to have an entire tree folded within it. Each seed could produce an entire tree; since each seed was unique, so was the life within it waiting to unfold. The acorn was a primary image for the seed of life waiting to awaken and unfold from within each soul. The "acorn theory" suggested that viewing one's life from its later stages could reveal the nature of the inner spirit trying to be released and find its way into the world.

As in the African tale of the soul's origins, the inner guide and spirit companion appears in connection with a remarkable tree. The words *tree* and *truth* happen to grow from the same roots and the inner guide and divine companion would keep us close to the truth and the inner pattern of the life trying to grow out of our souls. At a mythic level, true liberation involves learning the inner language of one's soul and being able to release the inner spirit in one's life. Unfolding the story within the seed also requires that we learn some tricks of the trade and develop enough character to contain the spirit that carries us as much as we carry it.

Fairy tales were once called "fated tales" and the word *fate* shares roots with *fairy* and *fee* and other elements that enchant us from within. Fairy tales deal with fateful issues such as problems at one's birth; or spells that keep a person asleep; or curses that must be defied if life is to progress and love is to prosper. We also live within spells and near wonders like the characters in fairy tales. We know it when as children we desire to hear certain stories over and over again. Folk and fairy tales contain images that preview issues we are fated to struggle with throughout our lives.

Like the young student we wander in search of the rare bird of our own spirit. We cannot become who we truly are unless the genius in us becomes recognized and released. If we keep the inner spirit bottled up too long it can turn against us and make our lives miserable. If we accept it as we find it and learn to work with it, everything changes. Spells are broken, gifts are revealed and our talents serve their true purpose. The genius can fill us with power and vital energy, yet it can also overwhelm us and fragment our lives.

While in the grip of the genius we can experience a sense of release, but we can also find ourselves being mercilessly driven. That's why there are so many old warnings about shining too soon and flaming out. As they used to say, the first problem is that we do not know what our genius in life might be. That leaves us bereft of meaning and genuine purpose in life. The second problem occurs when we do come to know the nature of our inborn genius. That produces the inevitable problem of how to handle the inner powers and gifts of the soul. Being by nature divine, the inner spirit can place "inhuman" demands upon us. Where there is genius there will always be issues of character and containment.

The Problem of Tuning In

We are each imbued with a resident spirit and called to a divine connection; that is the source of the longing that eternally plagues and delights the human soul. The real problem is not that people lack a life calling, for each soul is seeded within and called to something meaningful. The typical problem is that the calling comes in unpredictable and often surprising ways. Since the genius is essentially connected to the uniqueness in one's soul, the calling comes to each uniquely. There is no overall pattern and no general map to follow. Despite notions of a hero's journey with distinct steps, each calling comes with its own map that inevitably takes us off the expected pathways.

Responding to the call involves learning to listen to what is within and tuning into the presence of the spirit companion as well as finding ways to release its vital life energy. In the tale of the Spirit in the Bottle, the student receives great riches from working with the genius; he also becomes a great healer. In other words, there is healing involved as well as following a true calling in life.

Like the genie in the story, the resident spirit of the soul must be won over before it can become helpful to its host. Of necessity, we have secondary agreements that distract us from reconnecting to our original agreement and proper aim in life. The inborn spirit of our soul tends to be at odds with the ego or "little self" that develops to meet the immediate demands of the world around us. Eventually, we must loosen our ego attitudes and make room for the greater vision and more subtle scope of our own genius.

If the spirit companion within us is rejected or ignored for too long it can change from a beneficial daimon to an inner demon. The angel on one's shoulder can become a "little devil" that gets a person into the wrong trouble. Many an inner demon was once a guiding spirit that was bottled up too long. Many a genius has turned against its host as a result of the ego-self persistently turning away from the genuine orientation of the soul. What can bring us to spiritual fulfillment and *eudaimonia* can also demonize us from within. The demons that haunt us most are the perverse spirits that develop when we turn our backs on our natural inclinations and innate way of being in this world.

When it comes to issues of the divine, there can be no neutral condition; either we serve the "higher purpose" seeded within us or else foster a distortion of it that can become demonic. Until we tune to the inner voice of spirit and bend to the roots of our being we remain lost in the great forest of life. If we do manage to find and release the resident genius in our lives it does not mean that all our troubles are over. The genius of the soul would set us to the hardest task among all those tasks not actually impossible for us to accomplish. The resident spirit and divine companion is also the "taskmaster of the soul" that demands that we become fully alive and grow our soul until we stand like an old tree; until we learn to bend amidst the great storms of life and branch out and produce more seeds that grow more trees.

The resident spirit is the keeper of the inner pattern and the root of memory in the soul. It remembers what is essential to us yet is most often forgotten by us. Following the lead of one's inner spirit leads us to the aspects of the divine most in tune with our individual soul. Without being tuned into a genuine calling we are simply blind wanderers and dissatisfied customers on the roads of life. Once we receive a calling that resonates with the pattern woven within us we wander rightly, we find a path and enter a pilgrimage that suits our soul. Such a life-path requires that we risk ourselves continually in order to find ourselves more fully. The path may lead us far from all that we know, yet it can also to lead us to the dream at the center of our souls.

CHAPTER 7

THE FEET OF DREAMS

The soul is the beginning of all things.
It is the soul that lends all things movement.
                                    Plotinus

Each night dreams pound on the roofs of our lives like stars tearing at the darkness within us. They speak a language improvised just for us as they provoke and whisper, warn and even threaten in order to awaken us from the sleep of our common lives. They burn with information about the way our soul would incline us to live. They flicker in the night and settle in the soul's deep labyrinth only to revive and intensify when we approach major turning points in life. Our dreams are the nightly evidence that we remain part of the great drama and continuous pageant that the soul requires; for each soul is extravagant when it dreams.

We receive the strangely coded messages intended for us night after night; yet most fail to follow where their dreams might lead. Many drown in the commotion of life simply because they refuse to awaken to a dream they carry from birth. Many trade the dream that brought them to life for a life someone else dreams up for them. Yet the dream of the soul will continue to pull at the threads of our lives even when we dismiss it from our daily attention. For we are threaded through with the stuff of dreams; each person is a body wrapped around a soul imbued with a dream trying to awaken from within.

Despite the modern insulation of facts and statistics, at our core we still live in the dreamtime of deep imagination. Despite obsessions with rationality and narrow logic, our nightly dreaming sustains a vital connection to the great mysteries of life. Each life, knowingly or not, participates in the mystery of ongoing creation; for each is made of "such stuff as dreams are made of." We are tied to the unseen with the holy thread of dreams and cannot be whole or be holy unless we are somehow in touch with the dream trying to awaken us from within.

Dreams are both a universal human experience and an intimate mystery for each dreamer. The old argument goes back and forth: is a person most awake while walking about or more truly awake while dreaming? Is genuine awakening found by simply waking from night's realm of sleep or by waking up to the dream that is trying to live within one's life? What many call their "waking life" can also be seen as sleepwalking. Blindly going through the paces of life is not the same as following a dream or having a true calling and finding meaning in this broken world.

In dreams the mystery of life comes alive within us as we are carried to a necessary realm beyond the laws of gravity and the grasp of time. As dreamers we can be any age at all, appear young again or older than we have ever been. In dreams we change genders and have careers we are unqualified for; we run with horses and suffer nightmares, fly above our earthly cares or teeter on the edge of a bottomless pit. A dream can take almost any shape, just as we can shape-shift within it. Yet there is a dream behind the dreams, a dream woven into the cells of our being; it holds us close to a core pattern and unique message that our lives are intended to deliver to the waking world.

It is a dream or dream-like image that first calls the soul to life, and one's "calling" in life can come from a dream or seem like a dream. Those who awaken to a genuine calling stand at the junction of the dream and the waking world. For the dream of our life would connect us consciously and distinctly to both worlds and give us better vision in each. Dreams may arrive in the depths of sleep, but they intend to wake us up. Being fully awake means to become able to see and follow the dream of one's life wherever it might lead. Awakening means more than simply waking; it requires stepping out of the daydream offered to us and entering the greater dream that called us here to begin with.

Following that kind of dream means bowing to some mystery that knows us better than we know ourselves. The dream sewn within our soul calls us to awaken to another life already existing within us. It is the life we have received that must be risked again and again in order to find the life we came to live. The shape of such a dream speaks volumes about the soul of the dreamer. When in touch with the thread of our life-dream we know where we are going, even if we have never been there before.

It's like the story of the man who had the same dream three times over. He was an unassuming person who lived simply amidst common people in the village where they had all been born. Eisik, for that was his name, awoke one day from a dream in which a voice spoke clearly to him and told him to leave all he knew and all he had behind. The dream voice instructed him to leave his home and travel to a distant city. Upon arriving there he was to seek for a certain bridge and dig at the foot it. Buried there, he would discover a great treasure of gold.

When that dream came knocking on the roof of his little house it seemed so outlandish that he thought it foolish to take it seriously. At first he dismissed the strange voice that called to him to change his life completely. It was a wild dream; it didn't fit with his settled ways and it unsettled him to have such a dream. He had come to expect little enough from life and he had little trust in the world beyond the village he knew so well. So the dreamer ignored the dream and refused to heed the voice calling him to another life. After all, it was just a dream and his life felt real and solid and predictable, even if a little empty at times. He went about his chores and did his daily work; he lived the life he already had and said nothing about the strange voice calling him to change.

After a time the same dream came again. Just as before, the voice told the dreamer to leave all he knew in order to seek for a golden treasure at a distant bridge. Eisik wondered at the repetition of the same strange message. His life seemed squarely at odds with the dream and he wondered why it should come to him of all people. But there is no simple measure for the heart or for the soul inside a person, and a big dream can come to anyone at any time.

Eisik became less easy as he went about his familiar tasks. He became unable to dismiss the night message and less able to contain it within himself. One day he couldn't help but mention the dream to his friends. They dismissed it out of hand and reminded him who he really was and where he belonged. Of course, they thought he belonged where he already was, right where he had been his entire life and right where they all found themselves. Besides, it was just a dream and everyone knew that real life was a different matter and that it mattered more than dreams.

Dreams are a deeply intimate matter and no one else can hear the voice that calls from within our dreams. A great dream will separate us from others in order to unite us with something otherworldly within us. Telling others about it can make things worse; especially if those we tell never listen to the voice calling to them. In that case, they will resent us for reminding them of their unlived dreams. Some friends will instinctively support the dream in one's life, while others will deny any possibility of it coming true. Those who have long buried their own dreams cannot afford to invest in the dreams of others.

Hearing the Call

Eisik did not mention the dream again and nothing more was said of the voice that calls to life beyond what people commonly admit and allow to be present. Meanwhile, a dream can become a leavening agent working inside the dough of one's life. Eisik found that he could no longer dismiss the feelings and longings that began to rise within him as a result of his dream. He wasn't a greedy person, but the notion of a treasure waiting to be found stirred something deep within him. Time went steadily by; dreams pounded nightly on the roofs of the village, the night sky swirled with the milk of churning stars. And secretly, Eisik's soul sang of treasures that only he could find.

When the same dream came again Eisik could not ignore the message. The third time can be a charm and he could no longer deny that he had been called and had in fact heard the call. Although facing the unknown was fearful to him, remaining in the blind safety of his existing life began to present another kind of fear. Eisik worried over leaving everything he had behind and abandoning everyone he knew; yet he feared never knowing if his dream could be true.

The call that awakens the soul to a greater vision also stirs one's deepest fears. The little-self we call "our self" resists our true calling for it fears being overwhelmed by something greater than itself. The little-self fears failing and being rejected and typically prefers a familiar pain to an unknown joy. Yet there are times when the only security comes from taking the right risk in life; sometimes letting go is the only way to go.

Eisik found himself in the crux of life where he had everything to lose, but had everything to gain. The time comes when a greater life calls to us and existing ties must be cut. After all, a human being grows from more than one umbilical. Someone must cut the cord at the time of our birth or we cannot breathe. Later in life we must learn to cut the cords that bind us ourselves or fail to learn the reason for our existence in this world.

Eventually, Eisik left all he knew behind in order to follow wherever his dream might lead. One day, with nothing but the clothes on his back and the echo of the dream in his heart, he left his village and left behind all that he knew. He left all that he held dear in life in order to hold his own life more dearly. He put one foot in front of the other and entered the great adventure of his life. There was no certainty that he would ever arrive at the goal. He had no guide, no map, and no description other than the dream he carried as it carried him. He became a pilgrim with nothing to hold at all except the dream of the life he was called to find. Eisik walked out of one life to find another; he became lost in order to find himself.

Long before he ever reached the bridge he dreamed of, Eisik crossed a bridge within himself that shifted his life and opened it to the unseen world that is always just before us. Eisik joined the long line of dreamers and searchers and seekers that stretches back before time began. He set out on the road of dreams and having no other way to travel he walked on his own two feet. When the road became long he kept walking on. He walked so long that he wore through the soles of his shoes. His clothes became worn and covered with the dust of the road. For, it is hard to keep up appearances and follow one's dream at the same time.

The journey was hard at times and lonely and he felt unprepared for such a long endeavor. Having left those who doubted him behind, he found a deep uncertainty within himself. He began to doubt the validity of the dream's promise as well as his ability to see it through. Eisik became enveloped in a cloud of doubt that had been within him all along. He felt naked and exposed and he feared that others could see right through him and judge him to be a fool on a fool's mission.

The Journey Owns You

A certain kind of courage is required to follow what truly calls to us; why else would so many choose to live within false certainties and pretensions of security? If genuine treasures were easy to find this world would be a different place. If the path of dreams were easy to walk or predictable to follow many more would go that route. The truth is that most prefer the safer paths in life even if they know that their souls are called another way.

What truly calls to us is beyond what we know or can measure. It uses the language of hidden treasures and distant cities to awaken something sleeping within us. The soul knows that we must be drawn out of ourselves in order to truly become ourselves. Call it a dream or "the treasure hard to attain;" call it a vocation or the awakening of one's innate genius. Call it what you will, upon hearing the call we must follow or else lose the true thread of our lives.

A true vocation requires shedding anything that would impede or obscure the call. A true pilgrimage requires letting go of the very things most people try to hold onto. In seeking after what the soul desires we become pilgrims with no home but the path the soul would have us follow. As the old proverb says, "Before you begin the journey, you own the journey. Once you have begun, the journey owns you." After all, what good is a dream that doesn't test the mettle of the dreamer? What good is a path that doesn't carry us to the edge of our capacity and then beyond that place? A true calling involves a great exposure before it can become a genuine refuge.

In the soul's adventure we become a self unknown, a self unexpected, and in that way we find the greater self within us. Answering the call gives primacy to unknown places and foreign lands; it requires that we seek farther in the world than we would choose on our own. We enter our essential "creatureliness" and learn to sniff at the world again. We learn to read the wind and find our way by sensing and intuiting, by imagining and by dreaming on. Eventually, the dream of the soul becomes the only hope; it becomes a prayer and a map as well. In allowing the journey to "have us" we become lost; we lose our usual selves in order to find our original self again. Lost souls are the only ones who ever get found.

Meanwhile, in order to get a toehold in life most people follow plans made by others. Most people follow maps that have been made by others in order to avoid getting lost in life. They forget the old proverb that states: "It is better to be lost than to follow a map made by tourists." Those who fail to find and follow the dream of their life remain but tourists in this world, visitors who never fully buy into the essence of the life they have been given. The real adventures in life begin where and when we step off the beaten paths and enter unmarked territories.

Most educational paths simply follow where others have gone, most careers aim at obvious goals. Yet the soul has its own essential agreement with life and its own course to follow. The design set in the soul has more value in the long run than any plan cooked up by one's ego or career sanctioned by one's culture. Meanwhile, life arranges things so that all of us, young or old, eventually arrive at a point in time where the map we have been given does not match the territory we find ourselves in.

We are each Eisik in our own way; each called to an adventure that we cannot control and would best surrender to. We live on the edge of an errand that the divine sent us on and that our dreams try to indicate. Such a soulful errand necessarily involves a long road with twists and turns that can't be anticipated. Many things are lost along the way; especially we must lose any fixed notions about ourselves and about the true nature of this world. The reason for undertaking the soul's adventure is to become completely other than who we have been so far.

The greater life requires that we shed the false self that is fashioned simply for allowing us to fit in and get along. So the map of self-discovery leads away from the goal before ever turning to it. Until we become properly lost we have no way of knowing why we are alive. We must go missing to be found, become lost in the world, washed in the unknown, wrapped in confusion and hidden even from ourselves before we can find what we are truly aimed at.

If we could arrive in the same condition as when we departed, there would be no reason to go. If the genuine way was simple and straightforward, no vision would be required, no dream would be needed and no one's soul would be truly tested. If we could go directly there, there would be no *there* when we arrive there. Everyone would set out and arrive directly; no need to have one's assumptions defeated or one's illusions shattered. Point A would simply lead to point B and we would arrive just as we were when we began. That may be the desired effect when making regular travel plans, but it can't be the aim when seeking a greater life.

People say that what we seek to find in the world already resides in ourselves; there's truth in that, yet only after reaching some extreme limit can we locate what we carry all along. The necessary resources may lie within, yet we must go far out into the world before we learn how to trust what resides within. What we search for is both part of us and other to us; it is an "other that is also us," an "other self" that is the true self hidden within us. Before we can learn the other within us, we must experience the otherness around us. The hardest thing to trust in this world tends to be our own self.

The Divine Is Calling

Each life involves an essential errand, an adventure beyond the task of survival, a life-mission imbedded in the soul waiting for us to submit to it. In this life a pious journey is required. It is pious in the sense that a genuine path brings out our devotion, but also because it cleanses and clarifies our sense of self. The result may be pious, yet the process may look and feel like a stripping down to bare bone. From the common comforts, we must go to the edge of life; from simple self-assurance we must go to the extremes of our nature.

The inner thread of one's vocation began in the otherworld and it will lead us in that direction again. Each life is a once-in-a-lifetime experiment through which we attempt to decipher the errand the gods have sent us on. Any true calling has something of the divine in it; for our dreams and visions are given by the divine and the gods have an interest in the paths we take in this world. As the old saying suggests, "each person imitates as best he can the god in whose choir he belongs."

What waits to be found in the stumbling of each life are the divine connections that the soul already carries. This is not the pronouncement of a religious doctrine or the issue of believing in god or not. It is more a matter of recognizing that something divine is behind the whole thing and hidden within us as well. The point is not to prove or disprove the existence of one god or another; the point is to answer the call and learn where the divinely designed path might lead.

From the view of the soul, having a calling is not a matter of choice or just another option in the plan of life; finding one's calling is a great necessity. Until people hear the call they have no idea where they stand in this world. They may inherit wealth or gain great status, yet will have no genuine ground to stand upon and nothing to truly offer to others. Failing to answer the call of one's soul means living an unexplored life; it also means dying without having fully lived.

People say that "many are called but few are chosen." See it another way; each receives a calling, yet most choose not to hear. The usual problem in life is not the lack of a calling; the problem is usually a refusal to answer the call. The true problem is not the lack of a career, but the absence of a genuine vocation capable of provoking one's genius and inspiring one's heart. Out of fear of failing or being seen as foolish, most refuse to listen to what calls to them. Many go to the grave complaining of a bad fate, unjust treatment and great disappointments. The real appointment involves encounters with one's own destiny and each true destination involves something divine.

The lack of a genuine calling is the cause of great anguish and deep disorientation. Life can seem pointless and meaningless unless a divine connection and true vocation can be found. Of course, the second great problem involves hearing the call and answering it. Those who are called often look more lost than those who remain deaf to the whisperings of the soul and the voices of dreams. Answering such a call requires that we become both less and more than we appear to be.

Divine errands are intended to change how we see the world altogether and how we see ourselves almost entirely. Too many fixed beliefs, whether they consist of personal evaluations or religious doctrines, just get in the way. Inside the soul our god-given gifts, natural talents, and endless imagination wait to awaken and be put to greater use. In answering the call we learn how we are threaded and where we are aimed. Not responding to the call that comes to us leaves the soul aching and makes the mind anxious. Failing to heed the call can cause a depression of the spirit; for both spirit and soul are poised to respond and both are expecting the call.

The problem in most situations is not a lack of calling; but a fear of responding to the call. Besides the issue of leaving everything behind there is also the fear of being inadequate and the terror of being overwhelmed. Under the banner of practicality, most of life becomes arranged to obscure and distract us from what called us to come to life in the first place. Most people remain unwilling to be extravagant enough to wander where their soul would lead them, adapting instead to an endless series of short-term goals. People easily misplace their deepest longings and tune themselves to someone else's idea of life.

Eisik went another way. He turned away from all he knew in order to learn what the world was trying to say to him. He finally heard the call and joined the ranks of wanderers and vagrants who follow dreams and visions seeking something beyond the obvious levels of life. Like the seekers of old, Eisik became "god-struck;" not caught up in religious issues, but more responsive to hints of the divine. Eisik found himself on a divine errand that stirred all his doubts and raised all his fears in order that his soul might breathe and his heart might open.

Eisik was not a young man when he answered the call; yet it was the youngest part of him that took up the dream of his life. It is the eternal youth within us that responds to the dream no matter what age the dreamer may be. The youngest part of the psyche tends to be in touch with what is being newly imagined as well as what has been long forgotten. Certain aspects of the soul remain youthful and foolish in just the right way throughout one's life. The youngest part of the psyche is the true dreamer within us and the part of us closest to wising up to the true purpose of our life.

Remember all those youngest brothers and youngest sisters in fairy tales? Like the student in the Spirit in the Bottle tale, they wander off the beaten paths and listen when strange voices or animals talk to them. The dreamer within each of us is like them; an essential part of us is given to lapses and subject to strange visions. Under the rules of the daily world, that part of us is deemed to be stupid, foolish or mad, too dreamy or spiritual to be useful. Yet in the old stories when everyone else falls under some collective spell and life becomes stuck, it is the youngest one who stumbles into the solution and finds the path that redeems everyone.

Often they save the day by bringing forth a new imagination or else by reviving an old tradition that had been long overlooked or unwisely discarded. Only the youngest aspects of the psyche and the most ancient parts are foolish enough to question all the assumptions and conventions that pass for knowledge in this world of illusions and delusions.

The youngest brother-sister represents the spiritual side of the self, but also the great longings of the soul. While other parts of the persona seek careers and alliances in the outer world, the youngest part longs for the touch of healing and the breath of inspiration. Being too weird or dreamy to be of use, it becomes the forgotten part of us. Yet it remembers the dream hidden within us and understands how the right kind of foolishness can lead to genuine wisdom.

Whether we heed the call during youth. or it finally reaches us later in life, the calling is heard by the eternally young part of our soul. The eternal youth within us follows the threads of dreams; it sees with visionary eyes and trusts in unseen forces. Given half a chance the youngest sister or brother in the psyche knows how to connect to the dream and use it to sustain the entire life project. That part of the soul remains closer to nature and to animals because it remains tuned to our inner nature. Each time a crossroads appears in a person's life, the youngest part of the soul tries to awaken further in the psyche.

Younger and Wiser For It

The dream of one's life often seems the most extravagant thing one could possibly do and often a dangerous thing to attempt as well. *Extravagant* means "to wander outside or beyond," especially to wander outside the limits and beyond the rules we set for ourselves. For each human life is an experiment on the part of the divine and each soul is an extravagance produced by the greater dream of life. Each soul is on a lifelong pilgrimage and the secret object of every pilgrimage is the center of the pilgrim.

People set off to a famous shrine; they seek to enter a holy place or arrive at a natural wonder. The point seems to be to reach that distant destination and somehow be renewed and confirmed by the experience. Yet any renewal that happens must happen within the pilgrim and can only happen when the center of the self becomes awakened by the ardor of the effort or by the grace of the unseen. We may set out to reach a shrine or spiritual center, but we fully arrive only when we reach the center of ourselves.

A genuine path must lead us to the center of our own life; for our life is a pilgrimage to find our awakened self. Anything that awakens us is a call from the divine whatever shape it may take. The awakening that turns a journey into a true pilgrimage can occur anywhere along the way, even on the way back from the supposed destination. Any step that leads to the center of the soul is itself a pilgrimage and a full journey. The awakening occurs whenever and wherever the little-self finally surrenders and the original self becomes evoked. For the soul arrives with its own rhythm and in its own time.

The calling that calls to us aims at awakening and sustaining the weird way we each are shaped and aimed from within. That seems foolish to others, especially to those who have forsaken their own dreams. Yet those who avoid the uniqueness of their own lives turn out to be most foolish in the end. The greatest foolishness of all is to miss the calling in one's life and never know the true nature of the adventure that the soul came to life to live.

By the time he has worn out the shoes of his former life, Eisik seems a fool to the eyes of the world. Since the dream that carries him cannot easily be seen, he seems to be more empty and forsaken than others. In a world that believes only in what can be seen and be proven to be, it is a foolish thing to trust in the unseen realm. Yet again, a person may have to become more foolish in order to one day become wise. The youngest part of the self may look particularly foolish to those who would run the world; yet it is that internal aspect that knows where to turn when all else fails and the daily world runs out of ideas and inspirations and proper dreams.

That which is truly wise is first seen as strange and weird; were that not the case, everyone would have seen the truth of it right away. In answering the call we become strange by ordinary standards; we become both younger and older at the same time. The ever-young part of us remains foolish in ways that are secretly wise. We embrace what at first seems foolish and become wiser than we otherwise could be. Walking with the feet of dreams leads to being foolish in the right direction and becoming wise in the end. In order to become wise in that way we must accept and nurture the threads of our own weirdness. Becoming truly wise depends upon befriending the eternal youth as well as the sage within us; ultimately it means accepting the unique shape of our own soul.

Sole and Soul

We are called to become ourselves and since each self is unique, the calling comes uniquely to us. Learning one's true way of fitting into this world often requires becoming unfit for regular duties and common expectations. What truly calls to us would have us go beyond the usual limits. In responding to the call we join the lineage of those who are burning with an inner fire; not simply fired up with the heat of ambition, but awakened to a dream and flame that flickers in one's heart of hearts. A genuine calling further ignites the eternal spark originally carried into life by the soul and nothing can sooth that inner flame except that we fully respond and follow it through the world.

Although the first agreement begins in the otherworld it can only be fulfilled in this one. Throughout life the soul continues to descend and attempts to become incarnate more fully on this earth where we walk in the dust of the moment on the soles of our feet. *Soul* and *sole* are related words that also have shared roots. *Sole* carries the meaning of "being the only one of its kind" as with an exceptional item or a unique and extraordinary person. *Sole* can also refer to the bottom of one's feet. In order to become a unique and extraordinary person we must "walk our walk" and move the way our soul would have us move. We must find the original speech of the soul and become the vehicle of its true expression.

The Old English word *sawol* speaks with the same soulful tone of the "spiritual and emotional part of a person" that animates the person's being and also resonates with the song of existence. The purpose of life can be seen as an effort to create more soul and thereby bring more of the song of existence into being. The only way to accomplish such a lofty goal is to draw energy from the inner roots of one's soul and bring it up and out to the light of day. What then appears is the unique way each soul sings its inner note and the surprising pattern through which each pair of feet finds its way into the great dance of life.

The story of Eisik speaks to something ancient in our soul; for he is the immigrant of our dreams, the forsaken son and lost daughter secretly residing within each person. We are each his relative, some more distant than others; but each a refugee within ourselves until we find the way already seeded within us. Some dream brought us here and only it knows the way we are supposed to walk in this world.

Just as each set of fingerprints is unique, each pair of soles are distinct and cause us to connect to the ground of life precisely. The soles of one's feet give each person a unique stand in life. The soul within us is secretly connected to the spirit of the earth itself and the living earth has an interest in the growth of our soul. For it was some aspect of earthly life that first drew our souls down to this world where meaning and beauty must be shaped from the union of matter and spirit.

Walking with Eisik means going against the flow, crossing over where others fear to go and being foolish in the right direction. The treasure hard to attain includes the wisdom hidden in one's life, but can only be found after some foolishness breaks the spell of normality. We must feel the emptiness within us or else never find fulfillment. Only after we are worn down and turned back into the essential bones of our life can someone or something appear that can help turn things completely around.

Meanwhile, those who trade their dreams for the safety of a prescribed life make a false and foolish bargain with the world. They live in a sleeping village even as they pursue a busy life. They may have the trappings of outer success, yet they fall into the trap of following maps made by others. They may be clever, yet they cannot become truly wise. Wisdom can only come from a surprising self-revelation and from learning what it is that we truly love. Such a great learning must make us foolish before it can make us wise.

The treasure we desire most hides where we would never choose to go on our own; were that not the case many more would already have set out. Meanwhile, the soul sits at the intersection of time and timelessness, at the junction of dreams and waking life. It never tires of life's confusing journey because it finds hints of the divine in every event. Each night it shapes a bridge intended to bring the two worlds closer so that the divine might pour more freely into the mundane; so that the unseen might help us to see. In order to have such a soul vision we must be willing to be foolish for the sake of life's great song. Dreams can seem ephemeral and dismissible; yet they are an essential to both individual and collective life. Being foolish for the dream of our own life turns out to be how we help sustain the dream of the world.

CHAPTER 8

A SACRED AFFLICTION

The afflicted soul is always sacred.

By the time he arrived at the city of his dreams, Eisik had worn out his shoes and had shed several selves. He had become both a shell of his former self and a seed waiting to be cracked open. In that vulnerable condition he passed through the city gates and found himself in the great marketplace within them. Despite the nearby presence of wonders and goods foreign to his humble background, Eisik was blind to the distractions and impervious to their allure. His mind was set on reaching the bridge at the center and his heart only sought the treasure seen in dreams.

Just as the dream predicted, he came upon an expansive bridge set at the center of the city. The bridge made it possible to cross a moat and arrive at the entrance to a great palace. Clearly, a bridge is intended to be a crossing place, yet he could not even get near this one, as all approaches to it were guarded night and day. Eisik became afraid to go too close because of the presence of the guards. It was clear that any digging was out of the question. He had faithfully followed the map of his dreams only to become stuck before he could reach the goal and find the gold.

Having reached the end of his dream, he had no idea what to do or where to turn. Simply turning back was not an option; he had gone too far to return empty-handed. Yet he could see no way to go forward either. He had believed in the promise of treasure and trusted that he had an appointment with his destiny. Now he felt crushed with disappointment, all alone again and abandoned in a foreign place. Not knowing what else to do, he began to pace back and forth while staring at the bridge that was so near, yet so far.

The treasure was almost in his grasp, yet strangely seemed as far away as when he first heard the voice calling him to seek for it. No further dream or vision came to him and nothing stopped the growing sense that he had made some great mistake. He had followed his calling faithfully; yet now that the goal and gold were near, his faith was crumbling. His heart was breaking at the possibility that it was all a foolish dream that could never become reality. Something within him collapsed and all he could do was blindly wear a rut in the ground as he paced before the bridge.

Once again, Eisik became plagued by doubts and fears. He fell under the spell of his own uncertainties and into the grip of his deepest worries. Back and forth he went, dragged by dreams and doubts; crossing and re-crossing the same ground, unable to cross the bridge before him. Something else would be needed to tip the scales of life in favor of the dream and some sacrifice might be required before any treasure could be revealed.

Of course, this is an old scene repeated in many stories, as most treasures are found amidst great obstacles and dangerous circumstances. Before reaching the gold, whatever guards the treasure must be faced and something within that blocks the seeker from the goal must also be discovered and be overcome. Think of all the tales of treasures guarded by fearful dragons and poisonous serpents. Most people fear snakes as much as they desire gold. It seems a healthy instinct to fear something that moves without any legs and sheds its skin only to reveal another self hidden inside.

The snake that causes primal fears to stir within us turns out to be part of the treasure hard to attain. It reminds us that obtaining a great treasure requires facing our deepest fears. In addition, the presence of the snake indicates the need to shed whatever in our identity has become old and fixed and in the way of our growth. In order to qualify for handling the treasure, we must become like the snake: willing to shed old selves and able to grow a new skin.

A Bridge Too Far

Bringing a dream to life means changing everything and change is most often accompanied by fear and resistance. Living a dream requires the courage to cross not only where others fear to go, but also to enter where we fear to tread. The dream that calls us to a greater life is also a bridge between worlds, and the depths of one's soul must first be plumbed if the gold would be found. A bridge stands for all that is separated and divided and opposed in us and in the world around us. And a bridge reminds us that some essential union is trying to be forged.

Without a bridge opposing sides might run parallel forever and the opposites might never meet. A bridge teaches about both separation and union and says something about longing for the other, for the other side as well as the otherworld. There are old myths in both the East and the West about a bridge as sharp as the edge of a sword that must be crossed if one would reach the far shore and opposite world where eternity waits. The human soul harbors such ancient metaphors and can sense their symbolic meaning. The word *metaphor* means "to carry over, to go beyond."

A bridge is both a literal structure on which we can cross over and a symbolic image for going beyond the solid ground and seeming stability of the daily world. Lovers love a bridge for the way it suggests the mystery of attraction as well as the arc that can form between two souls. Each lover must cross a great space and risk exposure to find the other; the risk of stepping out and crossing over generates the intensity needed for union. A bridge in this world can act as a reminder of connections to the unseen realm beyond it and the ever-present mystery of crossing from one world to the other.

Meanwhile, the prospect of a greater union can also stir one's deepest fears of abandonment. Each person carries their own kind of emptiness within as well as a naked fear of falling into the void. For that reason, people also think of death when crossing a bridge, even if on a simple, everyday errand. A bridge simply makes the great journey of life and death more obvious.

As people move closer to the hidden gold and the genuine goal of their lives, they become a living bridge through which the time-bound and the eternal can meet. Yet being near the gold at the center also means drawing near our deepest fears and inner demons. The greatest issues and deepest wounds of the soul settle serpent-like exactly in the area where the treasure being sought resides. Being near the gold tends to activate our worst fears as the magnetism of hidden gold both pulls us closer to it and pushes us away. In the proximity of the treasure we seek, our persistent wounds become activated and often become exposed for all to see. Each step of self-fulfillment requires some self-exposure and some self-evaluation. Some emptiness must be bridged and some healing is required if we are to reach the treasure hard to attain.

At the level of the soul each person is gifted, but each is also wounded in some way. All of us have a wounded side, a little limp that holds us back or a weak wing that makes taking off in life more difficult. If our wounds were not intimately bound up with our gifts, we would find our inner gold more readily and share it more fully. As it is, approaching the hidden gold reveals what the seeker fears and will expose their specific weakness and way of limping in life.

Here on earth each soul carries and at critical times exhibits an inner defect, a sacred affliction and necessary wound that makes us truly human and full inhabitants of this world. For everything here is a little wounded, a little broken or cracked. Perfection may exist, but in another world, in the otherworld where eternal things reside and time cannot wound or hamper or limit.

Ancient artists often placed a defect in their best work in order to honor the necessary imperfections of life on earth. In making earthenware they left an area unglazed or allowed a small crack to be seen. The imperfection in the vessel made each piece unique, each a one-of-a-kind creation never to be repeated and all the more valuable because of that. Don't ancient stories say that humans are also made from the mud of the earth and from the clay of creation? Life on this earth includes precise imperfections as well as necessary afflictions. Each person may be a vessel where time and eternity can meet; yet each must also be cracked enough for the eternal to find a way in and for the inner dream to find a way out.

Although many people strive to be perfect, those who become wise know that perfection is a kind of death and that our weird imperfections actually keep us alive. The word *perfect* means "finished or complete," perhaps flawless, but also lifeless. Being fully alive means becoming more conscious of how we are already wounded. Becoming a whole person means learning how to live with our imperfections; for they too are ours to bear.

We are most whole when we are healing ourselves-- not just "walking our walk," but also limping our limp. We each carry an inner limp from the time before we learned to walk and becoming whole means accepting how we stumble inside our lives. Besides, being open to the otherworld can feel like having a great wound. Better to learn to carry the defects along with the gifts. Better to have a little crack that allows others in and lets the inner light of being shine out on occasion. What inner gold we have can only shine through the cracks of our being.

Don't be like the man who desired to be seen as holy by others. Each time he went to the temple to pray, he removed his shoes with great care. He made a great ceremony of taking off his shoes off and placing them at the entrance so as to be seen as pious by others. Yet his desire went in the wrong direction; he aimed at appearances in a place that asks for greater presence. Temples and churches are intended to remind us that the divine presence can be found in this world.

Removing our shoes before entering holy ground symbolizes the total nakedness required when approaching the divine. The would-be holy man forgot that the divine already knows our defects and can perceive the depths and the aim of our longings. Removing shoes represents baring our souls. Treating such an opportunity as an occasion for improving our status with others shows the kind of egotistical blindness that obscures real vision.

Such self-serving attitudes often appear when holiness is sought. Coming closer to the source of life can intensify pretensions and illusions just as readily as it can be a cause of deep humility. In this world appearances can be misleading; yet those who appear perfect now will one day be seen to be hiding a great defect. The pretender to piety sought to be elevated in the eyes of others; but the true seeker must become blind to outer appearances because he is devoted to unseen things. Once we take a real chance at life and follow the dream we carry within, it becomes difficult to hide our defects just to keep up appearances. True holiness often appears near where the holes in life become more evident, where the tatters and rents allow the afflictions to be exposed but also allow the inner wounds to be healed.

A Weird Foot

Eisik had long ago worn through his shoes and his clothes were in tatters. Feeling that he was near the treasure hard to attain, he no longer cared how he might appear to others. He was caught in his greatest fears and wearing his doubts on the outside. He was also wearing a rut in the ground and deepening the hole he was already in. He looked strange and foolish, yet it was an honest anguish that pulled him in two directions at once and left him at his wit's end.

Eisik was afflicted with great doubts and fears that kept him from stepping forward. His inner hesitation had long prevented him from awakening to the dream of his life. Now that he drew near the treasure of his dreams the old affliction of self-doubt and the inner scourge of worthlessness returned, and with a vengeance. He was caught in an old pattern of indecision and deepening the same rut that had held him back for most of his life. Although he did not know it and could not see it, he was in the breakdown that so often precedes a breakthrough.

Like Eisik, we are each on the verge of discovering the treasure of our being and we each can get in a rut that holds us back and keeps us stuck. Like Eisik, we are each secretly limping no matter how we present ourselves to those around us. We present ourselves a certain way and feel differently within ourselves. Being human, we must walk on two feet and we also live in two worlds. One foot is an adaptive appendage that allows us to fit into society and step up to the requirements of daily life. That foot feels for solid ground to stand on; it serves the ego's need for recognition and a sense of accomplishment.

Call it the ego's foot, for the ego forms by adapting to the initial circumstances of our lives. The ego-foot seeks a way to establish itself; with it we step into the world, we step up to life. The ego-foot usually leads the way as we use our ego's attitudes to face up to challenges and fulfill common expectations. We use it whenever we put "our best foot forward" or climb another rung on the ladder of success. Yet, our ego-stance can also keep us in a rut and block any emotional growth or genuine spiritual learning.

It is important to have an ego-self and a "leg to stand on" in this world where we have to stand up for ourselves. Yet that kind of stability is always one-sided and eventually leads to too many fixed positions and hardened attitudes. Strange as it may seem, it is our other foot, our less adapted way of being that holds the secret of meaningful change and the ability to grow.

Something in us fails to adapt to daily life and common expectations. This other foot is a bit dreamy; not simply a lazy bone, but an appendage not completely shaped for this world. This un-adapted or poorly adapted foot carries the weirdness in us; it has its own rhythms and its own reasons and its own way of walking. Call it a spiritual foot or a pilgrim foot; either way it is weird and *weird* means to have one foot in the otherworld. Being tied to the otherworld, it is a foot of longing that remains clumsy with unrealized potentials even if we appear accomplished and well established to others.

This ill-adapted foot drags a little and lags behind when we go too far in the wrong direction. This malingering foot carries our limp and holds us back, but it also remembers essential things that we keep forgetting and leaving behind when we rush ahead. Call it the soul foot, for it moves the way the soul moves; it wanders off in the wrong direction and slips into shadows. It goes where it shouldn't go; returning to things we thought we left behind us. It prefers the roundabout to the shortcut and circles around things most people avoid. It knows where the deepest wounds are and where our fears fear to go.

We may put our most adapted foot forward when practicality is called for; but when it comes to our actual calling in life, it is our mythic, awkward, and dream-bound limb that knows the way we must go. Because it causes us to limp and long for unseen things, it usually becomes covered up. We disguise our weirdness in order to seem like others or to get ahead in life. Yet the weird within us has its own ways of slowing us down and even stopping us cold. If we ignore this symptom-bearing limb too long it can cause an accident or an illness that stops us in our tracks. In the end, we can only go as far forward as we can reach back. And the weird within us would have us reach all the way back to the dream we brought to life and all the way down to where our deepest wounds seek to be healed.

In the common light of day our limp can be covered up; but truly walking our walk requires that we also limp our limp. On the path of our dreams and in pursuit of our greater sense of self, our limping becomes more pronounced. All true paths include dark stretches that expose the afflictions within us and make their healing possible. Surprisingly, when we find ourselves in a rut we are also near the area of hidden treasures. That which holds us back must be faced if we are to reach the treasure hard to attain. We must pass through our greatest doubts and touch our deepest wounds in order find the deeper self within us. When seen from the other end of life, our affliction is a sacred wound secretly connected to the hidden gold.

A Second Calling

Eisik could see no way forward and he couldn't simply turn back. He couldn't find a way in; yet he could not turn away. He became thoroughly stuck and there was nothing he could do but limp his limp and face the shades and shadows he had in his life. To the guards at the bridge he looked quite strange and foolish to boot as he continued to cross back and forth and deepen the hole he was already in. After a time the captain of the guard approached the rut where Eisik paced and spoke to him.

"We have observed you pacing back and forth day after day. You look harried and lost and deeply troubled. Friend, are you all right?"

Sometimes the only thing left to do is to tell the truth of the situation. When asked what the problem might be, Eisik had no way to disguise why he was there and how he felt about it. He told the truth for it was all he had left in him. He described the voice in the dream that came three times and explained how he had left everything behind to follow the instructions that led him to the center of the city. He confessed that he was supposed to dig at the base of the bridge where a golden treasure could be found. He expressed how he wanted to do just that, but also how he feared that he would be harmed or imprisoned by the guards. He exclaimed that he could not turn away; for he would not give up his dream.

To the regimented view of the captain of the guard the dreamer seems a sad and foolish soul. To the doubting dreamer the captain seems an emissary of defeat. Both stand near a treasure waiting to be disclosed, yet neither knows exactly what to do. It is a fateful meeting of opposing energies that creates a tension that cannot remain. As so often happens in stories and in actual life, a third thing is required in order to shift the tension and change the situation. The third thing, as they say, is a charm and nothing draws a charm close like the tension created by opposite forces.

The captain spoke again, "My friend, you are old enough to know better than to believe in dreams. Everyone knows that dreams are not real and that they can have no bearing on life in the real world." He went on confidently, "Why I myself had a dream last night. In my dream a voice said that a man named Eisik should return home and look behind the loose bricks of the hearth in his own hut. There, he would find a great quantity of gold. You see how foolish and mistaken such dreams can be. There is no treasure to be found in going that way."

For his part, Eisik said not a word. He only bowed deeply in gratitude for the captain's timely speech. He gathered himself together and turned away from the rut he was in. He left the bridge he had sought for so long, and began walking again. Without even looking behind him, Eisik began the long trek that led back along the way he had come.

Anyone overhearing the conversation between the captain and the dreamer would conclude that the pilgrim had come a great distance on a fool's errand. It would appear as if the wanderer finally came to his senses and recovered himself. He bows as if awakening from a foolish dream, as if accepting a more relevant vision or convincing argument. The firm admonition of the captain seems to clear things up, straighten him out, and send him on his way.

Yet something very different has occurred. Eisik is being called again, but in a different direction. This time he doesn't need to hear the call three times in order to heed it. Despite the messenger, this time Eisik gets the message right away. Strangely, this second calling comes to him through the dream of one who rejects dreams. Now, dreams are talking to dreams and the maker of dreams is speaking through believers and unbelievers alike. The message that reveals the truth comes from one who does not understand the nature or the meaning of the message he conveys. In the strange logic of the otherworld, the one who risked everything to follow a dream learns from someone who neither believes in dreams nor listens to the language of the soul.

While dismissing the dreamer and his dreams, the captain actually pushes him deeper within and closer to the genuine goal. Eisik learns the secret from one who guards this world against messages from the other one. While being called a fool the seeker receives the exact knowledge needed to continue on the path of awakening. The joke reveals that even those opposed to the unseen must do its bidding when the time for a genuine transformation has come.

A Deeper Message

The captain considers the night message he received to be complete and utter nonsense, further proof of the foolishness of following visions and dreams. But there is a method in this madness and those who listen with inner ears can hear the words within the words. The captain says one thing, while Eisik, cracked open by his long pilgrimage, hears a deeper language. Eisik has made the effort and has suffered the pain; he has surrendered to the unseen and brought himself to the point of no return. When things are truly ready to turn around even the naysayers begin to help out. The one who rejects all knowledge of the otherworld becomes the one who delivers messages from it.

The turning point did not come from digging at the base of the bridge; rather, things turned around when the seeker dug deep inside and came out with the truth. He faced his fears, bared his soul, and expressed his inner pain. At the point of painful revelation, help can come from any direction; then even seemingly discouraging news can open the way. When the two worlds are being bridged anyone nearby can be drawn into the exchange that secretly encourages the pious journey of life to continue. At the bridge where things cross between one world and the other, anything can become a source of knowledge.

Sometimes, offering the truth is a foolish thing to do; often it is wiser to withhold what one knows. And at certain moments, telling the truth is the only way to proceed; especially if the truth makes healing possible. Doesn't a patient have to indicate where the pain resides before the right treatment can be applied? At critical times the inner confusion and pain must be expressed for things to become clear. That is part of being foolish in the right direction and part of becoming wise as well. When it comes to the underlying affliction, exposure and airing out are part of the curing process.

In proximity to the treasure hard to attain, things become subtle. Everything can change with just the slightest false note. Imagine another seeker who is afraid to speak the truth to the captain of the guard. He fears being punished or rejected or else fears that the guards will take the treasure for themselves. If the seeker holds back the painful, foolish truth, the captain will fail to recall his dream. He guards against the night visions and would have others reject them as well. He can easily forget that he was dreaming of hearths and gold and a man named Eisik.

Instead of everything turning around, the dreamer might simply be turned away as something gets in the way of the transformation secretly trying to occur. Even on a proper path there are no guarantees that the message intended for us will actually reach us. If the seeker holds something back or becomes enveloped in fear additional struggles will be required before the information needed can come all the way through.

Meanwhile, for one who becomes ready to awaken, everything becomes a wake-up call. Something wise is being demonstrated here; for a person does not have to go the entire way to reach an important goal. If the destination is aligned with a true destiny it is the effort of the seeker that counts in the end. At some point along the way, and often when things become stuck, the otherworld begins to move towards the seeker. When that happens, helpers appear in unlikely forms. Eisik followed his dream as far as he could go; when he could go no further, the next dream came looking for him.

In the great turning points of life, anything and anyone can become a source of deliverance. In the proximity of genuine knowledge mysteries become revealed and in mysterious ways. The real Way is like that; help from an enemy, truth from those who believe nothing, release provided by those guarding the prison. This kind of self-awakening changes everything; it opens wide the gates of understanding. The captain believes that he is bringing a foolish man to his senses; meanwhile the pilgrim has received another revelation, one that turns things inside out and aims him directly at his own hearth and home. When a great turnaround is underway the seeker can accept the whole truth, even if it involves a complete reversal of direction.

The captain of the guard stands for all the dull ideas that guard against the possibility of genuinely waking up to the unique nature of one's life. He represents the certainty of the unawakened who willingly reinforce the restrictions of collective life. He believes what he has been told by those above his station and he wants you to believe in the same way. He wears the uniform that represents a uniformity of ideas as well as conformity to whatever the ruling "isms" might be. The bridge between worlds is subtle and delicate and those who dream are always less certain than those who keep a distance from their inner life.

The irony of looking but not seeing is epitomized by the captain who guards the bridge. He also stands near the place of understanding and the site of buried treasure, yet his fixed beliefs make any subtle presence invisible to him. Those who have no hint of the gift of life will often turn others away from searching for it. Being unaware of the treasures hidden within them, they try to prove that none exist at all.

The roads of life are cluttered with signs set to persuade us to become someone else, rather than strive to become as we are inside. A tremendous collective effort is made every day to insure that the limited perspective and common beliefs that sustain the obvious world remain firmly in place.

Despite the wild dance of dreams invisibly spanning the arc of each night and the pulse of imagination inside every soul, the daily routine requires that the false certainties and ruling orders be guarded zealously.

People talk of being realistic, of paying attention to the real world, all the while missing any connection to the reality of the deeper self and the wisdom that resides within it. Knowing nothing of the true situation, they speak with great authority of what is real and what is not. They consider themselves to be realists, yet they know nothing of the Real that waits to be discovered under the skin of common reality.

A Foot In Each World

The real treasure of life, the one difficult to find and hard to attain, is never far from us. That's an unwritten rule on this earth. What we desperately desire and need most is buried in the recesses of our innermost being all along. That is the open secret found in many traditions and told in many ways. Yet it remains a secret because trusting in oneself remains one of the hardest things to do in life.

We live within a paradox, within the restrictions of a fate that can trap us in familiar patterns and a longing for the eternal that won't leave us alone. Back and forth we go on the bridge of life collecting knowledge first from one side and then from the other. At times we must follow our dreams and undertake the errands of the divine; at other times we must become more fully incarnate and play a role in the earthly drama. If we fail to become established in this world, we can lose our footing and slip into obscurity before learning what our soul desires most. If we fail to awaken to the calling of the divine we can become mired in the mud of mundane errands and dutiful tasks.

The bridge of life stretches between this world and the otherworld. We have two feet and are required to find a way to live in both. We are servants of the unseen and keepers of the dream of life. Yet we must participate in the real world and play our part in the drama of life on earth. We serve both worlds and in moments of awakening become the living bridge that holds them together.

It's like the old story of the seeker who had the dream of becoming a saint and an accomplished ascetic. In order to transcend the entrapments of the common world he emptied his life and sought refuge in the realm of the spirit and in the heights of the holy hills. He spent all his time following spiritual practices in remote mountain caves. He avoided all the temptations of life and practiced austerities from dawn until night. He meditated and fasted and abstained in order to remove the stain of this world from his soul. He also sought to draw down the attention of the great god Vishnu. For it was Vishnu who first dreamed the cosmic dream and Vishnu whose holy breath sustains this world as well as all the dreams within it.

Narada, for that was the name of the serious seeker, sought a victory over the illusions and disillusionments of life on earth. Through severe practices, he became a bare flame burning naked in the empty heights of the sacred mountains. Eventually, great Vishnu noticed the "tapas" or holy heat emanating from the spot where the holy man executed his strivings. The gods have great interest in the striving of human souls, especially when someone begins to burn with serious spiritual heat. So the great deity of dreams decided to visit the seeker and grant him a boon as a way of recognizing the effort that he was putting forth.

Having dreamed the entire world into existence, Vishnu could appear in any form he wished. At times he appeared as a wise sage or else as a poor beggar. A powerful ruler might have to bend down to see the deity, while a poor soul might have to look up in a new way. The divine often appears in a form that the one receiving the visitation can learn the most from.

In this case Vishnu came before the bare-boned ascetic in a resplendent and dignified form; but he also came with a little desire, as we shall see. After commending the saint for his efforts, the god offered to fulfill any wish that the holy man might have. After all, even the gods like to play god. Meanwhile, Narada well knew that each god had particular powers. He knew that the deity before him was the original dreamer in this world and that if anyone could fulfill dreams, it was Vishnu.

When offered the fulfillment of his wish, the saint did not hesitate. He knew exactly what he wanted and what he most desired was to comprehend the power or *maya* of Vishnu himself. He wished more than anything to understand the magical power behind all of creation and all the illusions that shape this world. For *maya* means both matter and magic, both energy and illusion; both the stuff of and the play of existence. Like many before him, Narada wanted to know what the god of creation knew. He wanted to understand the power and genius behind all the manifestations of this earthly realm.

Vishnu was not exactly pleased by this request. He gently suggested that the holy man try another wish. But Narada was as single-minded on this subject as he had been in practicing his austerities. Even in the face of the divine, the saint would not budge. Vishnu had offered to grant a wish and the holy man had responded with his request. An offer had been made and it had been accepted; an agreement had been reached and even the gods are subject to certain agreements. A deal had been struck and there was nothing else for it; so Vishnu beckoned to Narada to follow him.

The saint and the god began to walk along together, the mortal and immortal almost hand in hand. They followed a lonely path and eventually entered a wide desert. As they proceeded under the intensity of the blazing sun, Vishnu suddenly announced that he was thirsty. He asked Narada if he would be kind enough to go on ahead where there seemed to be a village and bring back a drink of water to cool his thirst. The saint was familiar with service and with self-sacrifice and he knew that an errand for a god was not something to deny.

Narada hastened off to the village and went directly to the first house he found. He knocked on the simple door and waited in a heightened state of devotion due to his errand of seeking water for the divine. Yet he also felt his own great thirst. When the door swung open before him, a graceful young woman appeared. She greeted him kindly and welcomed him inside. As he stepped across the threshold he gazed upon the beauty of the woman standing silently before him. She seemed to be the most beautiful being he had ever laid his eyes upon.

As he drank in her beauty, Narada neglected to ask for the drink of water. He simply followed her into the coolness of the house. Once inside, he was graciously received by the young woman's parents who treated him as an honored guest. They made him comfortable, brought him sweet drinks and made friendly conversation. Time began to pass as they all enjoyed each other's presence. Soon enough, in the cordiality of that house and amidst an exchange of glances with the young woman, Narada simply forgot that he was on an errand from god.

After a time, and how else could it be, Narada and the young woman became engaged and were married with the blessing of her parents. The saint soon learned the joys of marriage as well as the hardships of a peasant's life. With one thing after another, a dozen years passed somehow. Narada found himself with three children and many responsibilities in this world. When the old parents passed on, Narada and his beloved wife inherited the farm and worked hard to preserve the land and sustain the family.

A Rock and A Hard Place

One year, they were assaulted by a great flood as torrential rains poured unceasingly from the sky. On a harsh, storm-driven night, their herds were drowned in the flooding waters and the house itself began to wash away. Water rushed everywhere and solidity was nowhere to be found. Narada took the hand of his wife and those of his older children. He placed the youngest child on his shoulder and struggled to lead them all through the raging waters to dry land and safety.

In the midst of the deluge the burden became too great. Narada could not hold them all together against the flood and the youngest child slipped into the rushing waters. Letting go of the others, Narada tried desperately to save the little one. As the torrent swept the child away, he saw his wife and the other children disappearing in the opposite direction. Torn and pulled in two directions at once and caught in the dark turbulence, Narada began to fall and soon could not rise again. He fell into unconsciousness and became as inert as a piece of wood.

His body drifted along on the current until he was cast headfirst upon a great rock. The hard knock caused him to suddenly awaken. As he recovered consciousness, he remembered the great flood and the loss of his wife and family. Then, all the sorrows of the world came rushing at him and he began to lament and cry out in pain. In the midst of his wailing anguish he heard a familiar voice speaking to him: "Where have you been my child and where is the water you were bringing for me? I have been waiting here for more than half an hour."

Narada turned towards the voice and saw the vision of Vishnu again. Suddenly, they were standing next to each other on the deserted path. All around them the earth stretched dry and cracked and parched by the blazing sun that poured heat down upon them. There was no flood, no torrent, no river and no great rock; there was no water to be seen anywhere.

"Now do you understand the secret of my power and the *maya* of this world?" asked Vishnu. The god of the dream of creation had granted the petition of the holy man and the great seeker had been given a little taste of the divine power. He had received the gift of knowledge that he desired most and found himself waking up between one world and the other. He had asked a question and found himself caught amidst a flood of additional questions.

Is it all a dream and nothing but an illusion? Was the lifetime in the village real? Did the god truly come near? In the midst of many other agreements, both sweet involvements and heavy responsibilities, do we all forget some divine errand we were on? Or in longing for the otherworld or following a dream do we lose all connection to the world around us? The story asks of us, do you understand now?

The gift of life takes us in contrary directions; we burn with holy longings and we thirst for earthly delights. We stand at one threshold and then at the other; we live in both worlds and must learn to serve them both. We undertake an errand for the divine only to find ourselves back in the common village of life. A door before us opens; in service of something divine and also driven by thirst, we must step through it. In a simple step and a single moment that suddenly become momentous everything changes. We are swept up in the dance of creation; we give ourselves to it body and soul; we enter it fully and lose ourselves in it. We become part of it all, and it all seems solid and real and meaningful and necessary.

Then, the hard times come and the floods of change wash over the land. All the solidity of daily life slips away and reality rattles all around us. People we held close begin to drift apart and things we held dear fall from our hands. All that was so real and so beautifully and damningly immediate becomes remote. All that we had gained seems lost and we find ourselves amongst the rocks and in the hard places. We wake in anguish between one reality and another soaked in our essential aloneness.

Surprisingly however, even as we wail at all our losses and decry the pain of life, we are close to the divine source again. Having lost all that we loved and labored for, we are near the errand of the soul again. In the anguish of loss we are near the first agreement of the soul; when all else has slipped from our grasp we may be closer to grasping again the original aim that brought us to life. How else to understand this world where everything is temporary and all agreements subject to change?

We are on an errand for the divine all along, even when we knock on doors and forget why we were knocking. We climb the ladders we find before us without considering which wall they lean against. We sit with the neighbors and dream of distant treasures. We fall in love with the wonder of this world and with the beauty in the souls of those we meet in it. How else could it be, how else should it be? We succumb to the magic and *maya* that create the world we see each day and we also dream at night of other worlds and other lives.

The point here is not to dismiss the beauty of earthly life, the allure of sensual love or the importance of children and family. Love has its own kind of magic and *maya* and power. Love plays an essential part in each person's fate and also has a part to play in the destiny of every soul. The old alchemists, seeking for the magic that turns common things into gold, had a saying: "Without love, the work cannot progress." We need many life experiences in order to learn how and who and what we love in this world.

Wasn't it the god of creation who sent the seeker to the threshold where he found beauty and discovered ways of being and loving and serving the desires of this world? The point here is not to dismiss the delight of being alive on earth. The door of life is there to be opened and the wonder of earthly life is there to be discovered again and again.

Like Narada, we enter the next village or the next stage of our lives and forget again why we came to life to begin with. There's no help for it and no simple escape from it. Isn't that part of what Vishnu is revealing to the saint? It was precisely while he was on a direct mission from god that he fell in love with beauty, with life in the world, with children and with being a contributing member of the human community. The conversation with the divine also leads the soul of the seeker to an immersion in the dramas and delights of life on earth.

Places of Awakening

The moment of greater awakening only comes after some life experience, not from completely avoiding it. Narada awakens in the midst of the human dilemma, in the most human place, between the proverbial rock and a hard place. He wakes to the message that we are here to live and love and lose and suffer in the "real world." And in awakening he recalls that he has forgotten his agreement with the divine. On one hand we must know what it means to be alive in the human drama that alternates between love and loss. On the other hand we must seek to know the divine and serve something that transcends all of the human experience.

Narada is another form of Eisik, for both are seekers and servants of the divine and each becomes lost while on an important errand. Both inhabit the village of life and each finds a way to awaken further when the time comes. Eisik finds an awakening when he fears that all has been lost; Narada must actually experience loss before he can awaken fully. Narada is the saint who remembers the divine errand and also the sinner who forgets everything but the immediate demands of life. He is the saintly sinner and the lost seeker and the suffering pilgrim in this dream of life that can appear as one thing and then become another.

Whatever we achieve in life can also be lost again. Despite all our good intentions and caring dedication, one day we lose what we love, we lose those we love. We fail our families or lose the whole farm. Whole empires disappear; armies are destroyed, and cities fade into dust. Everything that arises in the great drama of life must one day disappear as if it were all an illusion; there is truth in that. Yet again, the world around us is and will continue to be the Grand Illusion.

Call it illusion or call it reality, life is the dream that must be dreamed and we are all dreamers trying to awaken further. For it is the divine that dreams up the world and sets each threshold before us. And it is the divine that waits for us to awaken and recall our soulful errand again no matter what roads we have been on or what losses we have suffered. What seems like a lifetime to us is but a short time where the divine is concerned. When it comes to the divine errand anytime could be the right time to awaken.

Whether it be the loss of everything we thought was ours or a message that says the time has come to turn everything around, most awakenings do come as a shock. The saint asked for knowledge equal to what the gods know and the deity answered by sending him back to the door of life's entanglements and illusions. The answer indicates the necessity of both worlds; for both errands are part of the magic and power and *maya* of creation. Only after entering the door of life fully and experiencing both the reality and the illusory nature of this world can the saint fully awaken to the conversation with the divine.

The continuous illusion of this world is precisely next to the divine source that creates and sustains it. Two different orders of being, both flow from the same source. Life is the necessary illusion from which we drink as well as the circumstantial waters in which we drown again and again. That is the truth as well as the illusion of it. We are each on a mysterious errand and the great beauty of this world requires that we both forget and at times remember it.

The two worlds are close to each other and a person can cross from one to the other in a single step. That kind of crossing over can happen at any moment and can be precipitated by seeing beauty, by receiving an unexpected message or by waking up with a compelling dream. It can come through a sudden shock or a hard knock; but can also be found through spiritual devotion and practice. In this world each wake-up call is an opportunity to turn back to the conversation with the divine.

We are each a certain question being asked of god and asked of life.

Only over time can we learn how to wake up and dry out and take our rightful place in the divine conversation. Just like Eisik, we are closer to an awakening and to a turning point whenever we reach the end of our rope and feel that we have lost everything again. At that point, we either fall apart or else we find the thread of destiny that pulls everything together and opens the path before us again. One way or another, a deeper calling begins to surface and a voice gently asks: Do you understand now?

CHAPTER 9

THE ARC OF RETURN

*All our forgetting exists that we might remember
essential things more vividly.*

What is truly ours returns to us when we become ready to return to it. Having received the critical message from an unlikely source, Eisik turned completely around and the long pilgrimage was reversed. He had gone as far as he could go in one direction, now his calling called him back and he began to retrace the steps he had taken while first following his dream. Eisik had entered the arc of return that comes after a person has wandered into the world and finally stumbled in the right direction.

Each life has an outward arc that engages the world and an inward, more introspective path that produces understanding. On the return journey, the seeker has more insight and sees things differently. On the returning arc it becomes clear that nothing has been wasted; for the soul doesn't waste anything. No proof is offered for that, it's just a sign posted on the path of return where everything encountered can be tinged with revelation.

By the time he reached the old village, Eisik had gathered the pieces of his life and had gleaned a greater understanding of his fate. Standing at the edge of the village he could view his old life with new eyes. He could see all that had held him back and had kept him in his expected place. He could also imagine all the dreams floating through the village each night only to be forgotten when the common rounds of day began. He had returned to the same old place, yet he saw it all with different eyes.

There was a time for travelling out, but now the time for digging in had arrived. Eisik entered his old hut looking for a treasure to be found within. He went directly to the hearth and to the heart of the matter. Just as the dream of the captain described, there were loose bricks at the back of the humble hearth. As Eisik began to loosen them further the glimmer of gold began to shine forth. Breaking through the inner wall, Eisik found the treasure hard to attain right where it had been hidden all along. The gold he sought at the distant bridge was near at home, waiting for him to return and turn to it.

The gold glowed from behind the fireplace as if it represented another kind of burning; as if it symbolized a fire within a fire. It is useful to notice how close *hearth* is to *heart*. Remove a single, almost silent letter and a fireplace becomes an inner organ. Remove the first letter and the place of the fire becomes *earth*. An unseen fire burns at the very center of the earth and an inner flame burns at the center of each heart. The heart is also a hearth; it can burn with emotion but can also illuminate the world with inner knowledge.

In this world everyone is on fire; an inner body-fire keeps a person warm even when the temperature drops outside. Yet if the issues of the heart become too dark or suffer great neglect a person can be cold no matter what the outside weather. The inevitable troubles of life cause stones to grow around each heart. Something valuable and golden waits to be found within us, yet something must be loosened to reveal it. The time comes when that which protected the vulnerabilities of the heart must be loosened and removed for a deeper sense of self to emerge.

Many old stories convey the message that what we seek for most was within us all along. Someone says: "This is an outrage; why weren't we told about this at the beginning? We could have stayed home and saved all the trouble and travel, side-stepped all the trials and tribulations." Not true. Gold is buried in dark and forbidding places and only found after a great amount of searching has occurred. If the discovery of gold was a simple matter, people would find it more easily and value it less.

The treasure we value most has been sewn in us and the knowledge we seek can be found within. That is the message trying to get through all along; yet it only arrives after we have exhausted all other avenues. We carry what we seek, but it takes a lot of bumping and scraping, losing and loosening to reveal it. We must receive a few hard knocks ourselves before we become loosened enough to value properly what was hidden within us all along.

The treasure is hidden where we are least likely to look and less able to go at the beginning of life's journey. Although it waits to be found deep within, it cannot be revealed until outer extremes have been experienced. In this world it is necessary to go all the way to the end of our dreams in order to learn where the dreaming comes from. At the far end of our waking and walking, of our worrying and working, we begin to turn back to the deeper self and our original agreement with life. On the arc of return we turn within and find what has carried us all along.

Be Here Now

The real journey of life aims at revealing something essential and original within us; yet it can only arrive at the source after leading us away from it. The answer is within, but the call comes from somewhere beyond. Going out and coming back are both required; for there are two worlds involved and two arcs of life that call to each of us. In order to truly "be here now," it turns out that a person must be everywhere else first.

Those who state that the present moment is all that counts are telling the truth; yet they didn't start there. They are telling the story of arrival while many are just departing. For those about to go on a long journey, it is not very helpful to know that the treasure is found within. Like most important things in life, finding genuine knowledge involves timing. Those starting out need reasons to leave home or they might fall asleep and miss their star. They might mistakenly conclude that there is no reason to enter the greater world and thereby miss the exact adventures that the awakening of their soul requires.

There are subtleties and surprises on any path and only after traveling far can the seeker hear and understand the words behind the words. Only after being driven by the unseen can we begin to see into our own confusion;

only then can the messages about the inner life begin to make genuine sense. Because it takes enough experience of being lost to learn how to find one's way, the dream of life both misleads us as well as leads us home. If the way were simple and straight forward, no dream or art, no true practice or surprising revelations would be needed. Everyone would set out and arrive directly at the soul's destination.

The distance to the center of oneself may be short; yet the road that leads us there is much longer. Those who take shortcuts at the beginning will find themselves going the long way round later on. The path to the center requires several kinds of surrender; we must stretch and change in many ways and suffer our greatest doubts. It is the willingness to surrender that allows the pilgrimage to the self to begin. It is the willingness to sacrifice and be vulnerable that allows us to reach the treasure. It takes a certain amount of courage and even some heartbreak to learn what one's heart already knows.

The great adventures as well as the deeper reflections of life both aim at the revelation of the deeper self within. A true education serves to break the fetters on the soul and crack the shell of the self and reveal the heart within it. A hearth is the figurative center of a house just as the heart can be seen as the center of a person. From the heat of a fire that burns, to a light that glows and illuminates the way, that is the progression of heart-learning. From the burning questions and searing emotions to the clear light of one's spirit, that is how the forging of the inner gold proceeds.

Eisik was a friendly fellow and a good soul, but something essential to life had been walled over or blocked with stone. Some old heartbreak had become walled in; some deep longing had been walled off. Something hard in the heart of the seeker had to be loosened up in order for the inner way to be found. Loosening the walls around the heart brings up many fears; it feels like dying or being torn apart. Most prefer digging for treasure on foreign soil or behind other walls. Beyond our fears of the world around us, there waits the greater fear of encountering our own self.

Eisik had to leave all that he knew and go far into the world in order to learn how to look closer within. In turning back we learn to see with different eyes and know our self in a new way. Until the outer arc has been travelled, the inner path cannot be believed. Always some sacrifice is required for the inner gold and original self to be revealed and be accepted. Meanwhile, people keep making the mistake of thinking that the experience of others can relieve them of the requirement for fully entering the world and finding their specific way to be in the here and now.

The Tiger's Whisker

It is reminiscent of the old village tale of a young woman who feared that she would never truly know love or learn the ways of her own heart. The one person to whom she had given her heart had become distant from her and she became afraid that she would never love again. The trouble began when the one she loved most in all the world went off to the latest war and only barely managed to survive it. When he returned he was no longer the same person. Whereas they had been so close as to be of one heart, he now remained distant from her. When he did come near, he was either quick to anger or taken to sudden dark moods. She longed for him to heal and for them to find the source of love again. Over time however, she became afraid that she would never know love again.

Fear can keep us too long in the same place and it can also drive us to places we otherwise would avoid. The young woman's fear drove her out of her normal patterns and caused her to seek far and wide for a remedy. Her search led her to the great marketplace where she wandered amongst those who sell salves and potions intended to cure the aches and pains of life. When she found no remedy there she went to the temples and listened to the sermons and lessons that were offered.

One day she heard mention of a sage who lived far up in the mountains that surrounded the town. People said that the old sage had deep knowledge and could fashion cures for all that could ail a person. So the young woman decided to climb the mountain and find the cave where the wise one was said to dwell.

The next morning as the sun rose in the sky, the young woman began to ascend the mountain path. In due time, she arrived at the opening of a cave. She stood for a moment in the bright light of day, then stepped into the dark opening. Once her vision adjusted, she could detect the flickering flames of a small fire at the back of the cave. Seeing the outline of a person against the light of the fire, she cleared her throat and apologized for interrupting the stillness of the place.

Having received no response, she went on to say how she had come in search of a cure. But before she could finish her request the sage interrupted her in a loud voice. "A cure, a cure; the whole world is looking for a cure. Tell me this, what is the cure for a world that has become sick?"

The young woman was thoroughly surprised and only managed to say, "I did not come here ready to answer questions, but only came seeking for a cure myself."

The old sage seemed to recover and gently asked, "What then is the ailment that troubles you and brings you all the way here?"

The young woman explained that she had lost the one she loved most in the world and feared that she would never love again. Was it possible that the sage could make a potion that could bring back her love? The old sage began to lament again, talking about the loss of love throughout the world. Then he caught himself and stopped. "Come back in three days and I will know if there is a cure for this condition or not."

The young woman bowed and made her way from the dark interior of the cave back into the light of day. She spent the next three days the way you spend time waiting to learn if there is a cure for you or not. When the time was finally up, she rose with the sun and climbed the path to the cave again. She entered the darkness and made her way to the fire at the back of the cave. She greeted the old sage and asked if he had found a cure.

The sage said that indeed there was a cure and that he had gathered all the necessary ingredients--except one. A final ingredient was needed and he wondered if she would be willing to seek for it. She said that she would gladly seek for the missing ingredient whatever it might be. The sage explained that the only ingredient remaining to be found was a whisker from the head of a tiger; more exactly, a whisker from the head of a living tiger.

The young woman was aghast. What kind of request was that,

what kind of danger was she expected to face? She asked if all the other ingredients were as dangerous to gather as a whisker from a living tiger. The old sage reminded her how she had just stated that she would gladly seek for whatever the cure required. What could she say? What could she do? She had asked if there was a cure and could hardly refuse when a solution was being offered. She would now have to face her fears and risk more than she had imagined if she would find a remedy for lost love.

She left the cave and stepped back into the harsh light of day. She followed the path down without a clue to how she might acquire the whisker of a tiger. She had set out looking for love and found herself searching for tigers. Back at her little hut she felt more alone than ever before. Evening fell all around as the young woman stirred some rice for dinner contemplated her dilemma. She watched the steam rise from the simmering pot and suddenly remembered that people used to talk of a man-eating tiger that roamed the hills nearby. In was said to reside in a remote cave at the end of another path that led into the mountains above the village.

Now she knew where to go, but had no idea how to approach such a dangerous place. It occurred to her that tigers must also get hungry. Not knowing what else to do, she placed some rice in a bowl and set off for the mountain as the sun sank in the sky and darkness began to chase the light from the world.

She found the path and went as far as she dared to go; all along the way she feared that she might actually meet the tiger. When she could no longer contain her fear, she bent down and left the bowl of rice on the path. The next night she prepared the rice and climbed the path again. Reaching the place where she had placed the rice, she could see plainly enough that that the food had been eaten. She stepped past the empty bowl and went as far into the teeth of her fear as she could manage. She left a bowl of rice as before, retraced her steps and returned home.

Each night she prepared the rice and carried a bowl up the mountain path in the fading light of evening. Each time she returned she would find an empty bowl. She would step past that marker and enter further into her fear before leaving another bowl. Each time she went as far as her fear would allow before descending to safety.

One night, in the light of a waxing moon, she ascended the path in her accustomed way. Just as she stepped past another empty bowl, she saw the tiger coming towards her. Stopping cold in her tracks, she gathered her courage and placed the bowl before the terrifying beast. Despite overwhelming fear, she spoke to the tiger as it bent its great head to the bowl and began eating. She offered an apology for what she was about to do, took a deep breath and plucked a long whisker that stuck out from the corner of the tiger's mouth. As she leapt back full of fear, the tiger seemed not to notice.

Holding the key ingredient in her hand she could not resist dancing with joy and lifting the whisker up to the moonlight as she descended to the village. When morning came she rose with the sun and carried the precious ingredient up to the cave of the old sage. He asked for the whisker in order to examine it and verify that it was indeed a whisker from the head of a living tiger and she gladly handed it over to him.

The sage held the slender hair up in the light of the fire; then suddenly let it drop. The whisker that had been acquired after such diligent effort fell quietly through the smoke until it reached the flames where it was instantly consumed and turned to ash.

As the missing ingredient became lost in the ashes the young woman became inflamed at the injustice of it all. She railed against the sage, asking if he had ever suffered in the way he now caused her to suffer. She released whatever pent-up angers, frustrations and fears she had. Then she demanded an explanation. The sage responded with a question of his own. How, he wondered had she accomplished the task of facing the tiger and getting the whisker?

She was happy to tell the whole thing, in detail. With intense emotion, she described how she carried bowls of food into the darkness each night; each time stepping further and further into her fears. She recalled the shock of actually encountering the tiger and the terror of reaching out to grasp the whisker.

The sage then asked if the heart of a person was more dangerous than that of a tiger; if such a practice worked when approaching a man-eating tiger, could it not be used to reach the human heart? At first, the young woman did not understand the question; then the sense of it began to dawn upon her. After some reflection, she began to see how in facing her fears she had found the way to open her own heart. She had found the great courage within her and her desire to heal.

Without replying any further, the woman bowed to the sage again, this time in great gratitude. Then she turned from the fire and returned to her little hut back in the village. She took up her life again; although nothing is told of whether she was able to rekindle the old way of loving. It is clear that something had opened within her and she saw everything with new eyes. She found the courage and wisdom of her own heart.

What the Heart Loves

The heart is a vital organ, but also a great territory. The heart is where true imagination resides and when it opens we find that there are mountains and caves within us. There are tigers and sages as well and the woman of the soul walks there. She is searching for love and for healing; she knows that the cure only comes after the deepest fears have been faced. Love, like life, cannot be tame. Each approach to what the heart truly loves is likely to raise some level of fear.

Fear and love are opposing energies, yet they are often found together. The struggle between fear and love is an old one; for one would separate where the other would unify. Meanwhile, that which we love is much bigger than anything the little-self understands. The ego-self formed around the earliest fears we felt and it continues to feel the way it did when we were small and helpless. The path of discovery will inevitably raise the exact fears that hold the heart captive.

The old sage and the young woman set on finding love are two parts of the wise and loving heart that harbors the inner gold. But the heart also harbors a tiger that must be nourished or it will attack its own host. All of us have fierce issues that will devour us unless we learn to face and make peace with them. The tiger has the missing ingredient and is willing to help, but can only be approached after the little-self relinquishes its fearful and controlling attitudes.

Remember Eisik digging his rut before the bridge? He set out to dig for a treasure and was close to the gold; but something in him was still closed and fearful. He had made the effort and gone the distance, but another opening was needed. It was no accident that guards were involved in the pivotal events; for he was still fearful and overly guarded. He needed to receive something from the hardhearted captain just as the young woman needed an encounter with a dangerous tiger.

The young woman had to be patient and loving towards herself as she learned to face her deepest fears. Later, she did not need the tiger's whisker because she had tamed the tiger of her fears and found her own inner brilliance. The missing ingredient was within her all along as was the devotion that love requires. It takes courage to open the heart and learn what anguish it has and what remedies can be found within it.

Courage is a heart word that derives from the Latin *cor*; it refers to the core of one's deepest feelings and innermost thoughts. For the heart harbors thoughts and dreams as well as feelings and emotions. The heart can be mined for enduring courage and living imagination; yet we must often be driven there by fear or despair or loneliness. Remember the old thief trapped in his dark dungeon? He had the golden seed all along, but only found it after he faced a period of great loneliness and deep despair. Then he became a tiger of truth-telling and others had to face their fears and failings. He found the seeds of liberty in the midst of darkness, just as the young woman found freedom and joy after bravely facing night after night of fear.

Our deepest fears form at an early age and at a vulnerable time when the heart is naturally open and unprotected. Each child comes to the world with something golden to give; each soul is ready to shine in its own way and give of itself. Yet when the golden sense of self is rejected or met with fear or coldness, the heart begins to close around itself. The gold of the self is there, but surrounded by fear and guarded by stubborn walls.

When the time comes for the heart to open fully again, the old fears will awaken and the inner walls will tighten up. Although fear can become terrifying and paralyzing, what we most fear is where we must go. "Fear is the guide for the true direction of the heart," they used to say when considering the courage required to become oneself. Our way of loving and healing is seeded within us, yet it takes more than one breakthrough to reach the inner treasure. A long road made of longing and self-discovery is required in order to re-open the heart and reveal the gold within it. Another old proverb states that "what the heart loves is the cure." Life is the ailment and what we love provides the cure for what ails us.

A Broken Heart

The problem is not that people have nothing genuine or meaningful to give. The problem involves the pain of opening the arteries of imagination and veins of genuine love that became closed and fettered early on. What tries to live through people is so big that it becomes heart-breaking for them. To become equal to the dream sewn within us, our heart must break open and usually must break more than once. That's why they say that the only heart worth having is a broken heart. For only in breaking can it open fully and reveal what is hidden within.

The deeper self is capable of great love, yet the walls around the heart are kept in place by habits hard-held by the little-self. If the greater self within would be found and the inner gold would be released, the core issues must be faced and loosened up. Breaking through usually requires a practice that fits the problem and can move the heart as well as focus the mind. Often a guide or teacher must be found before the right practice can be applied.

It's like the seeker who found a teacher and asked for a practice that would help open his life to wisdom. After observing the fellow, the teacher surprisingly advised him to begin giving money to those who insulted him. The practice being recommended required him to reward insults with payments of money. If he accepted this strange education, he would have to pay for insults for a period of three years.

What could he do? He had asked for direction and he had reached a point in life where something had to change. Either he would surrender and pay the price for waking up or else remain as he had been. The fellow decided to make the agreement and submit to the strange practice. Although deeply confused at first, he learned to return mistreatment with a reward. Each time someone insulted him, he responded by paying that person for the offence. Since he tended to be an arrogant and abrasive person, he had ample opportunities to attend to his new practice.

At the end of the three years, the student returned to the teacher and reported on his odd success. He had managed to give away a good deal of what he possessed and distributed it primarily to those who gave him insults. The teacher applauded him and announced that he was now ready to learn wisdom. He told the fellow to undertake a journey and visit a certain city. The disciple of insults lost no time getting going. He enjoyed the trip, being at ease in the knowledge that he had already paid his dues.

As he approached the gates of the great city he saw a man sitting near the entrance, as both holy ones and beggars are inclined to do. Although the man had the appearance of a saint, he had the behavior of a lout. He loudly hurled insults at each person who came or went through the gates. No one, high or low, was allowed to pass without suffering some humiliation. The strangest thing of all was the uncanny accuracy with which each insult was delivered. It was a kind of a greeting in reverse that most people found difficult to shrug off.

When it came time for the disciple to receive his greeting, the insult landed firmly. The difference was that the disciple burst out laughing and seemed to find great joy where others felt offended and abused.

"Why do you laugh when I accurately insult you," asked the gate guardian, "most people feel wounded when their hidden weakness becomes revealed."

"Because," answered the disciple, "for three years I have been paying for this kind of thing in hopes of finding wisdom and now you give it to me for free."

"Enter the city my friend," said the gate-keeper, "all within it is yours."

The student of insults entered the city and enjoyed the place because he had found a place in himself that needed to open and be healed and become clear. All indications are that the fellow had originally had trouble dealing with criticism of any kind. He took any suggestion that he change as an insult. Of course, that is often the case with those who readily criticize and insult others. Once he had to pay for insults his attention became focused on his own weakness and habitual condition. By the time he reached the city, he was like Eisik at the bridge. He was ready for a breakthrough and only needed one more insult to be released from his inner prison and become free to enter the shining city.

Each person has a complex of issues that surrounds the heart of hearts and blocks its full expression. There's no telling what might open a particular heart and reveal the gold hidden within it; but there is always some accuracy inside the circumstances that keep us stuck. Eventually a practice is needed to approach the problem and loosen the defenses.

The young woman who feared she would never find love was secretly a great lover. Her fear surrounded the love in her heart. She had to become more like a tiger in order to grasp her own loving nature. In stepping through her fears she moved closer to the fierce love that first set her seeking. When she went far enough into the teeth of her fears, the tiger came to meet her. When she became willing to grasp what she most desired, the fearful beast pretended not to notice. Just so, the otherworld moves closer whenever we face the tigers of our innermost fears.

The man who paid for insults had an unconscious way of berating and belittling himself. For what we do to others we tend to do more so to ourselves. With his insults he made others pay for his own discomfort and lack of acceptance. His joyful presence was hidden behind his insulting behavior. Only after he learned the true cost of offensive behavior could he learn to laugh at himself. Once he broke through the inner walls, he became able to enter the shining city of life open-heartedly.

An adventure becomes meaningful when it forces us to become ourselves. Sometimes that means going far out, sometimes turning deep within. Along the way we are bound to encounter old fears and infantile attitudes. A person must break several inner spells and awaken more than once in order to enter the gates of awareness. The problem involves our inability to truly trust what resides within us. Only after certain bridges of disbelief have been crossed does the door to the heart within the heart begin to open. Meanwhile, it helps to know that there is a resident sage in the heart, that the tiger within is inclined to help, and that the inner gold is always nearby.

Inner Alchemy

Just as the heart is more than a physical organ, gold is more than a valuable metal. Some brilliant ore exists in the inner tabernacle of the self. It waits to be revealed and become polished and be shown to the world. This "real gold" can only be found in one's own heart and soul; yet we must first see outside ourselves that which we would find deep within. Thus, the sense of spiritual gold being hidden in the heart permeates all the great religions and spiritual paths. Golden tabernacles, shining statues of deities, and saints with golden halos all stand as symbolic reminders of something that secretly exists inside each prayerful devotee. The message is sent through many channels because it intends to get through to us.

The golden aspects of the deep self are part of the natural epiphany that occurs during youth as each god-given talent is also a conduit through which inner gold can flow out into the world. Every young woman feels that she is golden at some moment; each young man feels brilliant in some way. Even a depression is evidence of something shining and bright that has disappeared from awareness. All people have their "golden moments;" for the inner gold cannot remain completely hidden. Being an essential part of one's life, it must become revealed, at least for a moment, or the soul will wither away.

For some, the first occasion of making love brings a stunning realization that a golden self exists and can awaken to a loving touch. Loving and gold go well together as so many lovers' gifts to each other can attest. Gold has qualities of endurance and malleability and people seek for the same things when it comes to love. Gold represents lustrous beauty unearthed, precious gifts revealed, and symbolizes fidelity to what is loved above all else. What a person truly loves is golden for each one, and we love those who in some way help us to find and better understand the hidden gold within ourselves.

Meanwhile, some people find the sense of gold within them the first time they climb a tree and see an entire forest before them. They feel the presence of the divine in the tree and in the breathing, living pulse of the forest. Nature can pull the gold in the veins of the heart into sudden awareness and trees can appear as a green fire and a spiritual presence. Others find their gold-connection the first time they speak spontaneously as words seem to flow forth and tumble out from a shining river at the back of their throat. For them, language is a stream flecked with golden nuggets that reflect an inner sun that can warm them and hold them near the unique flow and rhythm of the self within the self.

Some find a sense of inner gold the first time they touch a musical instrument. Their fingers already seem to know where the golden tones can be found and how to draw them out. The chords they shape resonate in tune with invisible cords already strung within them. Yet others awaken to a golden realm the first time they commit their entire body to dance. Some inner knowing and essential exuberance awakens in them when they hear the call of life's essential rhythms. They feel drawn beyond themselves, pulled on by secret sinews that cause them to leap. Leaving all else behind, they *become* the dance and in doing so enter into the depths of themselves shining forth.

The gold within the heart is a universal and essential truth about individual human life; it is an open secret waiting to be discovered over and over again. When such a secret becomes known it also becomes felt; for the open heart holds and harbors both our primary thoughts and deepest feelings. Gold represents a living spirit that can awaken at any time and reveal one's innate gifts and inspire the true work of one's life, the opus waiting to be created.

More often than not, the golden self makes a brief appearance; it goes unnoticed by others and lacks a meaningful confirmation. Later, the sense of a golden self must be sought for and sometimes be fought for before being found again. The inner gold must be mined from the dark matter, the "prima materia" or inner lead of one's life. Changing inner lead into gold requires a kind of rite of passage on a psychic level. It involves changing that which is dense and base into something noble and illuminating.

The finding and losing of the golden self is part of an inner alchemy and process of transformation that must be unique for each person. It involves the arc of return through which we view the course of our life the other way around. The returning path includes a life re-view and a chance to re-collect oneself from the road of lived experience. We step deeper into the same prints and find patterns that were there all along but hard to perceive the first time out. The second calling calls us to the inner arc of self-awareness and a reorientation to the original agreement of the soul and core imagination of the heart.

When the heart within the heart opens, the issue becomes not simply *who* I am or appear to be, but *what* is hidden within me. The *what* within each soul is the hidden gold, the core pattern and imagination from which the *who* of us grows and from which we draw inspiration for our intended life. True freedom means finding the essential *what* that we are and learning to live with and serve the divine elements sewn within us. Liberation occurs when the inner gifts become available and can be freely given.

Each person receives at least one experience of the gold buried in their heart and most have to go a great distance and pay a price to find it again. For Eisik it was the golden thread of dreams that led him all the way out into the world and finally back to the home ground of his soul. By following the feet of dreams Eisik found his gold again when he listened to his dreams and learned to open the heart within his heart. He also found his heart-work and core practice.

Eisik used the golden treasure to build a big house at the site of his old hut. He didn't build a bigger home to be self-important or to pretend to be something beyond himself. The point of the larger dwelling was to have a hall big enough for all the people of the village to gather together and talk. The great hall grew around the hearth of the old hut. When it was completed, Eisik invited everyone in.

Once they were inside, Eisik asked people to share their dreams. Having found the dream of his life and having followed where it led, he became a dream worker who tended the fires of imagination that burn even within the most humble of people. Eisik would listen carefully and encourage their dreaming. He helped people find the threads of their life-dreams and the callings that called them to become their true selves. In the alchemy of the soul those nearby also receive benefits when a person's dream comes to life; the inner gold increases rather than diminishes from being shared.

CHAPTER 10

GIFTS AND WOUNDS

Behind the wound lies the genius.
C. G. Jung

Because each soul is secretly tied to the Soul of the World, each culture, large or small, modern or traditional, must fashion a cosmology that somehow accounts for the entire universe. The smallest tribal group must have a story big enough to account for the planets and stars that swirl above, the forests and waters all around and the endless dreams and dramas that live inside people. Cosmology and mythology are as much a part of human nature as biology and logic.

Each group must shape origin theories and philosophies of life and some tale to tell about the nature of the soul, about the inspirations of the spirit, and the strange presence of an otherworld nearby. And each must consider the basic oppositions of life that appear as light and dark, as night and day, and also as the conflicts and contradictions found in human affairs and in each human soul.

The drama of light and darkness plays out every day and at every level of life. It can appear as right and wrong or even as good and evil. Yet the best stories keep a third element in reserve so that the opposing forces do not simply destroy or cancel each other, so that life cannot become completely stuck. In stories they say that "the third time is a charm," for the drama of opposing forces secretly intends to produce the unifying and healing energy of a third element. The missing third thing can often be found in the betwixt- and-between areas that are neither one thing nor the other.

Dreams and visions are part of the betwixt and between that keep life moving and make meaningful change possible. Members of a small tribe in South America have a keen interest in betwixt-and-between things, especially the time between night and day when the dawning light of day dismisses the dark cloak of eternity. They awaken early and begin each day with a communal and emphatic sharing of the night messages that came to them in sleep.

Because they are great singers, they sing their dreams to each other. They believe they are participating in the eternal reverberation of the song and sound of existence. The notion that "in the beginning was the word" rings true for them; but they imagine the "living word" of creation to be a continuing resonance and resounding vibration inside each life. Dreams and songs are ways of touching the deepest parts of oneself. Without them people can lose their natural rhythm as well as their true orientation in life.

Their big story about life includes the notion that the center of each soul remains essentially connected to the center of the cosmos. They consider dreaming to be the vehicle through which the human soul renews itself by returning to the vital source of life. Nightly dreams are seen as the free-of-charge, life-renewing, life-shaping messages that can be opened and shared and learned from. Each dream brought back from the cosmic center can carry important knowledge about the individual dreamer as well as the current condition of the world.

Wise and Crosswise

The tribal members consider the human psyche to have three separate elements and they describe each aspect of the soul as an essential inner word. The first soul element is called the "good word" or the "wise word." This seed word dwells at the center of one's life where it forms the core of the soul's language. The wise word carries the essential message a person is intended to deliver to the world. It is also the life-song, the feelings and imagination that the soul longs to express and contribute to the song of creation.

The second element is called the "word placed crosswise" on the soul.

It resides right next to the good or wise word set at the center of one's life. These two inner words are said to be entwined in such a way that they always move together. Each movement of the wise aspect within the soul activates the word-crosswise as a countermovement. Thus, each person has both wise and crosswise characteristics, both inner wisdom and something that can obscure or even cancel it. They use the sense of opposing words and opposite vibrations rather than the abstractions of good and evil.

Each person has an inner capacity to bring goodness to life and a natural wisdom to offer to others; at the same time, each has something cross-wise that can obstruct the goodness within. This inner dynamic helps explain why and how so many people act against their own best interests. It also elucidates how it could be that everyone on earth has something valuable to offer, yet most fail to give fully what they naturally have. The word-crosswise forms an inner shadow that darkens the light of the soul and can obscure the underlying goodness of life.

It creates deep doubts and acts as an inner critic that can cancel instinctive intelligence as well as drain the vital energy of one's life. As with fate, a restricting energy limits the intended expression of the soul. The threads of confusion must be disentangled if the wise-word and true destiny of one's life would be released. Fortunately, a third element exists that can alter the innate opposition between that which is wise and crosswise within each of us.

The third element is called the "word held in waiting" or the "waiting word." This third aspect of the soul appears as the inner charm of each life; it is the key to unlocking the opposition between all that is wise and crosswise within us and in the world around us. The waiting-word appears in dreams, in visions, and sudden inspirations that can lift the weight on the soul and shift the inner conflicts of one's life. If it were not for the word held in waiting, life could become truly stuck. The light and dark forces might cancel each other out and create a stalemate in the soul.

The waiting-word is what we are waiting for when life has lost its sense of meaning, when we have lost all sense of direction. It creates a middle ground of the soul, a place of understanding and distinguishing what compels us and what restricts our growth. It makes learning possible, especially learning what the underlying message and core imagination of one's life might truly be.

The essential play between elements of the soul is acted out each night when a person dreams. While the body rests in the arms of sleep, the first element or wise-word takes flight. It enters the unseen realm that exists at the edge of the waking world. Of course, it must be accompanied wherever it goes by the word-crosswise. Traveling together through the dream world, the two elements of the soul have various encounters and adventures. Eventually, they make their way to the center of the cosmos where all things and all dreams share a common origin.

The wise and crosswise elements return from their voyage beyond the daytime carrying messages they have collected on their night journey. They have witnessed things in the otherworld that have relevance to the dilemmas and troubles found here. At the moment of waking from sleep, the waiting-word is activated and receives the dream carried back by the other elements of the soul. In the betwixt-and-between state of awakening all three elements of the soul come together. They unite in the uncanny space between sleep and the waking world through the act of holding the dream in the present moment.

The night message becomes the opportunity for the inspiration of the waiting-word to penetrate the puzzle of the soul. The tension between that which is wise within us and that which is contrary about us forms the crucible in which the waiting-waking-word can break through and produce genuine meaning. The heightened state of true awakening is both inspiring and therapeutic as it involves both an experience of the wise-word within as well as insights into that which sits crosswise upon one's soul.

Through the word-waiting a person develops a capacity for true insight and an ability to find hidden meanings in daily events as well as in nightly dreams. The waiting-word helps reveal aspects of the wise self within that would otherwise remain hidden. Making the inner wisdom available to our consciousness makes life more meaningful and purposeful. Because the good word within is also the echo of creation and the song of one's life, revealing more of it also causes a renewal of one's vital energy. The thread of dreams becomes a channel for drawing energy from the center of the cosmos and the core of creation.

Disentangling the wise and crosswise threads woven within helps to reveal the underlying meaning and innate character of the soul. Such inner work is required if we would awaken to the destiny hidden within ourselves. The word-waiting acts as the sage in the soul, the natural dream interpreter and inner counselor that can awaken within, grow wiser and learn to solve the exact dilemmas of one's life.

The good word in each life waits to be uncovered; the wise word within longs to be expressed. However, on the way to revealing the hidden gold and expressing the wisdom of one's soul, we must become conscious of the contrary elements. Complicated issues will have to be disentangled. If it was simply a matter of expressing what lies at the core of one's being, everyone would already be wise and be living closer to the soul's essential aims. In the depths of the soul both the wise and the crosswise aspects of the self demand our continual attention. In order to truly awaken, the inner shadows and contrary elements must be faced. Each soul is wise as well as crosswise, gifted as well as wounded, and ever in need of the third thing, the charm that makes healing possible and makes each life surprising and ultimately meaningful.

Maggots and Gold

There is an old story of a young sister and brother who unexpectedly found themselves in a deep place where the opposite sides of life could be closely observed.

On a fine day they set out on a journey together and soon entered a wide field bathed in the light of the sun. Suddenly, they saw their father walking before them and were greatly surprised because their father had died some time before. Now, he was standing only a short distance before them. When he gestured for them to follow, they of course obeyed. What could they do; he was their father who had passed away and now returned before them.

The father walked in silence, while the sister and brother followed along behind him. Soon he came to an opening in the ground. Without saying a word, he entered the hole in the earth and began to descend out of sight. The children followed and found themselves on a road that took them steadily down into the depths of the earth. After travelling some distance, the sister and brother could see what seemed to be a village, right there, under the earth.

When their father entered the town below ground, they followed him. He led them to the center of the village and stopped. They could see that no one else was there. Suddenly, the father began to speak. He instructed them to enter some bushes that grew nearby. He exhorted them to stay hidden and silently observe everything that happened in the center of the village until the time when he would return. Since it was their father, since he had seemingly returned from the dead, since they were in an unfamiliar place, the sister and brother did exactly what he instructed them to do.

After they were well hidden in the bushes, the sister and brother saw a crowd of people enter the clearing. They gathered in the center of the village and seemed to be waiting for something. Then a noble-looking person appeared and walked directly to the center of the crowd. The people made room and the chief or king stood quietly amongst them. When the noble person turned to one side the brother and sister could see that his body was covered with rotting flesh and crawling with maggots.

The people began picking the maggots from the body of the chief and cleaning off the rotting flesh. They continued cleansing him until he turned and walked away. Then all the people dispersed and the center of the village became empty again. After that, the darkness grew and night seemed to swallow all the visible aspects of the place. For their part, the sister and brother kept still and remained quiet in the bushes.

When the light returned and chased the darkness away, they observed the crowd beginning to gather once more. Soon the chief appeared again and strode to the center of the village where the people made a space for him. This time he turned to the other side and the brother and sister could clearly see how that side glimmered like gold. The people began to anoint the golden side with oil; then they polished it until it shone like the sun itself. After a time, the chief turned and walked off and soon enough the entire crowd dispersed and the village became quiet again.

Just then, the father returned and gestured to the children to come out of the bushes. As they stood together in the center of the village under the world, the father asked them to describe what they had witnessed from their hiding place. They told how the crowd appeared and at first cleaned the side of the chief that was covered with rotting flesh and maggots. They described how the following day the other side became revealed, how it was made of shining gold, how the people anointed and polished that side until it shone like the sun.

Then the father spoke to them again. He said that because they had come to the village on the day of maggots and rotting flesh their luck in the world would be bad. He stated that it would be their fate to labor and struggle on the road of life and that little reward would result from their efforts. Had they only arrived on a day when the golden side was revealed first, their luck and fortune in the world would have been different. Their fate would have been much more favorable and the road of their lives much easier to travel.

Having spoken in that way, the father turned away and began to walk out of the village. Without saying another word, he went back up the road that they had all travelled down together. The sister and brother did not know what else to do but follow him. When the father arrived at the place where the road of the underworld opened out to the world above, he stepped to one side and stood in silence. The sister and brother passed quietly before their father and stepped from the underworld back into the daylight of the open field. Neither of them looked back as they continued on their journey together.

The story ends in the field where it began. Nothing more is said about what they thought or how they felt about the issues of fate or the wounds and blessings they had witnessed. It is left for each listener to decipher the meaning of the contrasting sides of the noble chief as well as the mixed messages that the dead father offered to his children.

The Inner Village

In the human psyche, down and back, under and within are more or less the same. The psychic village exists inside us as well as underneath outer events; it is below as well as behind everything that happens in our daily lives. The psychic village represents the collective unconscious and the shared imagination of the human soul. It contains ancient and valuable ideas and images just waiting to be unearthed and cleaned up and polished for our inspection. In the deep center of the psyche the young and the old, the living and the deceased, the immediate and the ancestral all meet. The wise and the crosswise, and the gifts and wounds of life all appear together as well.

All the members of the psychic crowd gather and meet at the center of the inner-other- underworld to consider what to do with the rotten issues and the golden gifts of life. Like the children observing from the bushes, like the dreamers awakening with night messages, we are invited to see into the center where the core issues of life and death, of maggots and gold, of fate and destiny wait for our exact attention.

At the center of the psyche a double ceremony occurs as the opposite sides of the soul's noble bearing become revealed. The members of the psychic village play the role of the waiting-word that attends to all that is wise and crosswise within us. They handle directly and cleanse thoroughly that which is contrary and wounded and rotten in the soul. Then they proceed to anoint the good word within and polish the noble side of the lord of the inner realm. Through the inner ritual of cleansing the wounds and polishing the golden aspects of the self an underlying ceremony of life and hidden unity of the soul becomes revealed.

Just like the wise and crosswise words upon the soul, the gifted and wounded aspects appear together. Each moves in response to the movement of the other as they alternate in the inner dynamic of healing and revealing. Both elements require some careful and accurate attention for the village to function fully and be dynamically balanced. If the golden self is properly attended to, the entire village brightens and shines as if to rival the sun.

Each person has access to the deep radiance of the noble and awakened self; but only after the rotten issues and suppurating wounds have been brought out in the open and have been thoroughly cleansed. In order to be a proper ruler of one's own psyche, one must face what is rotten inside as well as come to know the ways that one is naturally golden within.

The deceptive simplicity of the tale reveals a deep psychic truth about the gifted and wounded nature of the soul and about the core problems that face each community, each society, and each culture. Imagine the difference in most places if people fully realized that everyone they meet is both wounded and gifted, both burdened with some troubling issues and imbued with some golden qualities. Imagine the difference if powerful rulers and elected leaders exposed their own mistakes, brought their inner shadows into the light of day, and allowed others to help clean their inner shadows and cleanse their rotten areas.

The golden qualities of life wait to be found; yet some descent is required and a willingness to handle whatever has become poisonous or twisted or simply unwise. The core psychic ritual begins with a careful cleansing and healing of whatever is wounded and distorted, what has become rotten and corpselike within us. It is this other side, the darker area and wounded part of both personal and collective life that tends to be avoided and that keeps the inner nobility from shining forth with greater frequency.

Life cannot be neutral for very long; when the inner cleansing does not happen, the rot inside deepens, and both the individual soul and the core of the community become sick. Only after picking over the worst inner issues can the noble sense of self be restored and be able to shine at the center. The inner ceremony of the soul reveals the intricate and intimate relationship between gifts and wounds. Where there are great gifts there will also be deep wounds for they are two sides of the inner nobility of the soul.

The root of *nobility* involves the sense of "coming to know." We are noble in so far as we come to truly know ourselves; for then we learn both how we are gifted and where we are wounded. In knowing that we become able to heal within and be generous and generative with others.

Of Family and Fate

The tale of the young sister and brother facing issues of life and death in the underworld implies that visits to the deep psychic village will involve early life experiences. Because our inner wounds were first felt during the vulnerable periods of infancy and childhood, going near them later can cause a person to feel childish and abandoned all over again. Regardless of one's age, it is easy to feel like a helpless child when near the old, unattended wounds of the soul; yet it becomes necessary to go there if the golden side of one's life would be found again.

The business of gifts and wounds begins early in life and inevitably involves one's parents and the issues of family fate. Regardless of good intentions, one's parents are rarely the wisest counselors regarding the nature of one's soul and the inner shape of one's life. They have their own blind spots and crosswise issues and their own wounds to deal with. Parents can be most caring and protective; yet they can also be great obstacles to perceiving one's natural orientation and intended role in life.

Through our parents we first experience love and intimate relationships; through them we often receive our deepest sense of abandonment and most potent experience of misinformation. The father in the story manages to lead the children to a place where the central issues of life and death can be considered; yet the conclusions he draws may not serve their lives at all. Often unwittingly, sometimes mistakenly, but also necessarily, parents mislead and even betray the vulnerable souls of their children. And they do it with surprising accuracy, so that attending to the earliest experiences of abandonment and wounding will also bring people close to where their natural gifts reside.

Meanwhile, each family has its share of human tragedy and psychic residues that descend down the family line. Each family has its "specific gravity" that includes elements of fate and aspects of psychic weight that cannot be completely swept under the carpet, or simply be left behind. There may be elements of a family inheritance that make life comfortable, humorous or exciting; but there will also be shadows and inner gravities.

Each family has elements of fate and energies that run crosswise and contrary to the health and welfare of its members. The family shadow includes some "prima materia," some primal matters and core issues that affect the soul of each child born into it.

For each family represents an ongoing attempt to struggle with fateful issues, heal certain wounds, and make inner gifts more available. The inevitability of family shadows and inherited fates is the stuff of ancient tragedies that were played out on the earliest stages. The fates and shadows of royal families were acted out like the drama in the underworld village so that everyone could be reminded of the search for genuine nobility and reflect upon the maggots and the gold found within the lineage of their own families.

Call it inherited depression or a proclivity for violence; call it anxious tendencies or shared phobias; each family has its familiar, familial traumas and troubling patterns. Each family system includes characteristic ways of avoiding, denying or glossing over the very issues that need to be faced and healed and cleaned up. If the core issues and inherited fates are too deeply buried or too strongly denied, they become a toxic inner lead that can be poisonous to the entire family.

The family fate can include the heavy hand or poisonous atmosphere that overshadows the natural aspirations of its children and crushes dreams before they fully form. It can also manifest itself as a cool indifference to both the painful vulnerabilities and the gifted nature of children. While indifference may seem preferable to a heavy-handed fate, it will be experienced as a deep blow to the growing psyche of a child. For the natural expectation is that the presence of a golden self in each child will be acknowledged and be celebrated with fondness and encouragement. Indifference to the potential brilliance of growing children resonates deeply within them and adds weight to the cross-wise aspect that they naturally have.

The trusting and inquiring nature of children causes them to directly encounter and deeply feel the innermost shadows and hidden wounds of their family. Where there is no corresponding recognition of the gifts the children carry within them, the life-projects of the children can become largely overshadowed by the family fate. Did not the father in the story tell the children that they came on the wrong day and would have troubles all their life? That's how it feels and how it seems when the family fate takes precedence over the life-dream trying to awaken in a young person's soul.

When considering events in the psychic village, the sister and brother might recall that their father appeared at a certain time and called them to follow his lead. He was intimately involved in the timing that brought them to the village of revelations on the day of maggots and rotten wounds. He first beckoned to them on the unlucky day, so he is implicated in the heavy fate he later assigns to them. He invites them into the depths of reality; yet he insists upon determining what their future reality will be.

Like fathers the world over, he feels it is his role to interpret what the children see and how they understand their experiences in life. Remember old Oedipus? It is no accident that the story of a father misinterpreting the fate of his child becomes the foundation tale of the resurgence of psychology in the modern world. It is a rare thing for parents to perceive or understand either the personal fates or the inborn destinies of their children.

The story focuses upon inner gifts and wounds, but it uses the father's attitude and the family fate to frame the core issues. Parents may lead their children to the doors of knowledge, but what the children see when they open the doors is between them and their fate, between them and the unfolding threads of their destiny. The story depicts the inevitable disconnect between the experience of the children and the beliefs of their father. Many human experiences reflect a similar distortion.

When the children leave the inner realm and return to the daylight world, they must pass their father. He stands at the intersection of the outer world and the inner psychic village. Just so, most people encounter the shadow and the spirit of their father each time they take a new step in life or attempt to bring a new project to fruition in the outer world. Fulfilling one's personal destiny requires passing beyond the position one's father took in the world.

The story suggests that people must go to great depths if they are to break the family spell and awaken to the specific nature of their own fate and destiny. In order to get the whole picture of the inner realm, the children will have to see things with their own eyes and in their own unique ways. That's true in the story and true in the world, where parents so often feel that they know what is best for their children; where society so often limits the lives of its members. The father may have opened the way to the depths of the inner realm, but it will be the lifelong task of the children to discern what needs to be healed and what must be polished in their own souls.

Gifted and Wounded

A father often represents a knowing authority, perhaps more so than otherwise if he has passed away while the children are young. The sister and brother in the story were still young enough to be projecting the archetypal qualities of wisdom and guidance onto their father. Projecting inner gifts and powers onto others is the natural and necessary process through which we become able to see what most interests us in this world. Yet, in order to begin seeing the world with the inner eyes of their souls, children must eventually withdraw from their parents the typical projection of power and knowledge.

We are each the young sister, each the young brother of the psyche and we each must project before us what we long to claim as ours in this world of lost and found things. Repeatedly, we project onto others exactly what we need to find and recognize in ourselves. What begins as idolizing one's mother or father eventually leads to seeing others as kingly figures and queen-like personages. All people, to one degree or another, project their inner nobility and inherent power onto others until it becomes painfully necessary to reclaim and polish what was within them all along.

We all have access to the village under the world and we view the rituals of cleansing and polishing from the precise angle of our own inner hiding place. We perceive the symbolic drama from within our own psychic arrangement of gifts and wounds. A symbolic image like the maggots and gold manages to be universal in the sense that it speaks to everyone; but a true symbol is also specific as it can only be perceived by the unique angle of the individual soul. The eye of the self looks out through the window of the soul and the inner uniqueness provides a specific lens and a particular view of the world.

If everyone saw things the same way there would be no need for so many people and there would be no urge to individuate and truly become oneself. "I am your own way of seeing the world," says the soul, "each time you allow me to be present will be a sort of salvation." We are here because of our own mystical unrest and must learn to see the world before us with the penetrating view of our inner eyes. Despite the common notion that the world impresses itself upon our eyes, we are here to learn how the inner eyes of our souls already see and what path they seek to lead us to find and follow.

In learning to see through the inner eyes of the soul we shift the obscuring weight of all that is crosswise upon us. In removing whatever rots within us we become more noble and able to shine from within. Each soul has its own wounds and festering issues that need attention and each has its unique arrangement of gifts that are needed in the world. Gifted and wounded, that's how we arrive in this world that involves both the gifts of eternity and the wounds of time. Gifted and wounded, wise and crosswise, the human soul carries its complexities and seeks to unfold them.

Those who think they are not wounded in ways that need conscious attention and careful healing are usually the most wounded of all. Those who believe they are exempt from crosswise elements within have not yet opened their inner eyes. Those who imagine they have been fully cured of the ills of this world have usually not descended deeply enough. For the village of healing begins with personal wounds, but also includes whatever is rotten in the community and naturally extends to helping others who are wounded.

No matter who a person might appear to be in the outer world, they remain a complex mixture of maggots and gold in the inner realm. Gifted and wounded we are and must be if we are to understand the nature of this world that exchanges light and dark, night and day, life and death. By its very nature, life is both a gift and a wound; it is a gift that allows us to witness creation and a wound that separates us from the source of creation itself. To be human means to observe in our own unique way the village of life, to participate in the alternation of gifts and wounds, to grow by healing and to learn by giving away what is discovered.

Growing the Soul

In the eternal village under the earth the ceremony of the deep self waits to be found again and again. Each time an inner gift is grasped, an inner wound will need some attention; each time a wound receives the healing touch some golden quality of the self will shine further forth. Healing the wounds and polishing the gold; deepening the soul and revealing the great self within, these are the rituals of self-discovery and growing from within. In order to grow each person must become divided again and again so that a greater unity might be forged within. First one side, then the other; the inner rite of individuation shifts from touching the inner wounds and cleansing them to polishing the golden side of the self and further unifying the soul.

Each visit to the depths of the soul reveals another level of wounds that need healing and another aspect of the golden presence of the unified self that underlies all the divisions of life. The human soul is capable of reaching profound states of healing; yet we only remember and reach such depths when life pulls us to the edge of vulnerability again, when some new betrayal or old failing drives us back and down to the places of healing. For old wounds and deep losses wait for vulnerable moments in order to reappear and become further healed. Any shock, betrayal or loss in the upper world can serve as a catalyst that irritates old wounds and tries to instigate a cleansing and clearing of the soul. It is in this way that the suffering and injuries, illness and losses experienced in life truly become opportunities for healing and the growth of the soul.

Common wisdom would have us avoid trouble and seek comfort. Yet on the road of life and death, whatever troubles the soul but goes unattended will begin to rot within. What fails to serve life becomes as a corpse within that will make its way towards decay and death. People say it is best to leave the past behind; but the past travels with us and old wounds wait to be opened again in order to heal. Most people avoid the painful areas and resist the natural inclination to pick at the wounds. Yet there is a maggot capacity in each person. Maggots represent a deep process of separating and healing in the soul.

They may make people queasy and uneasy, but maggots are the expert cleansers and instinctive purifiers that remove the rotting flesh and precipitate genuine healing. Maggots appear wherever the tissues of life begin to rot; they instinctively know how to cleanse whatever becomes diseased. They will remove all decayed flesh yet never damage any healthy tissue nearby. Although commonly seen as the agents of death, maggots are secretly the agents of life and the natural healers of the earth.

In the story of the psychic village, they appear deep in the earth and at the center of the noble rites of healing. Those who have the gift of healing know something of the skills of maggots. Healers have to have some maggot qualities in them in order to help preserve life. In order for the healing to begin, the wound must be opened further. The decayed flesh must be cleanly separated and removed before the wound can be properly closed and healthy tissue can renew the wounded place.

Maggots are like the word-waiting that instinctively knows how to distinguish between what is healthy and wise within us and what is unhealthy and crosswise to our life spirit. Maggots represent whatever attends to our wounds and helps to clean up the inner mess of the psyche. Despite their creepy reputation they can be "exactly what the doctor ordered." As mini-surgeons they symbolize the essential process of healing and making whole as they separate the corpse from the living elements of one's life.

Once healed over, the wounded places often become stronger than normal tissue. Healing makes a person stronger than before the wounds were faced and treated. Thus, the "wounded-healer" remains the true model for all who would become healers. The process of revealing one's inner gold and pursuing one's destiny depends upon the companion practice of handling elements of fate and healing one's inner wounds. The sequence in the story shows how healing must often precede the time of anointing and polishing the gold.

Those who rise to great heights and handle power have great need for repeated healing if they are to develop and maintain some inner nobility. Whoever would become knowing and wise would be wise to face and resolve all that remains unwise within them. For whoever rises closest to the light must also cast the greatest shadow. Whoever would become anointed would best submit to continual cleansing and healing or else suffer a great fall when the shadow erupts and the inner decay becomes revealed.

Unity and Opposition

This world operates through polarities and pairings that both oppose and complement each other and humans are no exception. The heart beats with two sides, the lungs double up to breathe, breasts hang side by side and the testicles as well. The eyes and ears watch and listen from two sides of the same face and many have been known to speak out of both sides of their mouths. Sometimes one hand doesn't know what the other is doing and most of us suffer inner conflicts and are often at odds with ourselves.

A person is both a unity and an opposition, so is a marriage and so are most social relationships as well. A whole society works that way, with opposing political parties and with upper classes looking down on those trying to move up in the world. Each thing carries its own shadow and the inner oppositions in people repeatedly become reflected in outer conflicts that are even harder to get a handle on. Whatever we refuse to face within us will become a collective fate in the world around us. The wise come to know their own inner conflicts, while the unwise keep insisting that all the trouble is the fault of others.

Expression and repression are two sides of the same coin, just as knowledge and ignorance reside in the same person. This explains many things, including the common tendency to undervalue and undermine the exact things that are most important to us. A person feels the presence of inner gifts, but underplays them or defers to others who may be less gifted, but act more boldly in life. Whether it appears as debilitating fear or false humility, as false bravado or a rush to judgment, the word-crosswise within us is the source of persistent ignorance and blind self-denial.

Languages preserve this sense of close opposition in words like wise and crosswise or wit and witless. *Avidyā* is an old Sanskrit word meaning "ignorance and delusion; being unlearned or unwise." It is the opposite of *vidya* which means "to see, to know;" similar to the English words "vision" and "visible." *Avidyā* names the inner contradiction that can cause people to live in self denial and even defend their own blindness. The inner dream of life and the original agreement of the soul are there regardless of outer appearances; yet the word-crosswise and the inner shadows obscure their presence.

That is a cross we bear as humans. It is the crux of the matter when it comes to wisdom and healing and change. We all exist inside our own contradictions long before we face any opposition or enemy outside ourselves. Call it *avidyā* or the inner shadow; call it the inner demons or blind egotism; everyone suffers from it to one degree or another. Each has an inner radiance and each has distinct blind spots. The gifts are near, yet they so often seem far away and feel out of reach.

We all have our limp and necessary imperfections; we each suffer that which is crosswise on our souls and common society tends to sanction and sustain that which is most blind within us. Meanwhile, dreams keep pounding on the roofs of our houses and our callings keep calling to us. Our inner weirdness keeps trying to manifest itself and no one can remove the soul's desire to awaken to its own divine nature. The wise-word and the golden seed, the life-dream and the treasure hard to attain are all symbols representing the original agreement that our souls make before ever entering the womb of life.

Because our greatest gifts and deepest wounds reside in the same area; because the resurrection of old pains can be so fearful and painful, people need to be reminded in diverse ways that the inner dream of life, the wise word set within and the psychic gold are the natural inheritance of each human soul. Because it is so easy to forget what we so desperately need to remember; old stories talk of golden treasures and great dreams that call us to undertake adventures and pilgrimages that in the end reveal what was within us all along.

III

The Return of Wisdom

*The wise person allows universal imagination to
operate through them.*

CHAPTER 11

DIE BEFORE YOU DIE

Death has been separated from its original unity with fate.
Liz Greene

There are many stories of how the world began and many tales about how it all might end. The world is too surprising to be captured in a single tale; yet each story reveals something of the divine. In an ancient creation myth from India the beginning of the world comes as a surprise even to the one who creates it. The god Prajapati is credited with making the entire world; yet it appears suddenly, as an unexpected expression of life that bubbles up from within him. The great abundance of creation flows out as if from a sudden inspiration erupting from a hidden excess of life. The world, with all its complexities and diversity of life forms, comes pouring out full-blown into existence.

Ever since the original creative eruption, this world can be experienced as endlessly bountiful, as a place of constant wonder and awe. Creation continues in the surprise of each dawn that arises and unfolds from the dark reaches of night. It continues in the surprising birth of each child and in the many ways that people all over the world create more life by responding to inspirations, by fashioning art and by forging abundant relationships. Prajapati made the world through the surprise of creation and that way of making continues to occur throughout the world each day.

After the world was born in abundance and thoroughly elaborated, Prajapati experienced a new feeling, another strange sense from within. The creator suffered a post-partum depression on a cosmic level as all seemed to grow shadowy, empty and dark. In the aftermath of the overflow of life, the god of creation began to feel quite empty; he felt sad, lonely, even fearful. Something else was almost present and Prajapti was not the kind of god that would shrink from the presence of anything. So the god of creation created the world all over again, this time using the depths of loneliness and longing as the source of creation; this time using fear and trepidation as the way to proceed.

What had arisen out of joy and exuberance was followed by fear and by sorrow. What had been made of pure abundance was made again of pure loneliness. The creator made the world all over again, this time from the depths of negation, from the loss and longing he found within himself. Prajapati was so full and so empty that everything that was and all that was not came pouring forth from him. Life flowed from a hidden abundance to a manifest fullness and poured from the empty to the void as well.

Thus, Prajapati added a second layer and darker level of creation to the expanse of being and the overflowing joy of the world. And that is the world to which each soul is born, the world that keeps being born again and again from the overflowing fullness at the center and from the emptiness at the core of that fullness. The beginning keeps beginning and the ends keep ending; for fullness harbors emptiness within it and the void turns back into the abundance of the world in the ongoing dance of creation and in the secret exchange between life and death.

Light and dark are the contrasting, alternating partners of existence; they begin the dance through which joy travels with grief and through which fear can follow happiness in this ever-changing world. Some believe that god must be far above such negative emotions and seemingly faulty feelings; they have difficulty imagining loneliness in connection with the creator. Yet older ways of seeing considered that a creator must know all aspects of creation. Whatever exists had to be there in some form at the beginning or it cannot exist at all. If loneliness and fear, sorrow and death are in the world now, they must have been present at the very beginning when everything that was going to be began to be.

The old story shows two sides of existence and two hands of creation. It depicts the back-and- forth involving light and dark, positive and negative, full and empty that characterizes life from beginning to end. Abundance and fullness can only exist in contrast with loss and emptiness; one following upon the other and both being aspects of the ongoing resonance and reverberations that echo from the surprise of creation.

To this day, each person inherits this two-handed, double-sided, back-and-forth way of being in the world. Each has a hand of abundance and each is empty-handed at times. Each has the surprising gift of life and each life must one day come to an end. Death and loss must have a place in life or creation cannot continue. If we treat death simply as an absence of life, something essential to creation becomes lost to our awareness. When seen in the context of an ongoing creation, death can be found to have a place in the midst of life and even a hand in each occasion of renewal.

An old Celtic proverb boldly places death right at the center of life. "Death is the middle of a long life," they used to say. Ancient people did things like that; they put death at the center instead of casting it out of sight and leaving such an important subject until the last possible moment. Of course, they lived close to nature and couldn't help but see how the forest grew from fallen trees and how death seemed to replenish life from fallen members. Only the unwise and the overly fearful think that death is the blind enemy of life.

When death is denied or only given a place at the end of life, a kind of existential displacement takes place. Appearing only at the end makes death seem more devastating and fatalistic than it need be. A healthy awareness of death can make the breath of life feel more immediate and palpable and be all the more precious. Death used to be called the great teacher of life; for in knowing something about death people came to value life more distinctly. It is not morbid to consider the role of death in life; rather, facing one's own mortality may help clarify one's genuine role in life.

Ancient notions of where to place death might offer surprising hints for how to find the center of our lives. If the issue of death could become more central to life again, then life might become more centered upon meaningful things. When death is in the middle of life as well as at the end of it, more than one kind of death can be discerned and more of the secret of life might be learned.

A Conversation with Death

It's like the old story of the fellow who met death unexpectedly and surprisingly right in the middle of the great marketplace of life. He was the servant of a wealthy merchant in the old market town of Isfahan. The adventure began on a fine morning with the sun warming the face of the earth and with promise in the air. The servant rode off on his errands feeling content and carefree. His purse jingled with coins as he anticipated a feast being planned by his master. He was ready to discover what fresh items the market had to offer on such a fine and promising day.

As he moved amidst the teeming crowd, the servant suddenly saw the figure of Death. In the midst of the great marketplace of life Death seemed to beckon as if about to speak to him. Before a word could be uttered, the servant turned and fled with the utmost speed. He had heard the old belief that once death speaks to you, your life will end. He had no interest in having the final conversation at that time, so he raced off on his master's horse striking out on the road that led through the desert toward the distant town of Samarra.

By nightfall he had left Isfahan far behind and arrived on the outskirts of the distant city. Seeing an inn nearby, he drew the tired, sweating horse to the door. Using the merchant's coins, he purchased a room for the night. Exhausted in both body and soul, he stumbled to his room and collapsed onto the waiting bed. His fears and fatigue mingled with a sense of relief at the idea that he had preserved his life and had outwitted Death. As the night closed around him, the servant fell into the arms of sleep.

In the middle of the night he suddenly awakened at the sound of something moving in the room. When he looked up, he saw Death standing at the foot of the bed, smiling at him.

"How can you be here?" demanded the servant, beginning to tremble with fear again. "I saw you this morning far from here, in the midst of the marketplace in Isfahan."

"What you say is true," said Death. "When I saw you I tried to speak and say that you and I have an appointment tonight in Samarra. But you would not let me say a word and only ran away."

The tale ends in eerie silence as the conversation between Death personified and the fearful servant of life comes to an abrupt end. It's an old tale, one told in many lands and in different ways. The names of the towns change to suit the locale. Sometimes the servant is young, sometimes white of hair. Sometimes Death appears as an old woman, sometimes as a grim old man. There are old folk versions of the tale and more famous literary renderings of it. What remains consistent, however, is the sense of an inevitable appointment with Death and the irony of the servant trying to escape his fate. He thought he had left his issue with Death far behind him until he found it right before him. In trying to escape his fate, he ran right into it.

The servant cannot escape death and those who listen to the tale become caught in the puzzling questions of personal fate and the presence of death in the midst of life. The presence of fate is a great paradox in human life, especially when viewed through its connection with death. From one point of view, the servant was fated to meet his end in Samarra. His attempt to run away only led him more directly to what was bound to happen anyway. From another angle it could be said that he had to cooperate in order for the fateful meeting to occur. The servant went of his own will to the meeting in the dark inn. Thus, he contributed to his own demise; he willed it as much as fate decreed it.

As an African proverb states: "On the road where you will meet your death, your legs will carry you and your feet will go." The sense of death as a companion in one's life was common to ancient cultures. Our fate is unavoidable because it travels with us wherever we might go. "Death is in the fold of your cloak," they used to say in order to make clear how death is folded into life from the very beginning. The modern mind struggles greatly with the paradoxical nature of fate and often runs into it when least expected.

People avoid "end of life" conversations because they seem morbid or fatalistic, because they mention the unmentionable. The presence of death has become something to be avoided at all costs. When the end of life is simply attributed to "heart failure" or "lung failure" death becomes a "failure of life" instead of being seen as its inevitable companion. It's as if the old superstitions about avoiding the presence of death become even stronger when dying is considered failing to live. At times, the modern world looks like a harried and confused servant trying desperately to outrun the inevitable while claiming to be on the verge of a miracle cure for all that ails life.

The marketplace abounds with promises of cures for aging, drugs for whatever ails you and pain-killers that will make death's sting almost painless. Yet in making death a medical occasion more than a metaphysical event, life itself has become diminished. Many lose their dignity amidst overly heroic efforts to prolong life under any circumstances. Death has been separated from its connection with fate and has lost its place in life. Death has lost its place as the teacher of dark wisdom and as the metaphysical instructor in the course of life. When death becomes a final indignity rather than a necessary element in the human drama, something of the meaning of both life and death has been lost.

A Darker Knowledge

People forget that life is fatal, that agreeing to be born at a specific time also means agreeing to die one day. Without death there can be no road of life. Everything that happens to us occurs on the road that begins with birth and ends with death. We live between Ishfahan and Samarra; between the teeming marketplace of life and the dark inn of death. We run back and forth repeatedly, without even knowing it. There is a darker knowledge that involves an ongoing conversation between life and death within each of us. In denying death's presence in the middle of life people run the risk of denying life's ability to renew itself.

Isfahan was a renowned market town; it offered so much richness and wonder that people called it "half of life." It stands for the abundance of creation and all the brightness and freshness of life. It represents the great marketplace with its endless deals and exchanges that keep life pulsing and thriving. Isfahan is the brightness of life and the wonder of creation. Yet in the middle of the market of endless possibilities and amazing delights, fate and death will also be found. It is important to enter the marketplace, to accept and participate in the reckless dance of life; it is also important to know the other half of creation and learn how to die a little when the time for true change comes.

In order to be fully alive we must have more than one brush with death. Having a greater life means dying more than once. There are "little-deaths" that occur throughout the course of life; attending to them and learning from them secretly adds to the vitality and abundance in one's soul. Denying the presence of death and avoiding the little-deaths that make life meaningful means failing to learn the darker knowledge that comes from the other hand of creation. In the long run, there is no way to be entirely free of the hand of fate and no way to cheat death either.

The servant accepts the fearful superstition that any conversation with death means that life is about to end. Meanwhile, his death sentence becomes more pronounced as he runs as far as he can from the middle of life. The middle is where life and death constantly exchange with each other. The true point and darker knowledge of the old story may be that running from death also means running from life. When we fail to grasp the nature and shape of our own fate, we become ruled by it. In trying to escape our fate we inadvertently contribute to the hardening of it.

The real problem is that most people cheat themselves out of the promise of their own life. In trying to avoid fate and dismissing life's limitations in favor of seemingly endless possibilities, people fail to learn who they already are in their own center and how they might be called to a unique destiny. Fate limits us and even stops us in our tracks so that our destiny can find us.

Most people live their fate unconsciously, failing to sense an inner purpose waiting to be found within the precise limitations of their lives. Such is the nature of fate; either it becomes conscious and more malleable, or else it becomes increasingly restricting and fearful, and, finally, fatal. Either we face our limitations and find the meaningful thread that would unwind from within us, or missing our destiny, we blindly live out our fate.

If we stop the story at the point where death first appears but has not definitively spoken, the presence of death may have a different message to deliver. If we stand in the middle of life's great marketplace and look at the role that death plays, we may see how a little-death is required for life to continue. The presence of death is a tactic of life and a little-death is needed whenever life would grow greater. Death used to be considered the beginning of all philosophy. *Philosophy* means "love of knowledge" and those who truly love knowledge will search for it even at the door of death in order to better understand the mysteries of life.

Mysteries of Life and Death

All true stories try to touch the mysteries of life; where one story ends, another picks up the thread and continues on. The fearful servant ran away rather than learn what death might have to say to him. Yet there was a learned man whose search for knowledge caused him to purposely seek an encounter with the angel of death. People called him Luqman the Wise because he was so manifestly dedicated to the pursuit of knowledge, especially the knowledge of spiritual things. People also called him a prophet because he could see things that remained hidden from others. However, after years of perfecting his wisdom, one thing seemed to elude him: he had no knowledge of the time of his own death.

He was wise enough to consider that such information might be the privilege of god; he was also convinced that he could find a way to learn the exact hour of his death. The seer went looking for what most others avoid. He began a practice of deep meditation and vowed not to stop contemplating until he managed to ascertain the time of his death. The search for knowledge can be as compulsive and consuming as the search for wealth or for power, for that matter. Through persistent effort and deep insight, Luqman was able to determine the day on which death would claim him.

On the morning of the day on which his death was expected, the prophet left his home. He left behind all that he had and all whom he knew and made his way to a nearby cave. When the angel of death arrived at the door of his house, the wise man was nowhere to be seen. A small boy, whom Luqman had instructed, told the angel how to find the cave to which the prophet had retired.

The angel had his own commitments. He was on an errand from god and wasted no time finding his way to the mouth of the cave where Luqman waited in silence. He stood in the broad light of day and peered into the darkness of the earthly enclosure. He called Luqman by name and gave the customary salutation that begins with "Peace be upon you." For at that time, knowledge was considered a sacred thing and prophets were to be greeted with respect even by angels. It was a small courtesy owed to those who become wise in the ways of the spirit and the soul.

"Welcome," responded a voice from within the cave. Upon hearing the response, the angel stepped from the light of day into the dark interior and became unable to see for a moment. When his sight adjusted to the darkness, he saw standing before him, not a solitary prophet but a crowd of seers. There were at least a hundred Luqmans in the cave. The messenger of death was completely baffled.

"I am commanded to take the life of one called Luqman the Wise; so please show yourself," said the angel.

"I am here," answered a hundred voices.

"Yes, but I can only take one Luqman; which one are you?" questioned the angel. "That is for us to know," the answer came in a hundred voices, "and for you to find out."

Luqman the Wise had figured out how to multiply himself and how to hide himself within the multiplication of selves. He was there in the cave waiting for the time of his death, but he was also hidden amongst replicas of himself. The seer's time was up; yet he could not be separated from the crowd. Not knowing what to do, the angel of death went off to seek some guidance from god.

After hearing about the scene in the cave and the hundred forms of the one prophet, the creator instructed the angel on how to proceed.

"Return to the cave again. This time enter it before you make any greeting. Once your vision clears, greet the prophet in your customary manner and he will have to reply as his individual self or else he will offend the holy tradition. Before he completes his reply, take his life and be done with it."

The angel returned to the cave as instructed; he entered it silently and stood before the hundred forms of Luqman. "Peace be upon you, friend Luqman," said the messenger.

"And on you, angel of..." One of the figures began to give the customary reply. Of course, it was the real Luqman who answered. Before he could complete the response, the angel of death took his life.

Shortly thereafter, both the angel and the prophet appeared before god.

"Dear lord," said the angel, "there is something I do not understand about this strange occurrence. Only you know the time of each person's death. Although I deliver the fatal message, I only learn the name and the time of death when you reveal it to me. How did the prophet know when the hour of his death would come?"

Before the divine could have a say in this matter of life and death, the wise prophet offered an answer to the question posed about the nature of his own death.

"My friend, I did not know the exact time of my death. Had I truly known the hour of my death, I would not be here. What my seeking and learning revealed was only the time of your first arrival. Everything that happened between the time when I first saw you and when you came before me again was unknown to me. I knew *that* you were coming, but I could not decipher exactly when. In the end I was taken by surprise anyway."

Now, the conversation with death has become more specific and it extends all the way to god. Instead of an unwitting servant surprised by the presence of death, we find a wise man seeking to learn all about mortality and final things. Whereas the fearful servant sought to escape death at any cost, the learned man made the meeting with death the whole point of his life. Where one would run away under any circumstances, the other sought to have the final encounter on his own terms.

Through concentrated effort the wise man found a way to stand before death and not simply succumb to it. He learned what the wise often know, that here on earth everything has a limit, even death. When it comes to the human soul, even death must wait for the proper time to arrive. Death is the final distinction and as long as the wise man stood amidst the army of identical figures, death could not distinguish him. Death, like life, can only deal with particulars. Death may be the common fate of all who come to life, but death must come to each person individually. Even in a great catastrophe where many souls are lost, death must come to each one specifically, exactly and personally.

Each life is unique, each death is an individual matter, and what matters at the time of death is one's individuality. The prophet baffled the dark angel by appearing amidst false versions of himself. He kept death in the dark by hiding his true self. Since he could only live as Luqman, he could only die as Luqman. In the end, he could not be touched by death except in the unique form of his own life. In the end we can't hide in the crowd. Even if we fail to live our true individuality in life, we will respond to it and answer for it in the end.

What brings each person to life is unique to that person and it is that inner uniqueness that is called back to the divine when one's time on earth is done. Once again, the divine sends the message that the crucial element that unites this world of limitations with the unseen realm of the eternal is the uniqueness dwelling in the individual soul.

A Little Death, A Great Life

In a sense, we are all servants in this life, each having come to life in order to serve something greater than our little-selves. No matter what costume we may wear or what status we may achieve, we are all on the way to the dark inn or the old cave where the dark angel calls to us. In the meantime, there is an unknown territory, a mysterious area where the presence of death does not equal the end of life. There is an appointment with death that is separate from the final meeting with the dark angel. There is a "little-death" before death becomes such a big and defining event in life.

Death is the middle of a long life, and a little-death can lead to a greater understanding of the life one already has. Our little encounters with death, sorrow and loss are inevitable and if suffered honestly can become the darker wisdom from which a greater life can grow. The territory of little-death is where the ego-self dies a little and a deeper revelation of life becomes more possible. The question is whether we can learn something of our true essence from the way death brushes against our lives. The presence of death can be a teacher and guide that helps reveal the way of life waiting to be found within.

Remember the story of how the Buddha first encountered death? He was also on the way to the great marketplace of life when death appeared before him. The one who was to become the Buddha of the ages was in the midst of life's fullness when he first saw death and the suffering that can precede it. In his case, it was his servant who explained the universal presence of death to him. The encounter with death in the marketplace began his awakening to a greater path. Death was in the middle of the life of the one who would become known the world over for finding a "middle way" through the suffering and sorrow found on earth.

At the time he was still known as Prince Siddartha. He was the favored son of a wealthy and powerful family and his given name said as much. *Sidd* or *siddha* refers to achievement and practical accomplishments; *artha* typically suggests wealth and power in the material world. Prince Siddartha was in line to inherit his father's kingdom and become an even more powerful and wealthy ruler. Yet fate always has a say, even if a family is powerful and has distinct plans set in place for its children. Every family has its status and each also has its share of fate. Each child born will have its own twist of fate that can unwind in the direction of a unique destiny.

As with anyone else, the story of the Buddha's fate began before he was born. When the time of the birth of the prince was near, an ascetic sage mysteriously appeared. The holy man offered a prophecy regarding the life of the child. In fact, he described a puzzling fate that became the cause of great concern for the father of the prince. The sage announced that the royal child would either rise to be a powerful king who would rule far and wide, or else would become a saint who renounced all worldly power and wealth in favor of a spiritual path.

Of course, the king wanted a son who would follow in his footsteps. He longed for an heir to carry on his extensive legacy of wealth and power. Now he feared that the prince might one day become attracted to an ascetic path and turn away from his worldly inheritance. Because of that fear, the child was raised within walled palaces. He was constantly sequestered, not from the lures of the sensual world, but from any experience of spiritual things. The father controlled all aspects of the prince's world and kept him from any influence that might lead him down the road of philosophy or onto the path of spiritual learning.

Prince Siddartha grew up within a luxurious confinement; he lived inside walled gardens that isolated him from the ills and pains as well as the conflicts and troubles of the common world. For many years he remained unaware of the sufferings that plague most people. Yet fate has its way of slipping into even the most protected garden. The seed of knowledge early planted in the soul of the future Buddha began to grow. Feeling severely isolated and increasingly curious about the outside world, the prince yearned to see and feel the commotion of the marketplace of life. After earnest entreaties from the prince, the royal father finally gave him permission to step outside the garden walls and visit the nearby city.

Some say that in advance of the prince's outings, the king ordered that all the old and infirm people and all the dying and suffering folks be removed from sight. They say that no inauspicious object was left in view and only those who appeared young and healthy were permitted to be seen. Yet these precautions were in vain; for fate will have its day, just as death will have its due. Despite the arrangements made by the king, the prince became a witness to the suffering and death so common in this troubled world, where light and dark alternate daily and even moment to moment.

The prince left the garden of innocence and rode to the marketplace accompanied by his faithful charioteer. In quick succession he had four encounters that would alter the course of his life and in due course affect much of the world. The first apparition was an aging man, bent with years and short of breath. The prince asked the charioteer if the poor fellow was in a singular condition. The answer came that this was the common fate of all who grow old in this world. The next figure that appeared before them was someone in the throes of illness and immobilized with pain. The prince asked if this kind of condition was a frequent experience. The charioteer offered that illness comes to all who live, for that too was part of the fate of the human soul.

Next, they came upon a corpse being carried to the burning grounds. When the charioteer explained that this was a recently deceased person about to be placed in the funeral fires, the prince asked if he too would die one day. The answer sadly came that all people, royal or common, must one day meet their death. When the time comes, the breath of life will expire and each will be carried to the funeral grounds. The prince was shocked by the presence of death and dying in the midst of life's abundance and by the preponderance of suffering and illness that seemed to follow each life like a shadow.

After all the years of protection and all the distractions that wealth and power could provide, the prince had finally entered the marketplace of life where his fate could be encountered. He stood at the crossroads where life and death converge and where fate and destiny can become revealed. Once the prince began to live his own life, the hand of fate began to unfold before him. Fate is the drama we cannot avoid, the puzzle we must consider, the mystery we must attend to or else fail to take our true part in life. Fate waits for each person to step onto the road of life.

The prince was bound to become a significant person and destined to have an effect on the world around him. That was the message of the prophecy stated at the very beginning of his life. Having left the family compound and stepped beyond the family complex, the prince had arrived at the crossroads where his life had to go one way or the other. The fateful issues announced at his birth became the choices he had to face when he entered his life more fully. Fate weaves a certain pattern, but the soul makes choices when it comes to living out the inner design. What remained in question was whether it would be in the worldly realm or on a spiritual path.

Either he returned to the family estates to take up the role his father planned for him, or he went farther along the road marked with the knowledge of the suffering and death found in this world. Either he became a powerful ruler and a king amongst kings, or else he became a spiritual seeker and a potential saint. Either he remained Siddartha, the powerful prince, or he became a *bodhisattva*, a "Buddha to be." One way or another, the time had come for the prince to leave the life of innocence and protection behind.

Often, what must die before a person can truly live is the plan the family has for its children. Each child must be born to a particular family; yet the destiny of each soul rises from a different conception and often aims at a different star. Each has a family legacy of some kind; yet each also has a deeper birthright waiting to be discovered. There is a necessary tension between the family expectations and the destiny bequeathed to each of its children. Even if the children take up the family business, they still must enter the market of life on their own terms.

The elements of fate and destiny press from within and also call from outside the walls and doors of the family complex. Unseen threads and inner designs secretly pull each of us into the crossroads where meaningful choices must be made. Like many a soul in this world, the life of the prince could have gone either way. Before any decision could be made, there was one more fateful apparition awaiting him.

At the crossroads of fate and destiny, in the crosshairs of life and death, the prince observed a solitary ascetic sitting quietly at the side of the road. He exhibited a surprising calm and seeming serenity amidst the palpable suffering and confusion all around him. The fourth and final apparition came in the form of one who renounced earthly desires and the usual entrapments in order to find a path beyond the pain and suffering common to life. Once the eyes of the prince began to open to the conditions of old age, suffering and death, the path of his life appeared before him.

The very one who had been kept within elaborate enclosures and had not been allowed to see the world outside would one day spread his teachings all over the world. The walls that had held him back also compelled him to search for a genuine way forward in the world. The exact elements of fate that restricted him from early on also set the scene for the revelation of his destiny. For it is the within the twist of fate's mortal thread that destiny hides and waits for the critical time to unfold. Prince Siddartha would renounce his entire inheritance of power and wealth in order to follow a path that was also a thread unfolding from within. As he awakened further he both understood the common fate of humanity and recognized the unique nature of his destiny.

Paths of Destiny

Prince Siddartha could have become but a servant of his father's dream had he not awakened to his own path and thereby founded a way that others could also follow. The crossroads of history are marred by blind acceptance of duty and darkened by unlived lives and destinies ignored. Until we face the hand that fate has dealt us and pick up the inner threads of our souls, we are servants and beggars regardless of received status and inherited wealth. The prince had to renounce exactly what others struggle to attain; he had to relinquish his privileged position and become a homeless beggar to find his true way in this world. For the nobility of the soul is grounded in an inner inheritance rather than a received privilege.

The fateful encounters with illness and loss, with poverty and death serve to remind us how everything we touch is temporary and all we possess must one day pass. Meanwhile, an eternal thread has been woven within us; it ties us to a path of meaning and can lead to a way of being that is our true inheritance in this world. In order to find that holy thread and come to know it we must experience a brush with death, a fateful encounter that allows a little-death to occur.

In the case of the Buddha, the first encounter with death changed everything. Unlike the servant who tried to run from the dark apparition, the prince used it to awaken himself to his genuine purpose in life. For the "Buddha-to-be," the presence of illness and death provoked an awakening that opened the door of renunciation. In the threshold that appeared before him, he saw a *yogi* whose life was yoked to something unseen and transcendent. In that moment, the old life, the received life began to wither and die. At that point, the prince had to die to the life he had received in order to be born again to a path of destiny. From that symbolic death a greater life grew forth and a new philosophy for living was also born.

The desire to know more of life drove the young prince out of the garden of inheritance and into the marketplace of life. In seeking a greater knowledge of life, the Buddha encountered the presence of death. And death became the middle of the long road that has become the practice of Buddhism throughout the world. Buddhism, with its intricate and compelling philosophy of the illusory nature of both life and death, begins in the silent conversation between the budding Buddha and the presence of death in this world. No death, no Buddha; no illness, no Buddha; no poverty, no Buddhism.

The point here is not that everyone should become a Buddhist; that may be helpful to some but may be way off-track for others. The point is to find a genuine path that leads to the revelation of the life waiting to be found within one's soul. Because many plotlines exist in the great skein of life, there must be many instructive stories. Remember Rama, the noble hero of the ancient tales of the Ramayana? His story is still told throughout India where it continues to be seen as a contrast and counterpart to the tale of the Buddha.

Rama was also a favored prince and the son of a royal family and powerful father. Rama also renounced a great throne with all its attendant power and wealth. He went against the wishes and commands of his father when the king insisted that he inherit the throne instead of his brother. Like the Buddha, Rama saw a more righteous path and he denied his father's fondest wish. He shed his princely robes, left the palace, and willingly spent years as a homeless seeker. He wandered through wild forests, but also took up many spiritual paths where he learned what he could from a succession of gurus. All the while, he was searching for a particular sage who was greatly revered and widely recognized for his devastating insight and penetrating wisdom.

When he finally found the remote hut where the teacher practiced and meditated, Rama humbly presented himself and asked how he might find the truth. The blessed one responded: "What can I tell you? All truth comes from within. I cannot teach you anything you do not already know. The search for truth is really the search for one's true self. When people truly understand who they already are, they realize that they are part of the divine. This understanding cannot come from the intellect alone or be simply given to you by others. It must come from a place deep inside. Know yourself, noble friend, and you will know what you are searching for."

A rare shadow of confusion passed over the countenance of great Rama as he considered the answer to the question he had carried for so long. After a time, the sage spoke again. He said that although he could not in good faith give the prince any other answer, he did wish to give him a gift. The old sage disappeared within his hut to search for an appropriate gift to give. Meanwhile, Rama imagined himself receiving the present of a begging bowl or the kind of walking stick that he had seen saintly seekers carry.

The sage soon returned with a diamond-studded bow and a golden sword. As he handed the unexpected gifts to the prince he said: "Know yourself. This is who you are." Rama had followed the path of renunciation only to have it lead him back to the place of sovereignty and rulership. He gave up all wealth and power in order to search for the truth and found that which he could never give away or simply leave behind him.

For the Buddha to become himself, renunciation of worldly power was necessary. He will always be remembered for the wisdom of the path that passes between opposing beliefs and beyond all thrones. For Rama, being a ruler in this world was a true destiny; he will always be remembered for the grace with which he faced tragedy and the nobility with which he handled the powers of this world. Each had to find his true path and each had to search within to find where that way began.

The point isn't to blindly follow any path, but to act with the courage and deep intelligence that allowed both Rama and the Buddha to find his own way to be. Early encounters with fate and death are intended to awaken people to the exact value of the gift of life they have been given. Not necessarily the life given by one's parents, not usually the life defined by the marketplace, not even the life attributed to famous religious leaders. The point is to find the life seeded in the soul before one came to life. The point is to be willing to undergo a little-death in order to find the first agreement of one's soul with the genuine thread of one's destiny.

In the marketplace where death and life often change places, Prince Siddartha had to die so that the great teacher and spiritual leader waiting within him could be born. The Buddha was waiting to be born from within himself and his destiny involved making a new way. In following the way of his destiny, he left footprints for others to follow. Yet those who follow that path follow it best when they have their own conversation with death and learn where the thread of their life might lead. It may be part of their fate to be a Buddhist; yet it must be their destiny to become themselves.

Life, Death, Rebirth

Once we enter the great marketplace we are bound to encounter the particulars of our fate in life. We are also bound to encounter our mortality and experience a brush with death. Death is life's companion all along and at certain critical crossroads is as close as the next breath. That's just the way it is here on earth. Life occurs between the extremes of birth and death and both extremes are required whenever a renewal occurs. Besides being the final act of life, death is also the transformative agent throughout life. Death is the middle of a long life and it is a necessary ingredient of each big change in our lives. Life and death secretly conspire in order to make renewal possible. Knowing something about the nature of death leads to knowing more about the essence of life.

A little-death is necessary whenever life would become bigger. Genuine change requires that something corpselike be put down before the new way can be fully embraced. The failures, losses and mistakes in life are little-deaths from which the greater lessons of life can best be learned. When the little-self suffers a little-death, the greater self within can grow and find ways to shine forth. Those who fail to attend to the little-deaths and sudden endings inevitably encountered will also fail to find the life trying to live through them. Not everyone is destined to be a great teacher or spiritual leader; yet the failure to become oneself removes some pertinent knowledge and some spiritual essence from the world.

Our fate will bring us to a crossroads each time we need to transform ourselves. We each have an appointment with destiny but must suffer the disappointments of fate in order to arrive there. Fate would stop us in our tracks and strip us to the bone, so that we might discover the essential imagination and seeds of destiny sown at the core of our selves. Fate will ensnare and constrain the vitality of our lives until we learn where the wind of destiny would have us go.

In the end, the question is not whether death will come to us or not; for we will go to it. From the first moment of our birth, we began travelling towards our death. In order to avoid arriving at the door of death full of fears, blinded by anger and disappointed with life, a person must turn and face a little-death in the midst of life. Whatever death touches will certainly be transformed and those who accept the presence of a little-death in life are transformed the most and are least shocked when the hour of their death comes to them.

The mystics say that each exchange of breath with the world has a little-death in it. Death right there in the middle of each breath we take in life; each breathing moment silently repeating the pattern of life-death-rebirth. Death situated between birth and rebirth, a little-death in the middle of life ongoing. In the end, we all go to the dark inn. The true issue is not avoiding our death, but moving our fate. When we face our fate in life, we also begin to move it; and when fate moves, destiny can become revealed. Whenever we brush against the limits of our fate we also stand near the doors of our destiny. Facing up to fate allows the doors of destiny to open…. at least for a moment.

CHAPTER 12

THE DISCIPLE'S TALE

People fall victim to a fate they cannot control, precisely because they don't know that they are controlled by it.

Modern life takes place within the massive exchanges and rapid changes that constitute the worldwide marketplace. Amidst the great massing of material goods and seeming loss of cultural distinctions there also exists a complex exchange of new ideas as well as old traditions. Amidst the great confusion and the flood of changes, Western ideas and customs pour into the East at the same time as Eastern practices and philosophies penetrate the West. The radical individualism characteristic of the modern West can increasingly be found throughout the East, while ancient Eastern ideas and yogic practices pop up all over Western societies. In the wild exchange between the far East and the modern West two contrasting stories are also spread.

One tale involves the epic sense of progress and discovery as new inventions and ideas of evolution seem to triumph over all obstacles and natural limitations. The other story places more emphasis on inner discoveries and involves a greater acceptance of the limitations found in life as well as the repetition of tragic events that occur. Both views have archetypal roots and each forms a natural inheritance of human imagination. Both exist at the same time and have always existed together. However, to be alive at this time on earth means to be more exposed to all the uncertainties of life and to be more transparently suspended between the belief in progress and presence of collapse and decline. In a mythless world people believe that you must believe in one or the other; yet both take place at the same time.

The Western view tends to favor an unlimited sense of individual destiny and a drive to overcome all entrapments of fate in a single lifetime. The Eastern view tends to embrace fate as the rule of "karma" in which each action causes reactions that cannot easily be removed and that can affect even more than one lifetime. The West tends to work at finding meaning and making change by engaging the outside world. The East tends to engage the inner life in order to change all life circumstances. However, both views can be seen to share the sense that the limitations of life, be they called fate or karma, can be altered by choosing a proper course in life and finding an awakening by suffering the adventures that ensue. At the level of individual change and transformation, both approaches involve the archetypal ground of fate and destiny.

Whether an adventure is initially undertaken as a search for progress or as a pilgrimage for greater understanding, we reach a point where we must choose a path, take the first step and learn where the road of life might lead. No matter where we begin life's journey, certain moments become momentous and time opens before us and we begin to learn who we are intended to be. While we earnestly set out to find a pathway through the world, we are also being called to find a way that exists within us. The true way is already within us; yet as fate would have it, we must go a long way in order to learn our true way of being in this world.

It's like the old tale from ancient India that tells of a young fellow who had reached the age for choosing a direction in life. He had grown up in the simple way of life that his parents followed; but the time had come for him to undertake a quest to seek his own way of being in the world. They say that every quest begins with a question and the youth had been the kind of child that asked questions constantly. From an early age he wanted to know how things worked and why certain things happened. Now he desired to know why he existed and what way in life he should pursue.

Although his parents were simple folk and lived as peasants in their little village, they encouraged his questioning ways and supported his pursuit of knowledge. His mother was wise and patient with him. She would answer his questions if she had an answer to give; but might put the question back on him if she did not. As a result, the young fellow trusted his mother to be knowing and honest with him. So he brought the question of what to pursue in life to her. He asked her directly: "What is the best occupation in this world?"

The mother said, "Well, I don't know; except that people say that those who really seek in this world go in search of god or something divine."

"Where do I begin looking, then?" asked the questioning son.

"I don't know a practical way to begin," said his old mother; "but they say there are only two directions when it comes to searching in this world."

The youth was relieved to learn that there were only two directions to consider and asked what they might be.

"Well," said the old woman, "there's the way of solitary searching in the great forests of nature or the way of wandering in the centers and byways of culture. I've been told that those are the two great pathways for learning in this world."

The son was satisfied for the moment with that view of things. The next day he took leave of his old mother and set off wandering and seeking to learn more. Sometimes he would wander in the wide forests and even cross mountain passes. Sometimes he would search in the towns and even wander in the great cities. Sometimes, his patience would become exhausted, or his heart would be broken. Often he would be disappointed. Then, he would return home and visit with his old mother and father. They would care for him, nourish him, and send him back to the world to search again.

During one such visit, the son asked his mother whether there was any other way to go in this world than the way of wandering the paths found in nature and culture. After contemplating she said, "Well, I don't know. There are only two ways; although some people say that if you meet a teacher that might lead you to another way."

She asked if he had seen such a teacher. Well, he didn't know for sure, except he had seen one old fellow in the depths of a forest, surrounded by attentive pupils. Something about the situation had intrigued him and lingered in his mind. When the time came to leave home again, he went back to the place where he had first seen the teacher.

What Do You Love Most?

Upon arriving at that place, the young seeker observed that all of the students had their own little huts in which they rested and studied and learned to meditate. The young fellow desired to join the group and he wanted to have a little hut to dwell in like the others. He approached the teacher humbly and since he had a sincere and pleasing manner, the peasant son was accepted and given a place to stay. Immediately, he began to study earnestly along with the other students. One day, the teacher gathered all the students together and asked them to answer a single question: "What do you love most in the whole world?" All had to consider in a real way what it was that they loved in this world in which we all must love something. The students contemplated the question and began to offer answers. They named all kinds of things, truth and wisdom, love and family, honesty and devotion. Some even named the teacher. In due time, all of them had named what they loved except the son of those village peasants.

The teacher turned to him and asked: "Will you tell us what it is that you love above all things in this world?"

The youth answered that there was something he loved, but added that it embarrassed him to name such a humble and foolish thing. The teacher asked him again and he had no choice, but to answer. Only one thing had come to his mind, so he said it out loud.

"Of all the things of this world, what I love most is the cow I grew up with. I love the sound of its lowing and the shape of its great back that I used to ride upon. I love the swelling of its belly, its great teats, and the sweet milk it would pour out so freely. I love the curving horns on its head and its deep, dark eyes. Of all things, I love that cow."

The teacher then instructed all the students to go to their little huts and meditate upon that which they loved most in this world. Off they all went and it wasn't all that long before some began to wander back from the huts and gather in the teaching place again. Eventually, they all came back except the peasant son. The teacher arrived and asked if all were present. All except the cow lover, the students were quick to report. The teacher sent some students to fetch him, but despite repeated call he didn't come out of his hut.

The teacher decided to go over to the hut of the new student himself and all the other pupils followed. Even though the teacher knocked on the door and called out to him, the young fellow did not emerge. Finally, the teacher pushed the door open and looked inside. There, he saw the peasant son sitting quietly in the hut, immersed in deep concentration. The teacher spoke firmly to him: "All right, the exercise is over. You have meditated for a long time. Everyone else finished long ago; now it is time to come out and join the others."

The student answered softly, "I would love to come and join you. However, I'm afraid that the horns on my head are too big to fit through the doorway."

The teacher turned to the other students, "Here is something to truly contemplate; here is the living example of concentration and study, of love and genuine learning. People seek god and have no idea where to look; they work and practice, they argue and dispute and still can't find a path that leads them close to the divine. This one meditates on a cow and becomes the cow. His usual self is lost and he becomes what he loves. In loving completely, he finds something divine."

"Today, he is our teacher. He has become what he loves and that is the point of all genius and the destination of any real path in the world. Being lost or confused is not the problem; feeling like giving up is not the problem; but not becoming what we love, that is a real problem. In learning what our souls love we move near the divine, for love is a divine gift. Today, this one is our teacher, for he is not afraid to become what he loves."

The young seeker had found what he was looking for inside the hut of himself. He sat inside his joy and found the wonder of awakening from within. He had wandered far and wide only to reach a place in his heart where he kept his own sense of life and love. The cow was close to his heart and close to his deeper sense of self as well. It represented strength as well as sweet nourishment, full embodiment as well as gentle articulation. The object of his affection and concentration might seem strange to others, yet he learned something of his own orientation in life from the generous being that continued to nourish him from within.

Sacred Cows and Divine Presence

Of course, in India cows are quite sacred and having love for a cow could easily be seen as loving the divine. People wonder at the practice of revering cows rather than eating them, especially when so many people lack food and even die from hunger. It could be said that in India the hunger for the divine often remains greater than the hunger for food. Meanwhile, the cow was considered sacred because it symbolized the mother of all civilization with the milk of wisdom that makes culture and true learning possible.

The cow stood for the presence of the divine in this world and it can still represent the proximity of divine nurturing regardless of the poverty of circumstances. The word *symbol* can mean "to cast things together;" it can also mean "an outward sign of something else." A symbol combines unlike things in order to indicate something real, but hidden. In order to make the symbol of the divine real, all cows became sacred. In order to make clear that any approach to the divine must be respected, all cows were allowed to roam free. In order to remind that humans help to nourish the otherworld, as well as receive sustenance from it, it became a matter of good luck to give a bit of bread or a piece of fruit to a passing cow.

Cows were often associated with Brahma, the creator of the world. And a cow could stand as a symbol for the entirety of creation with each part of the sacred animal being related to a deity or some other kind of being. "All the gods are in Brahma as cows in a cow-house," went the saying. The horns, being the highest part and pointing to the bright heavens, were especially symbolic of Brahma's high place. The god Indra, who sustains all life and order in the world, could be seen as the head of the holy cow; while Shiva, who can destroy the world by dancing or with a sudden blow, could be imagined in the hind legs. All the people alive in the world at any given time were also said to exist in the inner body of the world cow.

The power of Brahma could be represented by the great horns of the cow, but Brahma's mind resided in the holy heart of the cosmic cow. The mind of each person alive was considered to be secretly connected to the great mind of Brahma. Thus, the boy meditating on his beloved cow could find himself in secret contact with the heart and mind of the creator. Brahma created the world and a part of the creator was considered to be present in all aspects of creation as well as being present in each person.

"Soul of the Universe" was another title referring to Brahma. It was used specifically to denote the divine essence and eternal breath with which the universe breathes; the source from which all things emanate and the place that all things return to. This eternal essence of all that exists was itself considered to be immaterial and invisible, but also unlimited and all-pervading. Thus, the source of existence is inside the cow and the cow can serve as a reminder that the divine is always nearby and exists in the soul of each person as well. "As above, so below" went the saying that deftly reminds us of the subtle integrity and hidden continuity of the universe.

Brahma was the Great Self and the universal presence, the divine essence and grand thought at the center of all existence. As a microcosmic replica of the macrocosmic arrangement, each person has a great self within and each is constantly sustained by the breath of the divine that sustains the living world. Since our true self was connected to the breath of the divine, the sages developed practices that would attend to each breath and meditate upon the presence of the divine until they reached the place of enlightenment and were absorbed by it.

They also created ancient rites that focused upon the notion of a rebirth from an inner womb where the essence of life could be found. The inner, spiritual womb contained the "golden embryo" of the deep self. In order to make the symbolic birth more real, initiates would be placed inside a golden replica of a cow. After being cleansed of the inevitable defilements of life, a period of seclusion and concentration inside the golden cow would follow. When the time of fasting and meditating came to an end, the initiate would be considered reborn from the breath of Brahma and the womb of the cosmic cow.

After this second birth, the initiate would be anointed with oil and be polished and praised as one able to shine forth with the inner gold of awakened spirit. If the expense of fashioning a golden cow for the initiation was out of reach, a simple hut could be used to replicate the uterine darkness and embryonic state that precedes rebirth. Since everyone was essentially connected to the divine, no one could be denied the opportunity of initiation because of class or social status. For the least among us is secretly connected to the source of all life.

The young son had found his way to a genuine initiation that awakened something deep within his heart. In concentrating on what he loved he also had been meditating on Brahma, the central source of consciousness and wisdom. His simple hut became the womb for his return to the source and his awakening from within. In attending to the cow that had given milk for his growth as well as food for his imagination, he found an inner pattern that could continue to nourish his growth and guide his search for knowledge. In doing the little exercise, the young seeker and common child of the world had found an image of the deity behind the unfolding story of his life.

Fate Intervenes

The young seeker had found what he was looking for in this world where so many become lost. Yet again, finding and holding can be two different things; what we seek to know must often become lost and found again if we are to know it well. At the beginning of a lifelong path there will be a revelation that opens wide the way; after that, some integration is required and some consolidation needed. The young student continued his studies with the forest teacher. He applied himself and learned what he could learn until he felt he was no longer growing.

After much reflection, he realized he had to continue his search elsewhere. After fully expressing his gratitude for what he had learned, he took his leave of the teacher and once again set forth along the forest paths and on the byways of the cities of this world. After a time, a short time or a long time, his fortune led him to the compound of an old sage who lived in the heart of a forest far from the mad rush and long reach of civilization. The sage recognized the willing spirit of the youth and welcomed him kindly. He offered him a place to stay, near his own hut, next to where the holy river ran and sang its way along.

The young student humbly served the old sage and his wise wife and began to learn what they each had to teach. He took his studies seriously and entered each new practice with the characteristic commitment he had brought to the exercise that focused upon what he loved best. He learned quickly and soon became a true disciple of the old sage who also became inspired by the presence of such a devoted student. Genuine study can make a person pregnant with knowledge; at the same time the presence of a true disciple can inspire new life in a teacher.

The sage and his wife were no longer young, but they remained youthful in some ways. They enjoyed certain pleasures despite their age and soon learned that they were to have their first child. Learning is a sacred and creative act that can affect the world on more than one level. The awakening occurring in the inner world of the student became mirrored by the impending birth in the family of the teacher. Each act of awakening involves a kind of creation and it turns out that the birth of each child is secretly related to the original act of creation.

When the pregnancy was far enough along, the sage developed a desire to make a journey to the source of the holy river that flowed near where they all dwelt. He entrusted the care of his pregnant wife to the young disciple and invited the wife of another sage to stay with her in the birthing hut. The sage instructed his student to observe carefully and guard the hut and not allow anyone else to enter during the time of labor. While the sage was away, the pregnant wife entered her labor. The woman friend stayed with her inside the hut while the disciple waited outside, protecting the space and praying for a safe birth and a healthy baby.

The old people in that area held the belief that Brahma had to be present at each birth in order to write a fortune on the forehead of the newborn. Brahma had been present at the dawn of creation and remains the source of ongoing creation. Since each birth repeats the creation of life, Brahma must be present there as well. As creator of all things that appear in the visible realm, Brahma had to attend the moment when the infant leaves the interior world of the mother's womb and becomes visible to the naked eye.

Part of the job of being creator involved putting in an appearance at the crowning moment of each birth. In that critical moment the god had to use a magic stylus to write the fate on the forehead of the infant as it takes its first breath in the new life. Although the god had to be present for the appearance of the child, he remained as invisible to most people as does the fate written on each forehead. For those with eyes to see, they say, the deities pass amongst us at crucial moments and all that is hidden might be revealed.

As the moment of birth drew near, the disciple saw what looked like an old Brahmin or priest approaching the hut where new life was pressing hard on the doors of this world. The sage had told him to observe everything, but had also taught him to truly see rather than simply look at what appeared before him. The young disciple's eyes were no longer those of an ordinary person. In fact, he had learned to perceive what others cannot see. With his acute vision the disciple recognized that it was in fact Brahma in the guise of an old priest coming to attend the crowning moment and mark the fortune of the new child.

The disciple knew enough to recognize that the god of creation was approaching; he also was aware that he had a serious responsibility to the one who had taught him to see in this way. He had taken up a serious path of learning and had taken on a responsibility to his teacher. He felt a great reverence to the presence of the divine and he felt a deep duty to protect the birthing hut as he had promised. Humans are frequently caught between one thing and another. The child nearby was laboring between this world and the other and the disciple felt himself to be between a rock and a hard place. In each case something had to give.

"Stop right there," said the disciple to the disguised deity. "What do you think you are doing entering a hut where a woman struggles to give birth? You can't go in there, no one is allowed."

Brahma patiently explained that as god of creation he had a divine task that had to be immediately attended to inside that very hut. The infant was about to slip from the womb, he had a job to do at that moment and there was no time to waste. He had to go in at once or some great error might occur that could imbalance all of creation.

The disciple was still uncertain about what to do. Then a thought appeared as if from nowhere. He bowed respectfully to the god and agreed to step aside and allow the deity to enter the birthing hut, on one condition. Only if he revealed the fate he intended to write upon the forehead of the newborn could he proceed. Now, the deity had to consider what to do. Pressed for time, Brahma quickly explained that even he did not know what his divine stylus would write. "At the moment the child enters the world, I place the stylus on its forehead and the instrument writes by itself. It draws upon something already existing but hidden within the child. It is not I who decides the fate; I only bring it to the surface. Now, don't try to stop me; I must go in at once."

However, the disciple persisted. "I too have been entrusted with a sacred task. If I do let you go in, you must tell me on your way out what was written on the forehead of my teacher's child."

Even a god can become trapped by necessity and time, especially if the issue at hand involves the hand of fate. Whatever he might have felt or thought about the situation, Brahma had to agree to the condition and bow to necessity or else fail to perform his divine task. He accepted the terms of the deal and entered the agreement with the disciple, then quickly entered the hut.

The child was just at the crowning moment of birth when Brahma arrived and applied the divine stylus to its forehead. Being busy with the labor, neither the mother nor the midwife saw the god appear and bring the inner fate out into the light of day. The child, of course, was busy adjusting to the outside world and like everyone else would remain unaware of the fortune being born along with it. Nonetheless, the first breath we each take in this world breathes life into the fate we each carry and which carries us throughout our lives.

The god departed from the hut as quickly as he had entered and found the disciple waiting with great attention. Brahma spoke to him directly: "As agreed upon, I will tell you what was written on the forehead of the child. However, I will now place a condition on you: if at anytime you tell another soul what I reveal to you about the fate inscribed of this child, your own head will split into a thousand pieces. The child is a boy and he has a hard life before him. A single buffalo and a sack of rice are his allotment and will be his share in life. He will have to live on that. Don't blame it on me; for you wanted to know and I did not choose this. I only raised up what was within him."

"How can this be his fate," cried the disciple, "this is the child of a great sage?"

"What have I to do with it?" said Brahma. "Remember, if you ever tell this to anyone, your head will explode in a thousand pieces."

The god vanished, leaving the disciple bewildered and pained by what he now knew of the hard life awaiting the sage's child. The seeker had encountered the god of creation and learned more of the secrets of life than he wanted to know. Not only that, but he could not share what he had learned with anyone. He had asked to learn about fate and soon found himself bound by it. He had sought to gain knowledge only to learn how isolating it can be to see what others cannot see and know what most do not know.

Dealing with Gods

The crowning moment of life awakens a mysterious force already present in the one being born. The magic stylus writes of its own accord, but what it writes is in accord with a previous condition in the soul, an existing life sentence waiting to be evoked. The limitations of fate become the defining issue of life as the force of creation pushes the child into the world of time and place. When it comes to this world, even the god of creation is bound by the rule of necessity and the hand of fate. Surprisingly, the deity must also bow to the sacred duty the disciple has towards his teacher.

At the moment of birth many things are being revealed and more than one fate becomes activated. The disciple learns the fate of the child, yet we learn something of his fate as well. The fortune of the disciple seems to involve an ability to perceive what is mostly hidden and that includes the fate of other people. This increase of knowledge and expanded vision of life turns out to be both a blessing and a curse as he cannot reveal the knowledge given to him. The disciple has encountered the precise twist of fate that places him firmly on the path of revelation, but that also puts him in a double-bind. For what becomes revealed in the first deal must remain completely secret as a result of the subsequent agreement.

In seeking to learn the fortune of another the seeker also provoked previously hidden aspects of his own fate. He now knows something profound about life; in fact, he knows what the god knows. However, unlike the deity, he cannot share what he knows for fear of fragmentation and disintegration. Ignorance may be a kind of bliss, but genuine knowledge can be its own kind of danger. The teacher's son must face a difficult road in life; but his student's fate seems to include a hard education about how knowledge can be a burden.

The teacher and his wife may have taught the disciple to see in penetrating ways; yet neither of them could perceive the trouble he now carried inside. Nor could they discern the troubling fate written on the forehead of their own child. Maybe that was just as well as little might be served if parents were to learn the fate of their own children. Parents suffer great enough responsibilities without knowing the strange limits inscribed in the lives of their offspring.

Eventually, the old sage returned from his journey to the source of the river. He found the old mother and newborn son both healthy and happy. The infant grew rapidly and everyone delighted in seeing the generative success and prosperity of the old couple. For his part, the disciple said nothing to anyone of his encounter with Brahma and the stylus of fate. He continued to dedicate himself to the paths of study and learning. Time went on and the river flowed by. In the course of affairs and in the learned company of the old sage, the disciple soon forgot his sorrowful experience.

The old couple continued their own practices and to the amazement of their friends, they somehow managed to conceive another child. When the pregnancy was far enough along, the old sage again conceived a desire to visit the source of the holy river. Once again, the teacher placed the disciple in the position of guarding the birthing hut and protecting the laboring mother and the child about to be born. Once again, the student took the task seriously and brought his full attention to the situation.

Just as before, when the moment of birth drew near, Brahma suddenly appeared in the form of an old priest. Before he could enter the hut and activate the child's fate, the disciple blocked the door. He refused to allow the god to proceed until he again agreed to reveal whatever fate was written on the forehead of the newborn. The disciple was hoping to ease his heart by learning that at least one child of his teacher might have a fortunate fate in this world.

Once again, the god was trapped by the devotion of the disciple to his duty and the pressures of time and fate that so often rule the events of this world. In the interest of time, the deity agreed to the terms. Then the god entered the hut just at the crowning moment and applied the stylus to the forehead of the infant. Mother and child were both healthy and sharing in the warm embrace of life as the god retraced his steps.

Just as before, the disciple waited to learn the news. Brahma informed him directly: "This time the child is a girl. Don't hold this against me, but the stylus has written that she will have to earn her living as a prostitute and sell her body every night. There is nothing I can do about it. In the meantime, remember the rule, if you tell what has been written to anyone, your head will immediately split into a thousand pieces." Having restated the deal Brahma walked off, looking to the casual observer like an old man on a common errand.

The disciple was in shock. He was so deeply hurt he could not even find language to express his pain and disappointment. Besides, if he could express what he knew and how the knowledge made him feel, he might explode. Where he had hoped to find relief from the sad burden of his knowledge, he found himself instead in a greater and more perplexing situation. He tried to console himself with philosophical considerations and he tried to relieve himself of the burden he felt through various spiritual practices. However, neither approach was of any help when he would find himself in the presence of the two children.

Although they were healthy children who seemed to prosper and grow readily, he could not look at them without seeing the hidden fates that were bound to bring sorrow into their lives. Being near the children and their parents while being unable to speak a word of what he knew made having the knowledge unbearable. He had gained a penetrating insight into the mysteries of human life, but felt increasingly filled with pain and anger and troubled with sorrow and anguish over the unfairness and seemingly random cruelty of the whole thing.

How could it be that a child is born into poverty and becomes fated to live that way throughout life with no possibility of redemption or escape? How could it be that another could be born to do nothing but prostitute herself simply to survive and never know any better? He knew that poverty was everywhere to be seen and that in many ways prostitution was the oldest profession. But that knowledge did not ease his mind or diminish the pain in his heart when he saw the young children headed for hardships they could not imagine. In seeking to learn what the wise know he found sorrow, in trying to help others he became helpless himself. He felt he would rather know nothing if knowing must come with such a heavy cost.

The seeker thought that knowledge would be its own reward. Now, he learned the sad truth that knowledge can also be a burden that cannot be easily shared or even be used to change the painful conditions of this world. He knew the unseen burden of fate that others must carry and as a result felt his own fate more strongly. "Every increase of knowledge is an increase of sorrow," they used to say when speaking of the weight of knowledge and the pitfalls that can be found on the sacred paths of learning.

Knowledge is one thing and wisdom another and eventually the wide-eyed innocent must learn to see with a darker eye. For wisdom is a darker knowledge that combines the brilliance of the light with the darkness needed to embrace it and hold it. The disciple had the burden of knowledge and increasingly felt trapped by it. He feared that he would suddenly reveal the secret he carried and his head would explode into a thousand pieces; or else he would continue to hold it within himself and thereby implode. Try to explain what he knew and he would fragment; say nothing about what he felt and he might collapse with the growing weight of anger and sorrow and disappointment.

Teacher and Pupil

The old sage had been drawn to pray at the source of the river at the time of each birth. Now, the disciple found himself drawn to the flowing waters as he sought some relief from the burden of his knowledge. The local people imagined the river to be the living presence of Saraswati, the divine consort of Brahma and goddess of learning and creativity. Saraswati was "She who flows towards the divine," so that knowledge tended to flow easily where she was involved. Just as a river found its release by flowing into the great sea, Saraswati showed the way to "moksha" or divine release from the troubles of this life.

Yet, even the sacred river could not lift the weight in the heart of the disciple; for it grew heavier within him as he watched the children grow up and move unwittingly closer to their respective fates. Eventually, it became clear that things would only become more painful if he remained as a student of the old sage. One day the path before him became clear and he went to the sage and his wife and asked for permission to leave.

The sage was wise enough to see the writing on the wall and sense that there was an unspoken burden on the soul of his student. A teacher must have an eye that recognizes pupils as well as an intuition for perceiving what they need in order to grow. The old sage knew that the point of learning was to awaken the hidden master within the pupil. He knew that genuine discipline could not be imposed upon a person, but must be freely chosen. Imposed discipline serves only the outer authority, whereas inner discipline develops one's true nature and awakens the innate authority of the deep self. Unless the inner master awakens, an outer master cannot help transform the student.

In the long run, learning involves both obedience and disobedience and teaching involves giving freely and letting go when the time comes. The old sage knew that the presence of the disciple had brought new life to him and to his family. He knew that genuine learning involved love and that love involved letting go as well as holding close. As the old saying has it: "We can't use the feet of a teacher to walk where our own feet must go."

One day, after a small ceremony and with the blessing of the old couple, the disciple left the forest and the holy river that ran through it. He bowed to his teachers and left the children to their fates. Once again, he became a seeker on the complicated paths of life. Sometimes he would wander in the wide forests and sometimes he would search in the big towns. Sometimes the past would catch up to him and his heart would feel as if it would break from the weight of unspoken words. He had set out to find knowledge and now found himself more alone; not just lonely, but separated within himself.

CHAPTER 13

THE ROAR OF AWAKENING

Enjoy fully what the gods concede to you; never covet what belongs
to others: not their goods, nor their talent, not their success.
Isha Upanishad

Knowledge can be a light that clears the way and knowledge can be a blade that separates and divides. The disciple had been cut and pierced by the wound of knowing. His new knowledge may have brought him closer to the divine, but it also separated him from other people. Knowledge that cannot be shared tends to be isolating until a way can be found to integrate it more fully.

Once again he travelled the roads of life seeking what he could not see, but hoped to discover. "Like cures like," they used to say. Perhaps more knowledge could heal the wound of knowledge. "A child has more than one mother," so a student can learn from more than one teacher. Anything that nourishes life could be considered a mother, whether it be a beloved cow, a revered teacher or a river. The disciple had been nourished by all of those; in his heart he trusted that more of the milk of knowledge would come to him. Each time he found a teacher he found more of his own way to be.

He wandered through forests and traversed mountains; he visited towns and walked the busy streets of cities. When he felt that there was no more nourishment to be had on a certain path, he would take his leave and move on again. He examined the world as he found it and pondered the hidden ways of life. He noticed how the temples in the cities imitated the shape of the mountains beyond them. He imagined that those entering the temples were also seeking what the mountains held so quietly and firmly. During his wanderings he would sometimes think of the old sage and his wife. He had seen and learned a great deal during the time he dwelt with them and he continued to contemplate the issues of fate and destiny that troubled his heart.

While walking along the banks of a deep forest stream, the disciple recalled the time when the first child of the old couple was about to be born. He remembered how the old sage left to visit the source of the holy river, leaving him to guard the birthing hut. The sage had never explained the ceremony he witnessed at the water's source or why it had to happen when the labor and birth were so close. So much had happened at that time, yet so little could be discussed because of the danger of speaking too much and having his head split into a thousand pieces. He reviewed the scene many times and each time became caught in the depths of sorrow as the burden of his knowledge of fate would return like a stone in his heart.

The trouble had begun when he stopped Brahma on his errand of fate with his magical stylus in hand. He had interrupted the god and interfered with fate and now suffered for the arrogance and presumption of that act. Yet he grew tired of simply blaming himself for what continued to be a mystery before his eyes. As he felt his way through the events that he could not leave behind no matter how far he traveled, he listened to the flow of the stream that rippled nearby. Thinking of the holy river near where he had learned and lost so much, he recalled an old tale that the sage once told about birth and rebirth, and the nature of true awakening.

The Tiger of the Soul

It seems there was a tiger that was mightily pregnant. She was near the term of her pregnancy and the one inside her was pressing ever closer to the doors of life. What appeared as one was trying to become two and the tiger-mother had to eat for both of them. Food was scarce at the time and the tiger found herself climbing amongst the rocky outcroppings of a mountain in search of a meal. Fighting exhaustion, she hauled herself over some rocks and spotted a herd of goats foraging in a little meadow below where she stood.

Looking down, the tiger saw immediate nourishment for herself and for the one about to be born. At the same moment, the goats looked up and saw the shape of sudden death in the form of sharp teeth that can quickly separate one thing from another. Life and death hung in the balance as the great tiger prepared to leap in the direction of the terrified goats. As the mother-to-be leapt at the herd, the goats thought of nothing but escape and scattered in all directions. She leapt with the aim of using death to contribute to life; they scattered with the idea of continuing life by avoiding death.

As fate would have it, the tiger died before even reaching the ground. She was undone by hunger or overcome by exhaustion and she expired mid-leap. Not only that, but the shock of the leap induced labor and just as the tiger-mother struck the earth, the little life within her was born. Thus, death and life were each born in the same moment, the death of one being the birth of the other. It was a case of life literally growing from death.

Despite the sense of impending doom, all of the goats survived the scare. Eventually they all convened around the lifeless body of the tiger and the little package she had seemingly delivered to them. Once they felt assured that the great beast could not cause any harm, they became interested in the little presence nearby. The mother instinct is as old and as great as anything in life and the mothers in the herd recognized new life in its delicate and dependent condition. It was not long before they began sniffing at and nudging the strange shape before them. Since for goats as well as tigers loving consists of licking, the mother goats began to lick at the newborn that had fallen into their lives.

They say that a tiger, like any other cat, will lick every part of the newborn; if they don't the infant will die. Some say that something similar is true of humans; if a part of them has not been loved and licked into life they will fail to fully live. At any rate, the newborn responded to the love-licking and began to stir. Soon its own instincts awakened and it felt a pressing need to nurse on something. Having been licked into life, it wanted to nurse and suck on the sweet milk of existence. The goat mothers did not disappoint. After some experimentation, the little tiger was nursing on goat's milk and following the goat mothers wherever they went.

Nature has its natural cycles of life and death and creatures in the animal realm have natural adversaries and feed upon each other. Yet sometimes things go *contra naturum*, against nature and the exception proves the rule. Strange to say, the little tiger was eventually accepted by all of the goats. It fed on goat milk and received loving attention from several goat mothers. Like any child in this world, the young one began to imitate those around it. Soon enough, the child of the tiger began to act like a goat; it began to sound like a goat, and even feel like a goat. The little one learned the language and the ways of goats and began to act like any other kid in the herd.

One night when the moon was rising and shedding its light on the rocks, another tiger appeared on the mountainside. It was a full-grown animal with a great appetite and it had not eaten for a while. While hunting in the moonlight, it came over an outcropping and spotted the same herd of goats. While looking down and preparing for the next meal, the tiger was shocked to see a little tiger acting like a goat and participating in the activities of the herd. At the same time, the little tiger-goat looked up and found itself gazing into the eyes of a full-grown feline. As all the goats scattered in fear, the tiger-goat stood transfixed, gazing up at the apparition with a confused mixture of both fear and awe.

As the great tiger leapt down to the glade below, the tiger-goat thought in its confusion that the end of life had come. When it felt itself being clenched at the nape of its neck and held in the powerful jaws, it knew it would be carried off to be devoured somewhere else. It came as a great surprise when the grown tiger took the little one to the edge of a stream and held it out over the waters. Under the illumination of the moon, in the reflection of the clear stream, the little one could plainly see that its own shape was more like the strange tiger than the goats it knew so well.

In the sudden moment of reflection, the little one knew that it was actually a tiger. In the brilliance of that moment, self-knowledge flooded through every cell of its body. Something old and knowing awakened within the young one and it suddenly roared mightily and triumphantly. The transformation of a lifetime took place in that single instant as the young one became entirely changed from within. The moment before, it believed that it was a goat; that it would live and die as a goat. The next moment it had become a tiger; it began to see with the eyes of a tiger and left the goat world far behind. With guidance, the little tiger-goat became all tiger and soon began to prowl the forests and burn with its natural brightness.

To know is to be on the verge of being shattered; for knowledge breaks the shell of what existed before. In a single moment of awakening the would-be goat became a tiger and the world completely changed. It was not a case of adapting to outer circumstances or learning to see things another way, more a matter of an inner essence bursting into awareness. As he contemplated the story anew, the disciple began to see further into the circumstances of his own life. He recalled a similar sense of sudden realization that came to him while sitting in the solitude of the hut near his first teacher. As he meditated upon the cow he loved as a boy, he became that cow. As he became the cow, he awakened to his own capacity to love and he discovered his gift of imagination. Something already formed within him awakened as he became who he already was within.

He realized that another moment of awakening had been close by when Brahma revealed the fates of his teacher's children to him. He could see that those fateful moments carried a deeper revelation still trying to awaken something in him. At the birth of each child he had been in a position through which he could see his own true nature. His expectation of a glorious fate for the children of the sage had blinded him to the reality of the situation. Although he hoped each time for promising news, a darker knowledge and deeper wisdom were being offered.

Afterwards, his overwhelming disappointment held him in a darkness of his own making. Now he recalled the old sage saying that each person was set down at a place by the river that made most sense for that person's life. It may not look that way or feel that way; yet we must in some way be equal to our own fate. If not, thought the student, then this world would be a far more unfair place than even he was willing to contemplate. His fate involved an ability to see into the fate of others; perhaps there was a way to understand how fate can change.

He began to view all that surrounded the birth of the old sage's children with different eyes. He realized that he had been left to guard the birthing hut in full knowledge that the god of creation would have to make a visit at the time of birth. It was part of his fate and his education to be present in the moment when the mysterious workings of fate would be revealed. He began to go back through all that had occurred at that fateful time and began to realize how the thread of his own destiny had been pulled to a point of painful awakening.

Like the would-be goat waking up to the presence of its tiger self, he had to awaken to some greater awareness within himself. As he gazed into the stream nearby, he began to see something that had been near but had been hidden from him until then. Suddenly, he could see behind the life sentence written on the forehead of the old sage's son. He could see behind the cursed fate given to the daughter who had been sentenced to a life of prostitution. It was as if he had found his own way of seeing and it caused him to see everything anew. As he continued to reflect upon those indelible events he felt a great longing to see his old teacher again. As he listened to the endless song of the stream, he knew it was time to return to the banks of the holy river. The direction having become clear, he lost no time setting out on the path of return.

Let Go and Don't Hold Back

Eventually, the disciple arrived in the area of the old compound only to learn that the teacher and his wife had both passed away. Heaviness grew in his heart again and was only eased by the sense that they would have been as ready for the arrival of death as they had been for most things in life. After making a small ceremony of remembrance and gratitude, he felt compelled to seek out the children of the old couple. He wished to know how they were faring and if the fates revealed by the stylus of Brahma had been manifested in the lives they were living.

He set off to inquire for news of the son and daughter and soon encountered a poor man walking the road before him. The fellow led a scruffy buffalo on an old rope while carrying a sack of rice on his back. He recognized the son of his teacher carrying the elements of his fate and decided to follow him home. After a short distance, the poor man led the buffalo to a rickety shed leaning near a simple hut. There, the poor fellow lived with his wife and two children.

As the disciple watched quietly from a distance, the poor family prepared a meager meal from the sack of rice and ate anxiously, seeming to fear that they would run out of food if they ate too much. When they had finished their simple fare, the disciple approached their hut. He introduced himself and offered his condolences for the passing of the old sage and his wife. After introductions all around, the disciple drew the poor man aside in order to speak to him in confidence.

He offered the poor fellow this advice: "Do not continue in this narrow way of life. Rather, take the buffalo and the rice to the marketplace and sell them for whatever price you can get. With the money you receive buy whatever you wish to have; spare nothing, hold nothing back and keep nothing in reserve. Invite everyone you know to a feast and on the way back from the market feed the poor as well. If there is anything left, simply give it away."

The poor fellow was shocked beyond belief. "If I act in such a carefree and foolish manner, how can I possibly feed my family tomorrow? You disciples and seekers always advise poor people to stop being so desirous and fearful. It is easy for you to say give everything away. Listen, I can see that you are the ones on the receiving end of this celebrated charity."

It was as if a river had been released from a dam; the man went on about the difficulties of life and all the injustices and the oppressions he experienced every day. He lamented how no amount of effort or prayer ever seemed to change the conditions of his poverty. Clearly, the deck was stacked against him. He had never been given enough in life and it was all he could do to survive and provide something for his wife and children. "And don't get me started on politicians and all the promises they make while they simply line their coffers with gold gathered from the backs of all who are poor and oppressed. Why not take your philosophy of giving freely to those who receive more than their fair share and would benefit from giving some of it away?"

Before he could work himself further into what appeared to be a familiar frenzy, his wife entered the conversation and spoke quietly to her husband. She pointed out that the disciple seemed to have something of the manner of his own father, the old sage. She suggested that he might also have some of the wisdom of that wise man. She encouraged her husband to at least try the radical plan. "Why not try the new approach for a single day and night and see what might come of it; nothing ventured, nothing gained."

The poor man argued that the problem was that he had to venture everything he had in this world and stood to gain nothing from it. Trying it just once was the same as trying it for all time. If he gave away all that he had and it didn't change things immediately, he would clearly have nothing left at all. The problem with the whole plan was that it was an all-or-nothing venture. Just one act of such reckless abandon was all that was needed to wipe them out forever. For her part, the wife simply looked at him steadily and waited.

What could the poor man do? Between the disciple's earnest entreaty and his wife's pleading eyes he felt trapped. Besides that, he did feel truly miserable about his life. A part of him wanted simply to roar out his pain and anger at feeling so constrained and restricted. He was barely able to acknowledge that he dreamed at night, much less admit that he longed for something beautiful and more meaningful than his pitiful daily struggle to survive. Inside, he felt a deep anguish that his children might never know the true delight of just being alive. As he thought of the gift of life itself, his mind slipped the noose that tied it to the buffalo and he became strangely unable to refuse the request of his long-suffering wife or the startling advice of the disciple.

When daylight came and chased the darkness from the world, the poor fellow took the buffalo by its tether and grabbed what remained of the sack of rice and set off for the local market. He entered the marketplace where people hoped to exchange whatever they had for something better. He offered up the buffalo and the sack of rice and sold them for the best price he could get. With the money he received he bought enough food for a fine feast. Despite his great uncertainty, he invited everyone he knew to come to the feast and added a few strangers he met along the way. He struggled mightily when it came to giving what little remained to the poor beggars he passed on his way home. Somehow though, he found within himself a long-denied sense of generosity and soon gave away all that he had in this world.

After he arrived home all the food was prepared and everyone gathered for the feast. All who came were well served and they ate their fill. He watched with deep satisfaction as his good wife and children enjoyed themselves feasting as if there were no tomorrow. As on most human occasions, the event finally came to an end and everyone retired to the land of sleep.

The poor man woke suddenly before the light of dawn pierced the blanket of night. He found himself sitting upright in a state of blind dread. He felt certain that he had foolishly given away everything he had in life. What would he do now with no source of food, no income, and no way to feed his family? How could he face his hungry children? Why had he listened to that weird disciple? What a mistake he had made!

As the sun began to rise in the sky, he went out to the little shed where he had always kept the buffalo. That's what he had done on most other days and he didn't know what else to do now. His heart was heavy with the overwhelming sense of loss as he continued to berate himself for being stupid and foolish and needlessly reckless. He entered the old shed as the sun dropped its light on the bare boards. He fully expected to be greeted by nothing but emptiness and loss and further self-recriminations.

He was more than astonished to see a full-grown buffalo standing there as if waiting for him. Before he could get over the shock of that presence, he spotted a full sack of rice leaning against the wall. The poor man began to shout with joy. He called his wife to come quickly to see the amazing sight. He called the disciple to come and see the wonder for himself. The simple joy of being alive overflowed within him. "Life is indeed a gift," he said, "so why worry over it and care so much about what is given or taken away? How did I not see this before? Why was I living in such darkness until now?"

When the man finally calmed down, the disciple asked if he would like some more advice. Of course, the fellow said; he would listen to anything and probably try it as well. "Take the buffalo then and the rice and sell them again just as before. Buy what you desire and don't hold back. Feed your family and invite others as before, and whatever is left give it all away."

The poor son of the old sage was just getting used to the notion of having something when he was told to give it all away again. He gazed at the fine, healthy buffalo; then looked back carefully at the disciple. He looked at his smiling children and saw his wife's bright eyes. This time the poor man did not have to be convinced. He did it all again and held nothing back. After enjoying the new feast and resting quite well, he found that the buffalo was back and there was another sack of rice to boot. Thus it happened, day after day and night after night. He gave it all away and somehow received it all back again.

The disciple advised him to continue in this manner, only warning that if he reserved anything or held back from his giving, the good fortune could just as readily desert him. The poor man did not argue, for something had transformed within him and he saw the entire world with new and brighter eyes. He was a changed man in a changed world despite and because of the fate he carried unknowingly from the moment he was born.

Why Change is Hard

Something had changed in the disciple as well. Whereas he had been unable to face the heavy conditions placed upon the children of his teacher, he now sought to engage exactly those fateful details. Whereas he had found the knowledge of troubling fates to be an unbearable burden, he now seemed to find a hidden value in them. He saw a blessing where only a curse seemed to be and he began to understand how a fate could be turned around or be turned inside out.

Until the disciple came along the poor son had no idea of the fate written within him. Being unconscious of the inner situation he became completely ruled by it. His entire life became an outer manifestation of the inner sentence. No matter how he slept or what he dreamed, he woke each day inside the limits of a fate that he had not awakened to at all. No matter what time he woke up, his fate was there before him. The inner sentence was inscribed on his forehead and it preceded him wherever he went without his ever being aware of it.

What could anyone tell him that might slip past the fateful blinders that kept the world before him narrow and kept his own spirit entrapped within fixed inner attitudes? He was like so many others who wake each day within a prescription about life that they carry within them but never understand. "That's the way I am," they say; "what you see is what you get." "I am what I am," as if there were no other way to be. As if the point of life was to never change, but simply be the way they happened to be and even defend their right to always be just that way.

Until some hint of awakening appears, or a shocking event occurs anyone can be a tiger believing they are nothing but a goat. There is nothing wrong with goats; they have their own stories in which it is *their* essence that triumphs. However, they are known for being hard-headed and for always taking the difficult way, even if a smoother path exists nearby. The poor son's insistence upon the narrow restrictions of his life had kept him in the goat world where his unconscious fate decided everything beforehand. He was not truly himself; he was one-sided in his outlook and as a result, he felt continually blind-sided by life. He became unable to imagine any notion of genuine change, much less the idea of having a deeper self within that needed to find its own voice and learn its own way to roar in the world.

He was a poor and unfortunate man and that was a fact that he could demonstrate and prove to anyone. In the bigger picture that included his unlived life, it was as if the literal poverty of his fate had become an emotional and spiritual poverty as well. It should come as no surprise; the same thing can happen to an entire community or a country that loses the big story and becomes impoverished on more than one level. It can even happen to those who possess great wealth; for abundance on the surface can hide greater forms of poverty within. Until the inner poverty turns to generosity no real change will happen even if there are piles of food on the table.

The son of poverty could not see the greater notion of giving freely or even the surprise of receiving something from an unseen hand. He was stuck in a firm belief that he had never been given enough in this life. It was not simply that he did not trust that his own life could change; he had also convinced himself that he could not trust the world at all. How could he trust the world around him if he had no real trust in himself? His habitual fear and continual need to control things became the rope that tied him to his inner poverty.

The poor son had decided to remain small and control the little life he had. He put his little goat-self in charge and denied that there could be any greater self within. In remaining unconscious of the hidden value of his own internal life he had to remain impoverished in relation to the world around him. It's not to say that poverty doesn't exist or that it can't crush the spirit and turn a person's heart bitter. More to say, that a person can become secretly punishing to themselves and therefore become unable to be truly generous to others.

Something had to wake the poor fellow up or else he would live his entire life inside a story that kept his spirit small and threatened to turn him cynical and bitter in the end. In holding so tightly to his narrow fate he would fail to find the natural generosity of spirit that was also born when he first came into the world. The poor son had to give away all that he had in order to move past the inner constrictions and hidebound restrictions of his fate. He had to step beyond his usual ego attitude and cease to be so cynical and controlling. In order to find the blessing hidden in the curse, he had to enter his fate more fully before letting it go completely. In order to change his life and alter his fate, he had to truly let go and not hold anything back either.

He had to change from the inside out if he would have the world around him change. He had to change both his idea of himself and his views of the world and risk everything on a destiny as yet unseen. Only by letting go and not holding back could his fate shift within and allow him to awaken to a greater joy in life that had been waiting for him all along.

When it comes to awakening, the point is not "self-improvement" or simply a change in status. Changing one's fate means awakening to another way of seeing and *being*. Not simply doing things differently, but becoming a different person, both more aware within and more alert to the mystery of life. The point of change is to become as another, to become the other that was hidden inside all along. In order for such a thorough change to happen people must let go of who they think they are. Letting go of one's habitual self turns out to be one of the greatest difficulties in life. If that were not so, many more people would escape the common traps that keep life small and self-confining.

Unfortunately, most people settle for fixed attitudes and habitual behaviors, then become wildly disappointed when they keep falling into the same trap over and over. The sages in ancient India observed life carefully and noticed similarities between certain animal behaviors and the human capacity for self-entrapment and self-punishment. It's like the hunters who observed the behavior of monkeys and developed a foolproof method for catching them. Monkeys are quick by nature and clever enough to dismantle all kinds of traps. Yet even clever monkeys could be induced to ensnare themselves. The trap that they could not escape involved a simple trick that pinned them in the clutches of their own nature.

A big coconut would be collected and then be hollowed out. A hole would be made in the shell, just large enough to allow a monkey's paw to pass through. The coconut would then be pinned to the ground and some tempting fruit would be placed inside the hollow shell. Inevitably, a monkey would approach and become full of desire for the fragrant food it could smell and almost taste. As soon as the paw of the monkey slipped through the hole and grasped the food inside, the poor creature would become caught in the trap.

The fist holding the fruit was too large to pass back through the hole in the coconut shell. Of course, to become free of the trap all the monkey had to do was release the thing it held so tightly and coveted so much. More often than not, the monkeys would cling to the immediate goal and lose the greater freedom that was also within their grasp.

Freedom was right at hand and only required the act of letting go; yet the hand that held the desired object would not release it. The monkey was trapped by what it desired so strongly, but also by how it insisted on being. Of course, people are close to monkeys in many ways and can be just as self-destructive. It is difficult to let go of a familiar way of being even when it has become more of a trap than a satisfying way to live. Some hold onto another person long after the once fruitful relationship comes to feel like a trap. Others cling to a career that no longer pays off or hold onto some bitterness that keeps everything in place.

Any meaningful change must begin with recognizing and letting go of what entraps us. Yet the little self feels it will lose what it holds so dear. Even when life begins to feel like a trap and the pain becomes undeniable, the monkey-minded little self will not simply let go. Often enough it seems better to cling to a familiar pain than suffer a genuine change of state.

The Cure is in the Pain

In India, where cows are sacred and allowed to wander freely, people keep water buffalo to give milk and cream as well as to do various kinds of work. Those great-bodied beasts have wondrous horns that spiral out from their heads. Unfortunately, some buffalo develop horns that curve backwards and that over time begin to grow right into their ears. Being pierced by its own horns, the buffalo bellows in pain and rolls on the ground amidst tremendous suffering.

Even at the height of its pain the animal has no way to stop the process; a pattern that it cannot control has become the persistent cause of its torture and self-torment. The piercing pain comes from its own unconscious way of being and it is powerless to do anything about it. If left alone, the horns will continue to grow inward until they penetrate the brain causing the buffalo to die from piercing itself. Although the condition is brutally painful and potentially fatal, the cure is simple and instantaneous. If someone simply saws off the offending horns the entire descent into pain and suffering stops in a moment. For the animal, that moment of healing and release must seem a wondrous miracle as all the pain and suffering suddenly stop.

Those who tend the buffalo naturally step in before the piercing goes too far and the animal becomes the victim of its own unwitting nature. Naturally, they also draw some analogies to the troubles and torments, compulsions and obsessions that afflict most human beings. For humans can also be seen to suffer from penetrating inner wounds and persecutions that seem to be self-inflicted. Unlike the buffalo that cannot hide the cause of their pain or cover over the pattern of self-destruction, people become masterful at covering up what is killing them from within.

Everyone experiences pain and most suffer from patterns that continue to make life miserable unless something or someone intervenes. The pain we feel comes from the cross-wise energies that keep curving back and cancelling the wise self and the good word that wait to be expressed from within us. Persistent pain is usually the indication that we have become trapped in a life too small for our true nature. That is the usual human fate and the common predicament where the little-self obscures the greater nature behind it. Until people realize what harms them and limits them from within, they are unlikely to call out for someone to help stop the pain. The remedy may be nearby, but until the pain becomes unbearable most remain caught in the agony of one form or another of self-inflicted wounds.

The disciple could not simply cancel the fate of the poor son; he couldn't take the buffalo and sell it in order to stop the pain and change the situation. Despite knowing the inner condition, he could not remove the obstacles in the man's life. Even Brahma, the god of creation, could not do that. All the disciple could do was cut off the usual conversation and offer some accurate advice that could help reverse the curve of the fate that impaled the poor son. In order to help he had to first intensify the pain. As they used to say, "The cure for the pain is in the pain."

Once the poor son grasped the tiger presence behind his own stubborn and goat-like ways, he not only had a clear direction, but also had the vital energy he needed.

The poor son not only kept a buffalo, he was like those buffalo whose horns turn inwards and threaten their own lives. His narrow sense of life was killing him as well as endangering his family. In order to help him, all the disciple could do was try to cut through the resistance and move him closer to the source of the pain and hope that he would find the insight and the courage needed to let go of what kept wounding him from within. The thread of destiny for the poor son was found in the vein of generosity that happened to be right under the tight reins he kept on life.

Once he learned to let go, he found a way to be that was deeply generous both to himself and to others. He found within the exact limitations that entrapped him the inner gifts that could release him. The brightness of the tiger-self within us hides in the dull determination of our goat-like attitudes and habits. Once awakened from the blindness of the herd, the tiger nature knows exactly how to proceed in the world. The once miserly man became a tiger of generosity. The tiger image suggests the deep vitality that becomes available when the inner channel of the deep self finally opens. This inner gradient and innate way of being carry the vital current of one's life and connect to a deep capacity for renewal hidden within each of us.

Each re-alignment with the inner law of our being produces a greater sense of imagination and meaning at the same time that it provides a renewal of the flow of vital life energy. Call it a "natural law" or an inner "dharma." It is a law in the sense that it has been laid down within us; it is a dharma in the sense that it is a holy power that indicates our true role in life and our capacity to serve something greater than our little self. This inner gradient shapes a pathway of intrinsic value that leads to an awareness of genuine self-worth even as it opens a unique way of giving to the world.

They say that people truly become healers when they heal something in themselves. In finding a way through his own pain and suffering, the disciple had come to understand the nature of the pain as well as the need to cut off the habits that allow it to keep growing. The disciple had awakened to a deeper sense of self and had found a key that could unlock the tangled relationship between the children's fate and their greater destiny. Whereas he had formerly despaired of being able to help the ill-fated children, he now could perceive a deeper level of meaning in their burdens. Where he had seen just the limitations of their fates, he began to see the greater possibilities of their destinies. In seeing the destiny hidden inside the restrictions of fate, he also saw the unwinding of his own intended path in life.

CHAPTER 14

PEARLS OF THE FIRST WATER

What is fated to be yours will always return to you.
Chinese Proverb

The disciple felt relieved that the burden of the poor son's fate had been shifted. He felt he had fulfilled a duty and performed an act of dharma or "right action." Yet he continued to feel separated from others and to struggle with what he knew, yet could not share with anyone. Despite all that had happened with the buffalo and the rice and the great feasts, the disciple could not explain the strange workings of fate and destiny to the son of the old sage. All he could do was share the fruit of his hard-won knowledge in a way that the son could understand and use in his own life. After all, you cannot give people any more than they are able to receive.

Information may be transferred readily; knowledge can be communicated with care; but wisdom will test the patience of the teacher as well as the capacity of the student. For years the disciple had carried the burden of his knowledge of fate within himself. He had struggled mightily with the impulse to tell the whole thing as well as with the concern that if he did his head would break into a thousand pieces. At first, the condition set upon his soul irritated everything in him; eventually the secret became a seed around which other knowledge formed. That which irritated him no end to begin with now could seem like a gem at the center of his being.

The son and his family were now embracing the abundance of life with a newfound joy. After celebrating with the family and accepting their gratitude, the disciple knew that it was time for him to depart again. Before going on his way, he asked what had happened to the daughter of his old teacher. The sage's son choked with tears at the mention of his sister, but he would not speak a word about her. The disciple waited in silence for some kind of answer to be offered, and the son finally admitted that she lived nearby. She had a humble hut in the next town over. He stated sadly that she had become the town prostitute and that was all he knew about it. At that point, he became overwhelmed with shame and would not say another word on the subject.

Once again, knowledge proved to be painful and could be seen to divide things before it could ever unify them. The disciple did not need further explanation; he took his leave of the son and his family and set out for the town where the sister was said to be living.

Although the distance between the brother and sister had grown quite wide, the distance between the towns where they lived was minimal. The disciple found the town readily and only had to ask where he might find a prostitute in order to learn the exact location of the sister's hut. People thought it odd that what appeared to be a holy man would be looking for a prostitute; then again, stranger things happen in this life. When it comes to love and sex all must deal with their needs and desires in some way; so they pointed him in the same direction that many of them went on occasion.

The disciple arrived at the hut of the poor sister as evening was approaching and the shadows were growing longer. He waited nearby until night began to fall then knocked on the door of her little house. Without asking who it might be, the poor woman pushed the door open and left it for him to enter. She thought it must be her first customer of the night arriving a bit earlier than usual. So, she was thoroughly surprised to see a holy man standing at the threshold. It was an unusual sight; but she was used to seeing all kinds of men appear at the edge of night, so she simply invited him inside.

The disciple explained who he was and that he had been looking for her because of the old connection to her mother and father. Hearing this, the daughter of the old sage began to weep openly. When he reminded her that he had been there at her birth, tears poured from her eyes. She cried for a long time, overwhelmed with the depth of shame she felt. Here she was the daughter of a great sage, reduced to being a common prostitute. She tried to explain how poverty had punished her, how easily a woman could be reduced to nothing in the eyes of men, how she felt that she had nowhere else to turn.

True as it all might be the lament did not change the anguish of her situation, yet she felt some relief in being able to express how utterly miserable and trapped she felt. She knew that no one in the village respected her and that she had lost most of her self-respect as well. The disciple listened carefully; he consoled her and after a time asked if she would like some advice. She said she would like anything that might change the way she lived and alter the way she felt about it.

"Well then," said the disciple, "keep your door closed tonight. No matter who appears, no matter how many come knocking upon it, tell them that you will only open to one who brings you a bag of pearls of the first water. Do that for just one night and I will return and visit you in the morning."

The poor daughter was used to making deals and accustomed to making them quickly so as to not lose what little opportunities might come to her. But this was an agreement of a different order. On one hand the poor woman was afraid that if she refused anyone at all she might lose everything. She might hate the life she had, but she also feared falling into a deeper hole. She wished to change things, yet worried that any change might make the disaster worse. On the other hand, she felt ashamed and anguished and at times tormented enough to be willing to try anything.

Given the way her life had gone, she tended not to trust anyone. At the same time, it occurred to her that the disciple was not asking her for anything. Besides, why would a holy person take an interest in her welfare if she were devoid of any value? It was an unusual bargain, but she decided to make the strange agreement. After repeatedly giving herself away and often for practically nothing at all, she now agreed that she would hold out until she was offered the finest pearls. She told the disciple that she would try her best; he said that was all that anyone could do. He repeated that he would return in the morning to see how she fared.

Waiting for the Unseen

It was an exciting idea for the sister to consider that she might be worth as much as valuable pearls. At the beginning of the night it gave her a sense of confidence and a feeling of hope where she typically felt resignation and a shadow of despair. As the night deepened, her customers came calling as usual and they came with the usual needs. However, no matter how many knocked at her door, she refused to open it to anyone unless he brought with him a bag of pearls of the first water.

Upon hearing the outrageous conditions being required by a common prostitute, they concluded that the poor woman had lost her mind and all quickly went away. As the night drew on and became deeper with silence and isolation, the sister of sorrow became truly despondent. Towards the close of night when the darkest hour spread over the land, the daughter of the old sage began to feel that she had made a huge mistake. She became overwhelmed with an old anguish and the kind of fears she had as a child. She felt completely alone and certain that she would wind up with nothing but her empty self and a desperate pile of regrets.

This is a strange world where mysterious things happen all the time, and happen especially when the issues of fate and destiny are afoot and the time has come for one thing to change into another. In the small hours before dawn, when most are asleep, a noble young man walked straight to the hut and knocked upon her door. He stood at the threshold as night began to approach its inevitable meeting with the dawn. The daughter of misery uneasily made her demand for fine pearls one more time. To her great surprise, the latecomer responded that he had a full measure of pearls of the first water and desired nothing more than to spend the remainder of the night with her.

This time, she opened the door and stood there wide-eyed with wonder as the noble fellow placed a bag of stunning pearls before her. Nothing more is said of what passed between them; suffice it to say that delight replaced fear and beauty replaced shame and that which was torn and divided became healed and united again. This world can be but a string of fragile moments hung precariously against the impending darkness; yet time can be stilled and remorse can be softened and even the deepest pain can be relieved.

The anguished daughter had stated her terms and waited her wait. She maintained the tension between the old bargains and the new agreement and that was enough to change the entire deal that fate had imposed on her. What started in the first fateful moment of her life now found remarkable fulfillment at the end of the long night of waiting and wondering if change was indeed possible. Certain moments can open wide and break time apart and draw down enough grace to redeem even the darkest past. That must be the case or even the gods might become discouraged.

According to Brahma, a person's fate cannot be denied, but must be fulfilled in some manner. It was the sad fate of the poor daughter to be a prostitute and sell her body each night. That much had already been proven to be true. However, nothing had been said or written about the price to be asked or the method of fulfillment or the role of love in the exchange. In this world made of nights and days, fate had to be fulfilled, but the bargain could be made in many ways.

When the daylight returned and chased the darkness from the world, the disciple arrived again at the sister's door. When he asked how she had fared throughout the night, she told him of the long stretch of loneliness and torment and of the surprise that came at the end of it. The daughter of the sage explained how she struggled in the darkness with an old sense of isolation and an all-too-familiar feeling of worthlessness. She recounted the anguish she felt as she refused to admit those who knocked at her door with the usual offers. She confessed how she felt herself sinking into oblivion, fearing that she would give in to her desperation at any moment.

Since it was apparent that some great change had occurred, the disciple asked how she avoided total despair. Seemingly still surprised at herself, she explained that she began to meditate and tried to center herself as her father or mother might have done. Sitting alone in her hut she found herself remembering times as a child when she played by the river that ran through her parents' compound. She began to recall how much she loved that river as a girl. She loved the steady sound of the rippling water and the play of light on the surface. She loved the purity she felt when she entered the water that was always treated as sacred by those around her.

The River of Change

In the midst of her anguish her knowledge of the holy river came flowing back to her. She remembered how people considered the sacred river to be the source of life and the model for how life continuously renews itself. The river was named after Saraswati, the ancient goddess who was the source of learning and speech and wisdom. Saraswati was the "flowing one" through whom knowledge and wisdom as well as music and the arts find their true course. Saraswati was also the source of a specific kind of longing that led to a love for rhythm and music. Music could also become a river through which all pent-up emotions and feelings could be released.

The poor daughter had long forgotten the devotion she felt when she was a child, but now she felt the stirring of it again. She began to say the old name of the river that was also the goddess, just as she learned it as a girl. She repeated the sounds and the meaning to herself: *sara-swati*, *sara-swati*; *sara* is essence and *swa* is self. She tried to hold to the essence of herself in a way that she had not felt since she was young and still innocent and blessed by the sparkling river nearby. It was in that way she that she was able to calm herself and become strangely centered in the midst of her aloneness.

Although she had long felt herself unworthy of the old traditions, they now came flooding back to her. Saraswati was the river of life and the essence of the self; she was also the original consort of Brahma the creator. Yet in old stories Saraswati often appeared as a disinherited daughter or as an estranged wife. She would often enter a self-imposed exile and dwell in silence in order to preserve her primal sense of self. As goddess of wisdom and purification the deity could focus her calm gaze upon the past and wash away all residual feelings of anger and resentment, sorrow or despair. The act of deep purification that leads to a renewal of one's sense of self was Saraswati's greatest gift.

In the midst of darkness, in the depths of solitude, in the anguish of exile, the poor daughter of the old sage kept calling on Saraswati to diminish the shame she felt and dispel her fear of being worthless. Instead of abandoning herself to shame or despair, she held to the image of the goddess who could cleanse and renew with the waters of life. Unseen by anyone, a shift occurred in the heart of the poor daughter that made her worth her weight in gold or jewels. Call it a moment of grace or an act of mercy or an unexpected twist of fate. It was only in the light of day that followed that the daughter remembered that the river goddess would be often be shown with a string of pearls in her hand.

The disciple listened to all that had transpired in the dark night of the soul and found his own memories of the sacred river flowing back to him. He too had learned to honor Saraswati as the source of learning and wisdom. She was said to be the inventor of ancient Sanskrit and the muse of anyone who sought for the deeper meanings found in any language. However, he had not considered the role the goddess played in rites of purification and renewal. Now, he thought of his old teacher in a new light. He had to consider anew the question of why the old sage went to the source of the river when the time for the birth of each child drew near.

The old sage could no more see the fate of his own children than other parents; but he may have intuited a way to seek blessings for them from the deity that bestows wisdom and can cleanse heartache from the soul. It now seemed that the old sage understood more about fate and destiny than he let on. He may have been wise enough to seek the blessings of Saraswati for each child at the same time that Brahma was activating the fate they would bear in this world. The disciple began to wonder if the sage had somehow intuited what fate might have written on his student's head as well.

After thinking his own thoughts for a while, the disciple spoke to the daughter again. "Now, you are of the purest of people; for you were faithful to yourself when it mattered most. Few in the world can say that after facing the pain of life and sitting in the broken depths of darkness." He asked if she would like some more advice. She answered that she would love further guidance, especially if it led her in the same direction. He explained that whoever brought the pearls the first time must continue to bring them every time she refused to sell herself short.

"Don't open your door to any other," he said. "Only wait each time for the true worth to appear no matter what feelings or hauntings might precede it. In the meantime, spend the value of the pearls and give freely to those caught in the teeth of misfortune. Continue to cast out everything in yourself that diminishes the value of life and the importance of love."

The young woman was happy enough to adopt the new practice. She found beauty in the course of each day and waited each night for the beautiful visitor to arrive with the stunning gift of pearls. Her life changed completely and she knew more joy than ever she had before. As they say, those who are willing to follow sorrow all the way down receive a free ride back on the elevator of joy.

The Oldest Profession

The unconscious fate of the poor sister had continually caused her to "sell herself short." It wasn't simply that she sold her body for so little, but that she gave herself away before learning what true value she had within. Prostituting oneself means to indiscriminately give up one's natural "stature and standing." In that sense, prostitution is not only the oldest profession in the world, it is also the most common condition in life. For most people sell themselves for far less than they are truly worth. Some "sell out" simply to survive or make a living; others make distorted deals to acquire fame or fortune. We all sell ourselves short to one degree or another and frequently sell ourselves out just to receive some attention or to be loved in some fashion.

In this world where it seems that one more business deal or one more conquest will make everything right, prostitution occurs whenever people fail to stand up for themselves. It happens each time the genuine self is abandoned in favor of a false sense of self. The inner pearl or golden self is repeatedly sold cheaply in this world where all prostitute themselves until they learn their own true worth. Whether to gain power, wealth or love the true sense of self is commonly traded for some immediate gain that cannot last.

People look down hard on those who prostitute themselves openly partly because the state of inner prostitution is so common and widespread.

Those most willing to condemn the actions of others have usually lost touch with their own essence; otherwise they would have more compassion and understanding. What is most important most often goes missing and tends to hide in the dark places where most people refuse to look. Only as a last resort will most people look deep enough to find the hidden pearls of wisdom.

There is an old story of a great city that was almost destroyed because no one high or low seemed able to find the truth or state it openly. The true situation came to the surface when a mighty river began overflowing its banks and threatened to flood the shining city with its amazing temples and palaces. The city had been built on either side of a river as happens throughout the world, but especially in India where all the rivers are considered to be sacred and central to life. Each river can be considered an embodiment of the divine feminine force that flows through this world sustaining life and secretly nurturing the land and its people.

Of all rivers the Ganges was most revered; as sacred source of the flow of life on earth it was called Ma Ganga, the "mother river." The Ganges was a living, moving temple that flowed through the middle of life. It was the primal representation of the milk of nurturance as well as the promising waters of compassion. But too much of even a good thing can become dangerous and when a storm of torrential rains fell upon the city in sheets, the river began to rise ominously. When the downpour continued, it became clear that the rising river might overflow its banks and destroy the city of many temples and holy places. All the inhabitants feared for their lives, but none wished to leave the royal city and lose all that they loved about it and had invested in it.

Eventually, the trouble reached the ears of the emperor who lived in a magnificent palace in the center of the city, near where the holy river flowed. The king was a powerful ruler who had conquered many lands, but had recently converted to Buddhism. He had become the first Buddhist emperor and the royal city had become a religious center as well. Despite the ongoing downpour, he ordered everyone in the city to gather along a high bank of the swollen Ganges.

Soon, a great crowd gathered on the banks and watched fearfully as the waters continued to rise. Everyone stood in the miserable rain, while the king's ministers consulted with the military officers and the religious leaders. After a time they all could be seen to be shaking their heads as they concluded that none of them could find a solution for the impending disaster. Finally, the emperor asked out loud: "Can no one make an Act of Truth that can change the situation and cause the waters of the Ganges to flow back upstream?"

He was referring to an idea which professed that those who had fulfilled their life duty could draw upon something deep in themselves and of complete truth. Any who found a way to live in accord with their deepest selves would also be in accord with the essence of life. On the basis of such deep inner accord, such a person could become a conduit for the primordial energy at the source of life. If what they stated was true in essence they might make a request that could alter the immediate conditions that prevail in life.

The idea of an act of truth rested upon the ancient notion: "as above, so below." Each person was a small replica of the cosmos and the essence of each person was secretly connected to the essence of the world. The energy of the universe flowed through each soul and under certain circumstances, one could affect the other. Those who could draw upon their own essence could also draw upon the essence and power of the universe. Thus, they could produce a great change in the moment.

It was clear that the emperor knew the old idea of hidden continuities. He was wise enough to call for an act of truth; but he was apparently unable to make such an act himself at that time. Of course, he turned to his closest advisors, but they simply looked questioningly at each other. None of the members of the royal court seemed ready to speak up either and all began to look further down the line. Since the caste system was in full force at the time everyone had gathered according to rank. Everyone looked to the military leaders, but they only stood firm and quiet as they gazed into the distance. The depth of the silence became profound as everyone looked to the religious leaders for some solace and redemption from the flood. No answer was forthcoming.

The silence spread through the crowd as the request for an act of truth reached the merchant class who, for a change, had nothing to say. Amidst the soaking rain, the imminent threat of loss and the lack of available truth, the lordly nobles, the ranks of warriors and the throngs of merchants all hung their heads. Even the common people fell under a cloud of silence as the desperation of the situation became clear to everyone.

At the end of the line and farthest from the royal host above stood the "untouchables." They were the lowest of the low and were not even included in the caste system; they were in fact the outcasts. Amongst them were those who handled the waste products of animals and people as well as those who buried the dead. They were the "untouchables" that members of the higher classes avoided at all cost. Touching them in any way might produce pollution by contact. Amongst the outcasts could be found the prostitutes who sold their bodies, but were otherwise untouchable. Strange to tell, but the only voice responding to the request for an act of truth came from the mouth of a prostitute standing amidst the throng of outcasts at the end of the line.

By now Bindumatæ was an old woman. She had been a prostitute for most of her life and was considered the lowest of the lowly. She was avoided by most people if she was noticed at all. Yet she was the one person who spoke into the swelling silence. Quietly she said to those around her, "I have an Act of Truth." When people encouraged her to tell her truth, the old woman moved closer to the banks of the river. She closed her eyes and entered a state of profound concentration. After a time she pronounced what she had to say with a clear and convincing voice.

As the old prostitute spoke from the depths of herself at one end of the quay, the emperor at the high end of the crowd noticed that the rushing waters were beginning to slow down. As people watched in awe, the holy river appeared to stop in the midst of its reckless flow. Then the water reversed its course and began to run the opposite way. As the waters receded a roar of wonder and relief began to rise and spread its way down through the crowd.

Once the miraculous reversal of the situation became clear, the emperor asked who in the world had performed the act of truth. None of the royal entourage had any idea. They looked at each other, but gained no knowledge on the subject. Only after a time did the rumor that was flowing up through the crowd reach to the level of the royal court. Amidst the growing amazement in the crowd the emperor was informed that of all people, it was an old prostitute who managed to make the act of truth.

At that point, the great ruler himself began to move down the long line of people still standing in descending ranks along the banks of the river. Eventually he reached the area where the outcasts were gathered. People moved quickly aside until the emperor found himself approaching the old prostitute who remained in a state of internal reflection.

"You!" the emperor exclaimed. "A wicked old sinner and disgrace to the community! Am I to understand that you have an act of truth?" "Your majesty," she answered, "I possess an act of truth and I performed it at your request and for the direct benefit of everyone here."

The emperor became quite curious and asked the old woman what she had said to make the river reverse course. He wanted an explanation of how she of all people could manage an act of truth when so many above her could do nothing of the kind. The old prostitute replied: "When I spoke my act of truth, I said that whoever offers me something I treat him the same as any other. Whether it be a high Brahmin, and there have been some of those; a warrior or a merchant, and there have been many of them; I treat each one the same. Whether it be a person down on his luck or another outcast like myself, I welcome each in the same way and serve their needs with the same quality of attention.

"I make no distinction in favor of those who happen to be powerful; I show no disfavor to those whose fate has put them in a lowly condition. Being in this way free from both pretension and contempt, I have learned to serve in the way that I know best. Since I treat no one better or worse than another, I have learned to treat myself in the same way. It is from this inner sense of acceptance, your majesty, that I am able to perform an act of truth and alter the desperate condition we have all found ourselves in."

The emperor was satisfied with this account and he was even instructed by the old woman's explanation. All who were nearby also found themselves contemplating their own inner worth. On that day the old prostitute became a teacher for everyone high or low. Despite what people thought of her, she had found a truth inside herself and was able to draw upon that essence. When the hard times came, the one who had survived many hard times herself became able to share the truth she had learned the hard way. Having such an open heart and mind proved that she had cleared whatever resentments and disappointments, angers and conflicts she might otherwise have carried within.

The trappings of wealth or power become empty and meaningless when it is the truth that is needed. When it comes to the truth there is no higher or lower class. Of all those present, the lowly prostitute turned out to be closest to the pearl of the self and therefore nearest to the source of life's endless flow and capacity to renew. She had found a way to reverse the fate within herself and that made her capable of reversing the course of events that threatened others. All people are noble in the depths of their souls and each can become conscious of a truth that can free them from servitude and serve others at the same time.

Pearls Before Swine

Despite the common desire to rise to the top, moments of essential change can depend upon a willingness to descend. A deep connection may be drawn between those who face the truth in themselves and the discovery of valuable pearls in depths of the ocean. Those who desire pearls must dive into deep waters; once there they risk darkness and isolation and the confusions of the murky depths. Similarly, those who would find the inner pearl must enter the treacherous waters of the soul and face the darkness found within. They must crack the hard shell of their little-self and come to know themselves from the inside out.

There is a lonely wilderness in the soul that must be crossed before the center of the self can open and reveal the inner truth. The daughter of the old sage had to dwell in darkness and sit in the depths of her soul before pearls could be brought to her door. She had to find a genuine sense of inner value before the outer conditions could change. Like the old prostitute making the act of truth, the sorrowful sister had to find the pearl at the center of herself and begin the process of reversing her own fortune.

Many people believe that a prostitute cannot have inner value and that outcasts live in the shadows because of something distorted in their nature. Yet the destiny of each soul is wrapped in darkness until it becomes revealed. Like the pearl wrapped in its shell and hidden in the depths, the soul is a light that grows from a darkness within each of us. The pearl has always been a symbol of unique beauty that rises from the unseen depths of life. In the same way, a pearl reminds us that a hidden alchemy is taking place in the inner tides of the human soul.

Those who seek for pearls must be willing to dive to the depths time and time again. Once in the depths things appear differently and each descent requires an inner adjustment in order to see what is otherwise hidden from view. People expect beautiful things to come in an attractive wrapper; but the soul has it another way. The hidden beauty works its way from inside out and must be sensed within before it can be displayed for all to see.

Doesn't a pearl begin as an irritant inside the life of the oyster? The rare gem that becomes the gift of the deep waters begins as an alien presence inside its host. The same situation exists with the human soul; that which can become the most valued aspect of the self is an irritant to begin with. The inner seed of great value is not recognized or valued at the beginning of life and remains overlooked by those who see with conventional sight. There is an inner alchemy involved and that which is rejected or overlooked early on secretly holds the seed that becomes the pearl of the first water.

Remember the necessity of imperfection and having a weird and unadaptable foot that keeps a limp in each life? The weird foot keeps in touch with the inner depths; it both hides and reveals the forgotten essence. Genuine pearl-fishers know exactly that formula. They train themselves to notice weird traits. They seek shells with an irregular shape or stunted growth; for those are most likely to yield quality pearls. Don't miss this message regarding the uniqueness of the soul and its way of revealing inner truth and essential worth.

Those who claim to be perfect or pure are like manufactured pearls;

their glow does not come from the mystery that turns blemishes into beauty or wounds into gifts. In the deep waters of life one thing can become another, and what seemed worthless at first can turn out to be most valuable later on. First, some deep soul-searching must occur; something hard must be cracked open if the shining self would be found within. Most people avoid the cracking and breaking- open process, yet that which tears at the shell does not harm the pearl within it.

Like the poor sister, many fear they will turn out to be a common oyster that has little value and becomes cast aside. In the waters of nature a shell with a pearl may be rare; but in the waters of the soul each swimmer finds the inner treasure if the search is long enough. The inner pearl grows from the irritation of fate that tries to trouble us towards a greater destiny in life. It is the troubling seed of fate that eventually becomes the jewel of destiny.

Old traditions call the pearl "the child of lightning." Something quite foreign first penetrates and impregnates the interior life of the oyster. The organism responds by covering the seed of light with layers of its own secretions. Over time the inner seed begins to lose its abrasive contours. Eventually, it becomes smooth and round like the drop of a tear. The pearl grows as a secret within secretions that both hide it and protect it until the time for cracking open arrives. The pearl of the deep self represents a unity formed of the fires of longing and the waters of renewal.

The inner pearl develops from a similar cultivation of the hidden spirit of one's life; it also incorporates something that is most foreign within us, even contrary to our nature. Ancient people called pearls "the tears of the divine." The first agreement of one's life is like a divine teardrop that has fallen into the soul and irritates its host from within. Until it becomes clear that what irritates our life is an inner pearl trying to grow, it feels as if something is wrong and troublingly out of place. It can appear in strange desires that persist within us and resist being dismissed or as a strange dream that must be cracked open before it can shine light on our life.

Unlike gemstones that must be cut and polished to bring out their beauty, a pearl does not need to be cut or reshaped in order to be valuable. A pearl can be worn in its natural form and it is the precise shape and exact iridescence that makes each one valuable. A "pearl of the first water" is translucent and possesses a unique iridescence or "orient." Such an inner glow and specific luster are also characteristics of the individual soul that is also a light inside the darkness.

Since pearls appear fully formed with each having a unique iridescence and orient, the pearl became an ideal representation of the inner uniqueness of each soul and the surprising completeness of the deep self. The great self shines uniquely, yet it also represents the cosmic pearl at the center of existence. As cosmic center it can offer calmness and clarity; as unique essence, it offers the creative energy and true orientation necessary for a meaningful life. In order to be properly valued in this world, people must find the pearl of the first water in the depths of themselves.

Destiny Turns Fate Upside Down and Inside Out

Everyone enters this world with an inner seed or hidden gem worth "more than gold." That is the human inheritance that precedes and transcends all social systems and methods of evaluating people. However, the problem remains that the inner gold and hidden pearl hide near the most wounded and most rejected parts of ourselves. By the time the disciple found the poor daughter of the old sage she had almost reached the bottom. She could no longer imagine that something unique and valuable resided within her. The narrowing of her fate placed her in a desperate condition and the only way out was to find the pearl within the shell she believed she was and refuse to allow others to make her feel worthless.

Consider the old prostitute again. She knew what it meant to be undervalued; she also knew how people of all classes suffered and secretly longed to be loved. She knew that the little-self with its high pretensions and hidden needs typically rules this world that is always on the verge of being flooded. When the presence of a deeper sense of self was most needed, she knew exactly where to turn. Her little-self had become acquainted with the greater self within. Some insist that the ego must be removed for the deep self to appear; yet the little-self can also learn to work with the inner source of its own presence.

The little-self is itself a creation of the great self within; yet it cannot know that until something breaks the shell which hides the inner spirit. The little-self is both a shell and a spell. It protects and it hinders; it both hides and at times reveals what is hidden within. Early in life it hides the radiance of the deep self which only occasionally shines forth; yet it can eventually learn to turn to that deeper self for solace and calmness, for clarity and for power if needed. The deep self is a natural epiphany, a shining through of the gold sown and hidden within the personality that both knows of it and again does not.

Pearl fishers are known to work in pairs. One must dive deep into the sea while a partner stays above to hold the other end of a lifeline that connects upper and lower realms. Both are required to bring the pearl of great value from the depths to the surface. Some say that the deep swimmer represents the greater self, while the surface partner stands for the little-self that anchors one in ever-changing surface of life. Seen that way, the little boat of the ego-self helps anchor oneself in the common world while the inner life grows from within.

The ego is a double agent that often obscures but can also help reveal the presence of a deeper self within. When a life situation can no longer abide compromise and something deeper and more meaningful must be found, the little-self can learn to bow to the greater presence hidden within. As the shell of the little-self softens and allows itself to be cracked open, the inner radiance and iridescence of the soul can shine through. Then, ego-self can become the agent of the deeper self and can begin to serve the original agreement and greater destiny of the soul.

As in the case of the old prostitute, the shining through of the deep radiance of the self is both creative and healing; it has a mysterious effect on other people and can shift the conditions of the common world. The trick in this life is to become aware of the wise self within before the little-self hardens too much and becomes a fixed fate and a crosswise ruler that keeps one's life feeling empty and small.

Feeling that his work was done, the disciple prepared to depart from the area where the son and daughter of his old teacher resided. Before leaving he returned to the river nearby to reflect upon the two villages where the children struggled with their fates in life. The brother and sister not only lived in separate villages, they had contrasting fates and opposite attitudes towards life. The poor son held onto everything he had no matter what, while his sister gave herself away and often to the lowest bidder. Both lived their fates unconsciously; both being trapped in the fixed attitudes of the little-self; both clinging to unfulfilling lives despite the great pain and alienation they felt inside.

In order to find their essential connection to the vitality of the deeper self, the unconscious deals and familiar agreements that kept the little-self in charge had to be turned inside out. The brother had to learn to give freely instead of clinging to the bare essentials of life. He had to become generous despite and because of his impoverished circumstances. The sister had to learn to hold herself dear and not simply give herself away. She had to value herself before others would become able to recognize her inner worth. They both had to become conscious of the way that fate held them back and kept them blind. Each also had to learn to trust in something as yet unseen.

Only after facing fate fully could the hidden deals and self-limiting agreements become conscious to them. As long as the little-self with its persistent fears and narrow vision remains in charge, each of us tends to live like the poor rejected sister or like her overly restricted brother. The village of internal poverty appears whenever we fear losing what little foothold in life we might have. We all tend to take up residence in the village of low self-worth where everyone sells themselves short, where cynicism and disappointment rules and everyone believes that they never really had a chance.

In the village of endless need and low self-worth, the inhabitants fearfully accept whatever role they find or are assigned to by others. Like the poor daughter they bow to fate and give up on life; better to resign to whatever has been offered than to suffer an even greater rejection or abandonment. Of course, little growth can occur in outer life if there is no forgiveness and generosity within. Holding back one's deepest nature keeps the spell of fate in place; so does the mantra of self-recrimination and the torment of self-loathing.

In the end, life is a mystery that can only be solved one lifetime at a time. The poor son had to learn to give like a king. The poor daughter had to learn to demand what she was really worth. In doing so they found the inner nobility of the self. By making a practice of such self-awareness and self-respect they were able to shift the onerous elements of fate in the direction of the destiny hidden within them.

The poor son who clung blindly to his meager possessions had to learn to let go and give all that he had to life. The poor daughter who gave herself away too readily had to learn to value herself in order to be treated as the noble soul she was in truth. Letting go and not holding back was the secret to the destiny of one, while holding back and containing herself was the secret to the destiny of the other.

Some days we are like the miserly son who controls and restricts the flow of life and fails to find the inner generosity that makes life joyful and rewarding. Some nights we find ourselves in the sister's hut in the village of abandonment where love and self-respect seem impossible and the fear of rejection overrules all hints of self-worth. Most people spend time in each village; often running back and forth between fears of letting go and impulses to throw one's self away.

Meanwhile, destiny waits to be found where one's fate in life turns inside out and the inner pearl of the self is finally found, where it has been all along, seeded within and trying to grow and break through the shell of one's life. Finding one's destiny requires becoming whole-hearted, both willing to give all that one has to life and willing to trust that life has something valuable to give to back. It can feel terrifying to insist on one's self-worth and risk further isolation and rejection; yet such self-recognition can break the shackles of shame and attract genuine love. It seems naïve to give all one has away, yet when done at the right time such reckless giving can lead to a place of greater abundance.

The practices of giving all one has and fully valuing what one has to give are essential for breaking the spells of fate. Fate may set exact limits on each life, yet in this world ruled by limits, there are also limits set on fate. Despite appearances to the contrary, life has hidden abundance and an endless capacity to renew itself from the ashes. There are no guarantees except that each fate has a hidden destiny that can only be found by letting go of self-restricting attitudes and self-defeating practices. Like a pearl of the first water, the dream of life is always more extravagant and more surprising than the punishing limits set by the little-self. Wealthy or poor on the outside, each person must eventually swim in the waters of despair in order to find the true treasure of self-worth.

CHAPTER 15

THE RETURN OF WISDOM

We are most alive when in tune with eternal symbols;
wisdom is a return to them.

The disciple felt satisfied that he had found ways to help the children of his old teacher shift the troubling fates that restricted their lives. Some things had shifted inside him as well and it was time to begin another pilgrimage and learn what the roads of life could teach him. He woke well before dawn and could see the moon hanging in the dark sky like a pearl on the ocean floor. He took it as a good sign for setting out and began to walk. He was not far along when he perceived someone walking the night road before him. As he drew closer he could see that it was a young man in fine clothes with a noble bearing. He was leading a buffalo and carrying a sack of rice on his head. He looked overburdened with a bag slung over his shoulder as well.

"Who are you sir," asked the disciple, "that you walk the lonely road at night and carry heavy burdens?"

The man gladly stopped, threw down his sacks and almost wept with frustration, "Look, my head has become almost bald from carrying a sack of rice each night to that poor man's hut up ahead. Night after night I must lead a buffalo to his empty shed. Then I must dress up and carry pearls to his sister's house in the next town as well. I am worn out with the burden of these tasks and it is your fault that I suffer in this way. Granted, it was my stylus that activated their fates to begin with; but it was your advice to them that now causes me to suffer. I must continually supply what was secretly promised at their birth but hidden from their view. You ask who I am, when you can see with your own eyes who must carry these burdens and walk the night roads. The question now is whether you will relieve me of the burden that the fates of those children have become for me?"

At that point, Brahma began to weep, for even a god can weep at times, and it was surely Brahma in the guise of the young nobleman. The god of creation was walking on the dark side of the road of existence where even the gods can feel constrained. He was feeling the grip of the second hand of creation that knows loneliness and sorrow and even suffers fear.

Meanwhile, the disciple considered how the original situation had turned all the way around. The sentences of fate had long held both children captive and had entrapped the disciple as well. But by the time he encountered Brahma again, the hidden destinies had been revealed and the burden had shifted back to the divine. Moving fate towards destiny means that everything can and must be renegotiated.

The disciple spoke to the god again, "If it is my place to change the deal that we made in the moments before the fates of the children were set in place, then I will gladly make a new agreement. I will absolve you of any need to fulfill their destinies. They have each faced their fate and learned the inner nature of their souls. If they remain true to themselves they can find their own way now. I readily agree to that; however, I have two requests to make of you." Having come far along the intricate road of his own fate, it was time for the disciple to renegotiate some issues of his own.

Brahma was more than willing to make a new agreement with the disciple and asked what the requirements might be.

"First of all, I ask that you grant the sister and her brother some regular happiness in this world and a share in the joy of being alive." Brahma agreed quickly and asked what else.

The disciple then requested that the deity rescind the condition that threatened the explosion of his head into a thousand pieces. He asked to be able to speak about what he had learned regarding the intricacies of fate and destiny without suffering total fragmentation. Under the new circumstances, Brahma was willing to remove the penalty he had placed upon the knowledge of fate. All he now required was that the knowledge of fate and hidden things be handled artfully and not be used for simple gain.

Under the light of the moon, in the time before dawn, the new agreement between the deity and the disciple was made. Then the disciple bowed and expressed his gratitude to the god of creation. As he continued on his way, the subtle rays of dawn began to break apart the night and the world seemed to be born again. With a feeling of lightness in his heart and relief in his mind the disciple composed his thoughts about fate and destiny as he began his next pilgrimage toward the unseen.

The Tiger Self

The disciple had been seeking to learn the fate of his teacher's child when he first encountered the god of creation, but he was also unwittingly standing on the ground of his own destiny. Destiny means to stand apart from others, to stand out in some way; most importantly, to be seen standing in a relationship to one's inner spirit. Destiny means to be close to one's genius and in the proximity of the divine aspect originally seeded in the soul. The disciple was able to converse and even negotiate with the deity because they spoke the same language. Brahma had been near him all along, beginning with the beloved cow that he first meditated upon.

The more fully he accepted his specific burden of knowledge, the more clearly he perceived the dilemma of his fate in life, as well as the solution for it. Things changed when he realized that his intrigue with the fate of others was part of his own fate in life. Like the little tiger-goat that awakened to its true nature, the disciple realized that all along he held his fate in his own hands.

In order to help others, he had to shift his own fate; he had to learn what knowledge was for and how to use it wisely. The point of knowledge is not found in the knowledge itself. Wisdom means having knowledge and knowing how and when to use it. Wisdom begins with radical self-knowledge before it becomes wise enough to be helpful to others. Knowledge that is not integrated into the knower will eventually fragment a person rather than make him whole. The disciple had to move knowledge in the direction of wisdom and each move towards wisdom also moves us closer to the divine.

Wisdom is wise because it combines aspects of the immediate with elements of the divine. Wisdom may include common sense; but it depends upon the uncommon sense of the divine in the present moment. That's why it is so rare and less available than simple knowledge. Living wisdom remembers what keeps being forgotten; and what keeps being lost is the divine connection. Wisdom connects one's basic nature with all that is transcendent and supernatural. In becoming wiser a person awakens to the divine seed set within and develops an innate connection to the eternal realm beyond.

Old stories bring the gods and humans together in order to remind us of the divine connection that is the universal inheritance of the human soul. Since individual destiny was considered to be connected to a divine source, it made sense that the gods would become closely involved in human adventures. At the same time, the animal realm used to have closer associations with human instinct and experience. Humans inhabit a middle ground between the animal world and the divine realm; but not just in the sense of having feet on the ground and heads in the air. It is human nature to draw inspiration from the natural world as well as from the supernatural realm. Both realms are close to the human soul and each offers images of wholeness and beings with noble bearing and essential integrity.

In modern times it often seems that the animals are far below us while the gods remain high above and far distant from the struggle here on earth. Being modern seems to mean being more isolated from both natural instincts and spiritual inspiration; thus, feeling less able to grow from within and fully inhabit the world. In the story of the tiger-goat the little one adapts so thoroughly to the circumstances of its birth that it comes to believe it is actually a goat. It finds a way to survive and fit in, but at the cost of losing touch with its true nature.

In modern times such extreme adaptations seem to be the rule more than the exception to it. Our essential identity can be completely overlooked by others and years can pass while the tiger-self sleeps within. If it does happen to awaken, the primal intensity of the vital self can come as a shocking revelation to the goat aspect of ourselves as well as to those who believe they already know who we are. The second birth that awakens the tiger within the self can make us feel as if we are living with the wrong species.

The tiger metaphor is no accident, as it stands for the compelling beauty, essential vitality, and mysterious nobility of the deeper self. The striking appearance of power and beauty that attends a tiger are contrary to the notion of fitting in and camouflaging oneself in order to survive. A tiger survives by being manifestly true to its stripes. It wears its noble existence on its back and roars with the intensity of creation.

The notion of an inner tiger may seem dangerous, yet a basic point about the intensity and uniqueness of life is being made. The life trying to awaken and grow from within is by nature greater than the notions of the little goat-self and the conventions of the goat world. The roar of awakening is the sound of existence that clears the soul of basic confusions and residues of shame that otherwise obscure the innate brilliance of the inner self. The inner roar is also the song of the self that intones the original speech of the soul.

The tiger-self knows instinctively how to act and where it fits in the grand scheme of existence. Similarly, the core self doesn't fear that it might be empty or essentially mistaken or have no meaningful role to play in life. Each tiger is unique and as they say, a tiger can't change its stripes. The essential markings on each human soul are also indelible and unique; but it takes courage to embrace and manifest the nobility hidden within. A tiger wears its uniqueness on the outside, but people must look deep inside to find their true colors.

At the same time, the goat-self will resist the exact intelligence and specific longings that call us to a life of greater meaning. The entanglements of fate and the words set crosswise on the soul conspire to keep the primal self and our original agreements hidden from us. Until we awaken to the unique story trying live through us, we can become trapped in a half-life with an ever-growing distance between the little goat-self and the primal self within.

Early in life it is necessary to fit in somehow and we make the required adaptations and the second agreements in order to survive. However, most people over-adapt in order to avoid immediate dangers and get along with others. At first our adaptations save our lives, later in life the adaptive habits of the little goat-self become life-endangering. Later in life, the tiger-self tries to get our attention and bring us to an awareness of the stunning nature of our dream-laden, gold-threaded selves. Meanwhile, the goat-self fears greatly that it will be devoured and destroyed completely by the tiger trying to get our attention.

Typically, human societies cater to the goat nature of the little-self in order to keep everyone in place and benefit from the herd mentality. Most cultural beliefs and customs serve to keep the goats in line and fear is the great motivator. Few realize that the fearful little-self is the source of most fears, especially the fear of change. It is the little-self with its big idea of itself and its unwillingness to change that should be feared the most.

The intensity as well as the deep beauty of the genuine self threaten the self-limiting attitudes of the little-self which fears to step beyond its comfort zone. Typically, something dramatic or tragic is required for the little-self to become so shaken that it relinquishes its grip on life and allows the true and noble nature within us to come to the surface. Remember the young woman who had to grasp a single whisker from a living tiger? She went searching for a remedy for love and each step she took brought her closer to the tiger. She hoped for a helpful potion, but in the end had to learn of her own tiger-self. Finding greater love means getting past the infantile fears and recriminations of the little-self.

Like the little tiger, each person arrives in the world as a whole package that includes the greater self hidden within. At first the inner self must remain hidden and the needs of the social community must be served. Yet all along the soul harbors an inner expectation that we will awaken to what and who we truly are and become the whole package. Each awakening of the true self serves as an act of truth for the individual life. And each act of truth can turn things around and bring a greater sense of healing, love and understanding to this troubled world. Whether the deep self awakens or not is not simply a personal matter. When people fail to live the whole package the world becomes diminished and the well of existence can become poisoned by unlived lives.

Poison and the Truth Told

It's like the old story of the boy who was playing with a ball, as children do in this world that is itself a sphere rolling through the Milky Way. As fate would have it, the ball rolled into the hole at the center of an old anthill where a poisonous snake had recently taken up residence. Not knowing the situation before him and desiring to reclaim the ball, the boy put his hand into the hole. Before he could retrieve the object of his desire, the snake bit his hand. No sooner did he pull his hand out in pain, than he fell into a faint because of the strength of the serpent's poison.

The parents of the boy began to wonder where he was and became concerned for his safety. They sensed that something was wrong and went looking for their son. By the time they found their child the poison had spread throughout his body. Realizing the great danger he was in caused both parents to act with uncommon awareness and decisive speed. Since there was no doctor in the vicinity and no time to travel, they quickly carried the unconscious boy to the hut of a nearby monk.

Laying the child at the feet of the holy man, they implored him saying, "Sir, religious people are known to have the ability to make potions and charms; please use your knowledge and cure our son."

"I know of no cures; I am not a physician by trade and I am not that kind of holy person," said the local saint.

"Well, you are a man of religion; you follow a spiritual path. You must be able at least to make some kind of act of truth. Have pity on the boy, have compassion and perform an act of truth for the sake of his life."

"I know the truth of my own life and can only draw upon that," said the ascetic.

Laying hands upon the head of the boy, the monk composed his words of truth: "After I became a monk, I lived for seven days serene in my heart, pure of purpose and committed to seeking spiritual merit. Since then, for fifty years apart from everyone and mostly self-absorbed, I have lived against my will and in a state of longing for what I may have missed. By this truth, may health come to the child; may the poison be struck down! May this truth be as a blessing and the lad be returned to life!"

No sooner had this act of truth been made, than some poison came out from the chest of the boy and soaked into the ground. The lad opened his eyes, but his body remained still and he seemed unable to arise.

The monk said to the father, "I have used what power I have; now is the time for you to use yours. Can you not make an act of truth to save the life of your only child?"

"I will make an act of truth as well," said the father. And laying a hand upon his son's breast, he spoke aloud: "For gifts and goods I have cared not at all, yet I live the life of wealth and power. I entertain important people and have become known for both affluence and generosity. Neither the powerful people nor the good and wise visitors knew that I was restraining my true self. I was unwilling within my soul all the while that I gave to them. May this truth be a blessing, may the poison be stuck down, may the boy revive!"

After this act of truth, poison came from the small of the lad's back and sank into the ground. The boy became able to sit up; yet he could not stand or move from the spot.

The father turned to the mother and spoke, "I have used my power; now it is your act of truth that is needed in order that our son can arise and return to life again."

The mother said, "I too have a truth to tell, but in your presence I cannot declare it."

She looked to the monk as if pleading for an intercession, but the holy man stood deep in his silence.

"By any means," said the father, "make our son whole. Do not hold back because of me; don't think of me or of anyone except your only son."

"Very well," said the mother and she lost no time speaking the truth she carried in her heart.

"No more, my son, do I hate the venomous snake that came and bit you today, than I hate your father! May this truth become a blessing; may the poison be struck down; may my son revive and return fully to life!"

No sooner was this act of truth performed than the remaining poison flowed out of the son and sank darkly into the ground. Rising whole again with all his body purged of poison, the boy immediately took hold of the ball and began to roll it over the earth again. While the young one played with the roundness of life, the older folks each had something rougher to consider.

After an extended period of silence, the father asked the holy man how he could live the life of an ascetic for so long in such an unwilling mood. The monk explained that after taking the path of sanctity a part of him kept looking back. "At first there was the excitement of making a choice and dedicating myself to spiritual disciplines. After a week a voice within me began to say: "You fool; you idiot. You have left the world behind before you ever learned what it was and what it meant to you."

Ever since, the monk explained, he had lived the life of ascetic practices and renunciation, all the while longing to know more of the sensate, sensual world. When the father asked him why he did not simply release himself from his vows and pursue his true nature, the monk explained that he feared being called a sinner and a fool. He feared losing the admiration of learned people and the respect he gained simply by virtue of his saintly appearance. Despite feeling untrue to what he knew of himself within, the monk kept up the appearance that others expected of him. Despite longing to know more of the world, he kept himself within vows that denied his true nature.

The monk then asked the father how he, a well-respected and powerful man, could pretend to host the learned, the holy, and the wise while withholding his true feelings and dismissing his own sense of need and desire. His house, so widely esteemed for nobility and considered by many to be a model of generosity, must in truth be more like a common tavern than a genuine place of refuge.

The father responded that he simply followed in the footsteps of his own father and in the traditional ways of his family. He was born into wealth and high status and although the trappings and practices seemed increasingly empty to him, he feared creating a scandal or ruining the family name. He felt he could not face being considered a failure by others. He feared that they would judge him to have a perverse and degenerate nature. So, he also kept up appearances and lived a half-hearted life amidst all the trappings of power and wealth.

Having somewhat explained himself, the husband asked his wife how it was that she so hated him, yet never informed him of the matter. How had she lived unfulfilled for so long and with hatred so close? Why had she not acted in accordance with her true and loving nature?

After a pause, the wife stated that it was against the custom of society and the beliefs of both their families for a wedded wife to leave her husband and take a new mate. She feared that she would be condemned for being immoral and be punished for desiring what she did not deserve. Fear of recriminations caused her to keep things as they were and live with him in an unloving way. Only for love of their child had she finally said what had been so long unspoken within her heart. She only knew love in the form of her child and spoke the truth because of that. Receiving love herself and being "in love," that was another matter and not something easily attained in a world where passion his often dismissed and longing is too often denied.

All three became quiet again, all thinking their own thoughts and feeling what they must feel. When the husband finally broke the silence, it was to forgive his wife for any hatred she felt towards him and to ask forgiveness from her for his own ignorance and callous behavior. Under the unusual conditions and in the aftermath of the acts of truth, she found it in her heart to forgive her husband and they made peace with each other.

Turning then to the monk, the father said that he hoped that the seeker could find a way to walk in holiness with a tranquil mind, but he also wished him a heart full of joy. Anyone who could bring forth such a painful truth in service of a total stranger must have a great heart. Such a great heart should find a way to live its fullness and come to know its relations to both this world and the other.

Both the mother and father of the wounded boy expressed their gratitude to the monk. Then, the three who were brought together by the poison that endangered life parted ways. All had something essential to consider and each had a life change to contemplate. All, in their own way, had come to understand that those who fail to act in accord with their deepest sense of self not only fail their own spirit, but they secretly add to the poison that endangers this world.

There are no bystanders or onlookers in life; each of us either adds to the cure or deepens the wound. The fate of the innocent boy depended upon the honesty and truthfulness of everyone involved. Each had to reveal a hidden pain and a specific lack of fulfillment in order for life to flow freely. The boy was the one bitten by the snake; yet poison resided in everyone. It was not just the child who needed the acts of truth. Life had become stuck inside all the false exteriors and poisons were growing exactly where people pretended to be righteous or caring or successful. While sending the poison back to the earth, they called blessings down on the boy. Once again, the two-sided ceremony that cleanses and polishes was needed to bring the soul back to health.

They say that the truth can set you free, yet most people hold back the truth and imprison themselves. Telling the truth requires approaching the tiger-self within and that brings up all the old fears of being judged and rejected and being abandoned again. Not until it becomes a matter of life and death does the truth usually come out. Until it does, poisons silently grow within and secretly endanger everyone nearby. Even seemingly innocent acts of omission produce a contrary energy; nothing in this world is quite neutral and what does not add to the medicine will eventually become poison. In this world where poison can erupt at any moment and a small wound can fester until it becomes life-threatening, it is important to know what the truth is and when it needs to be expressed.

You Can't Help But Be Who You Already Are

Once again, the story indicates that the truth can turn everything around; now it is revealed that an act of truth does not have to come from a place of inner peace or life fulfillment. Truth is found wherever people truly find themselves, wherever they can't help but be at the given time. As an old poet and monk once said, "You can't help but be who and where you are."

Clearly the monk had received a calling from the spiritual realm. He had the moment of awakening that each soul is entitled to have. A golden part of himself became revealed and he felt it necessary to turn away from anything not deemed spiritual and lofty. Yet in turning away from the world he denied the full package given to him at birth. Despite his ascetic practices and outer demeanor, the fragrance of the sensate world followed him wherever he went. When asked to sacrifice for the sake of a child, his true courage and caring nature came out. It was the child in him that also needed to play in the world. Had he trusted the way already in him he might have turned much sooner towards a genuine destiny instead of living a half-life in a kind of spiritual limbo.

Pain and love brought the father to the point of self-revelation and caused the mother to embrace her own loving nature. Sometimes it is enough truth and enough wisdom for people to simply admit the poison they harbor and pronounce the longing hidden behind it. Being true in such revealing ways can clear the individual soul and create a turning point that can turn even a drastic situation around. Wisdom, so hard to find otherwise, can be found in the truth of the moment. Once the edifice of denial crumbles the ground of truth will be near at hand.

Remember the old thief, he found the inner truth when there was no other way to turn. Having descended to the depths he found the inner prison that exists behind all states of imprisonment. After looking deeply inside himself, he became able to reveal the poison behind the throne. The outer world may celebrate falsity in its many forms, but denial of the longings of the soul and the natural nobility of the inner life generates the hidden poisons that endanger the essential joy and exuberance of existence.

In a world where injustice often reigns and love often turns to hate, the problem isn't that no antidote is available. The problem is that the inner truth is so difficult for the little-self to face. When the monk claimed that he was no physician and had no remedy for the ailments in this world, he had to be reminded of the deeper pharmacy. "Physician, heal thyself," is the old remedy that applies in most situations. The problem is not the lack of medicine for the soul; rather it is an issue of being unwilling to pay the price. Remember the maggots and the gold? An opening of the wounds and cleansing of the rotting areas must precede the polishing up and shining forth of one's true nature.

Everyone would like to plant the seed that instantly grows the golden fruit and produces a miraculous blossoming; but a certain darkness and culpability must first be faced. The healing begins when the patient finally announces the nature of the suffering. Didn't the poor son of the old sage have to face his narrow fears and lack of courage in order to discover his hidden generosity? His cynical attitude poisoned the well for his wife and children as well as himself. The fact that his parents had wise practices did not provide him with the remedy his own soul needed. He had to find the inner generosity that kept opening wider until it became a benefit to others as well as a remedy for himself. The hesitant monk could have learned something from that instinctive expression.

Didn't the poor daughter of the sage have to learn how to love all over again? She had to become generous to herself. Having been trapped at the bargain level of love, she had to revalue herself and no longer give herself away. The mother of the snake-bitten boy could learn something from that. When the poor sister became willing to face her loneliness and lack of love, she found hidden knowledge and ways to love herself. Soon, the divine had to come to her. On the roads of healing there is no certain way to go, unless we find the way already seeded within us.

The Wise Self

The poison develops where the inner seed goes to rot and where the original agreement of the soul is dismissed in favor of conventional ideas and poor bargains with life. Meanwhile, simply naming the poisons set the sick child on the road to recovery. Pronouncing the truth also began to revive something essential in the parents and the monk. Each had an unlived life and that kind of holding back eventually stops all internal growth. An unlived life becomes a greater and greater inner shadow that eventually blocks one's basic vitality and turns things bitter.

The father had what others envied and desired; yet his true nature remained undeveloped. Secretly he was spreading poison even as he hosted others. The mother had a loving heart but was only able to love her child. She had a great capacity for loving and a great desire to be loved; but love that is not given can easily become hate. Until she got that out of her system, she too was spreading poison. The cure for the pain is found in the pain. Only after the pain has been named and been expressed can the healing begin. All are carrying medicine within them, but the poison must be released before the medicine can be found.

The true wisdom of one's life lies deep within and tends to appear when the truth of the situation is faced. In accepting the fate of the moment, a threshold forms and change becomes possible. True attention is part of the remedy, for genuine attention is a form of love. When the monk and the parents turn their real attention to the wounded boy, they also shower him with love. They sacrifice the comfort and control of the little-self out of love for the innocent child. They become selfless in a way that allows the deeper self with its natural medicine to rise to the surface. When people act from the deep self they appear to others as if they are being "selfless." Yet such selflessness begins with genuine self-recognition and self-revelation.

The whole thing trembles on the verge of our awareness; yet, it often takes a great failure or a tragic circumstance for the little-self to relinquish its blind rule. The deep self beckons to us continually, yet the little-self fears a loss of worldly power and social prestige. The little-self believes that letting go will lead to a great emptiness and a "loss of self." Believing itself to be the only self, it imagines life to be empty without it. The little-self is a necessary imposter unwittingly waiting for the true self to arrive. Once the little-self can admit its fears it can be a forerunner of the deeper self within.

The story written within the soul requires a drama of self-realization and self-revelation. At critical moments the veil between the little-self and the deep self thins and a meaningful self-adjustment becomes possible. If a person does not become paralyzed with fear or frozen in hatred, the wise self hidden within will rise to the occasion. It is in that sense that most ordeals encountered in life are also occasions for learning and opportunities for healing. The continual lesson involves the awakening of the deeper self and the living of the truth it already carries. When a situation feels like a matter of life and death the deep self is close at hand and it already carries inner medicine and its own life remedy.

When the deep self does manifest itself, we feel truly empowered, especially empowered to become ourselves. In becoming more ourselves, we fulfill a destiny even if it is only in the moment. For each moment of healing and becoming whole breaks the grip of time and opens us to the presence of the eternal. It also draws some poison out of the earthbound world. Acts of truth and moments of loving and healing bring the two worlds together and make it possible for life to regenerate and renew itself.

The Two Arcs of Life

The boy bitten by the snake was still at the beginning of life where it is important to play and grow and follow wherever the ball might roll. He was just stepping into life's first adventure and onto the path of growing up and learning how to play in this world. The parents and the monk had already lived much of life's first arc; they were ready for the second adventure of life and the path the soul would prefer to take. They were being called to the path of self-discovery. As the story shows, both adventures are necessary if the world is to continue and what happens on one arc affects what occurs on the other.

The first adventure of life traces a path through the events of the daily world. We enter the marketplace of life and become part of the great exchange and the endless deals. We learn to buy and sell and to speak as best we can the language of the day. We become wet with life and accept the rules of the game to one degree or another. We buy into a way of life and live it up or fall down trying to do so. We make our mark and rise in the world. We rule the day or else stumble in some alley or waste away in a prison of our own making.

On the first adventure there are no free lunches and all the deals have strings attached. For this is the "real world" where anything can be measured and everything has a price, where life is cheap and truth is rare and hard to find.

The second adventure goes another way; it speaks another language and seeks a different aim. It leads us back to the first agreement of the soul and would have us find the inner gold and deeper values in our lives. Seen from the hustle and bustle of life's marketplace, the second adventure and the first agreement of the soul seem unreal, not just foolish but irrelevant. What's the point, where's the payoff, how can you value what you cannot count or hold in your hand? In the modern world the inward, downward ways of the soul are less appreciated and more commonly dismissed.

As the value of life becomes increasingly measured by the literal yardsticks of the outer world, the inner life of the soul becomes undervalued and less understood. As the real world of facts and figures, of technologies and economics has come to seem the only world, fewer people seem to live the second arc and undertake the greater adventure of life. Many seem to reach the end without learning why the soul came to life to begin with. Yet all the while, the second adventure, with its mysterious dreams and wild projects, sings at the edges of all the deals being made and continues to hum when the wheels threaten to fall off the wagon that keeps the market of life in motion.

The first adventure of life involves the necessary path of growing up and joining the give-and-take that sustains the waking world. This outer arc, with its tangled array of second agreements, must be embraced and its inevitable illusions and disappointments must be struggled with. The second adventure takes up the life of the soul and it must also be sought for and be fought for or life will be incomplete regardless of apparent success. The second arc of life becomes the road of release through which people step away from strict adherence to the collective rules and social conventions in order to become truly themselves. The second adventure involves the paths of spiritual growth as well as the places of ecstatic experience.

On the second arc of life, the soul leads the way and the way of the soul involves deeper forms of both sensuality and spirituality. For the soul is connected to both body and spirit and would have us live the full package: become fully incarnate as well as spiritually awakened. The ambit of the soul naturally includes the heights of spirit as well as the depths of love. On the second adventure, we open the doors and windows of the body as well as the soul in order to let eternity back into the world.

This World and the Other

It's like the old story of two friends who happened to meet on a street in their village. They were headed in opposite directions when they came upon each other. One was going to a rendezvous with a lover, while the other planned to attend a spiritual meeting. The fellow heading to the spiritual gathering said, "Why do you want to go in that direction? You know that love and sensuality are always temporary. Come with me instead and hear the words of the spirit, the wonderful tales of the lives of saints and the stories of god. Come with me and improve yourself."

His friend responded, "Why don't you come where I am going? There is great delight in loving and it can bring a deep joy that continues to live in the soul. Simple happiness may come and go on a whim; but you should know that joy is also a path to the divine. You can just as easily waste your time at a spiritual gathering. The title of something does not guarantee that the substance will be delivered. If the transcendent moment fails to appear or if the teacher relies on orthodox ideas and dogmatic beliefs there can be a loss of spirit where its presence was promised. Come with me and at least be in the presence of beauty."

Neither could persuade the other because each had made up his mind regarding the direction in which the unseen could be found. So, each went his own way. However, the one who went to the spiritual meeting found that he could not concentrate on spiritual matters that day. All he could think about was the wonder of beauty and the allure of love and the time he might be having had he followed his friend's advice. He felt he was wasting his time listening to sermons when he could be learning the lessons of love and deepening his understanding of pleasure and delight.

Meanwhile, the fellow who was in the arms of his lover could not fully enjoy the occasion. He could only think of the spiritual meeting where his good friend was learning of lofty matters and probably enjoying the edification of songs and stories of those on the spiritual path. He had to admit that there was a temporary quality to his desires and joy seemed just out of reach on this occasion. It occurred to him that he might be wasting his time and that he had chosen the wrong path to follow.

Who can say which seeker is right? In a way, they are both correct. Part of us remains anchored in this world even when the realm of spirit appears close by. And for some, the sensual way of going and knowing *is* the spiritual path. Not only that, but as a person grows in spiritual terms, the desire for pleasure and beauty also tends to intensify. Why else would so many preachers and spiritual leaders fall into scandal? A part of us desires the natural delights of this world and another part longs for the realm beyond all affairs of the body. In the end, each direction can be seen to involve darkness as well as light. Strange, as it seems reaching for one can lead to embracing the other.

Remember the prostitute who saved the royal city? She reminded everyone that the truth hides in seemingly low places, exactly where most people decline to look. The issue is not so much choosing which way to go; rather the point is to be wholehearted in the direction that is currently being followed. We are creatures of both worlds and we are intended to serve both in creative ways. In making love a person may follow a manual or adhere to instructions from those more experienced. Yet the real lovemaking begins when a person puts their whole self and soul into the act. In doing so, they forget all the rules and even forget their usual self. Inside that forgetting they begin to remember something essential and spontaneous waiting to awaken within them.

People say: "I thought I had died and gone to heaven." Notice the intimate connection between death and the divine state even when the occasion involves delight and joy. Love requires that the little-self die a little so that we become our whole selves, at least for a moment. In that moment everything can change. Loving can also be an act of truth that brings the lovers close to the origins of life. In the midst of surrender the lovers move closer to the act of creation and secretly feel the creator's breath. That's why they say that without love the real work cannot progress.

We are each a friend to the otherworld and a friend of this world.

We must live in both worlds or else learn when it is too late that we have wasted our time in some essential way. How else could it be? There are two worlds and we are born to both of them and both of them need our honest attention and earnest involvement. There are two adventures to undertake, two arcs to wander on and two sides of the self that need attention and care. When the realm of culture seems about to unravel and even nature seems to be rattling, we must attend to both worlds and learn anew how to be a living bridge between the two. In troubled times we must be a friend of nature as well as a disciple of our inner nature. We are beings of both worlds and must serve each of them or fail to have lived life fully.

On the second adventure, we have the opportunity to become a disciple in our own lives and learn the nature of our fate and the shape of the destiny that calls us on. Yet our unlived lives can cut crosswise against the wisdom waiting to be found in the soul. Life is a mystery that cannot be solved by following a straight line or a single-minded purpose. The soul prefers a circuitous route that holds the two realms together, that repeatedly passes through the village where the maggots clean the rotten flesh and the friends of the self polish the inner gold.

Ultimately, the second adventure leads back to the first agreement that the soul made before entering this world. Awakening the greater self within and seeking to live out the original agreement of the soul is our deepest responsibility as well as the essential longing behind all the quests in life. We have little choice in the end; either we follow the dream that calls us to a greater life, or we take up residence in the village where people keep forgetting what life is all about. There are no guarantees on the paths to the unseen, yet the dull outcome in the village of forgetfulness is quite predictable. Despite the trap of time and the limits of fate, each day has moments of eternity waiting to be found and the opportunity to return to the original agreement of the soul is continually at hand.

Our Fate In Time

Meanwhile, if those old enough to know better deny the basic truths of their own lives and fail to live the inner adventure, the next generation must absorb the poison that is produced. It may have been the fate of the boy to be bitten by a snake and have his life hanging in the balance. Yet there were poisonous circumstances all around him. The story makes clear that he also suffered a fate not completely of his own making. Those who fail to face their own issues of fate put heavy burdens on those who are younger and unprotected. In failing to live fully, they put others in danger as well as themselves. They leave the ball of the world unattended and rolling towards an even deeper hole.

People worry over the fate of the world at a time when it seems that we have poisoned the water and polluted the air enough to endanger the entire planet. The river of life keeps flooding before us and a tide of poisons threatens both culture and nature and can tarnish the dreams of those who are young and as yet innocent. No need to mention the spread of wars and terrors and the increasingly obvious ways in which those with the power to help others indulge instead in their own greed or poisonous obsessions.

Our collective fate involves being alive in a time of great tragedies, in a period of overwhelming disasters. The snake-bitten condition has already spread throughout the collective body. Amidst all the fear and confusion, it becomes easy to forget that the real battle is inside; that history is made in the depths of the individual soul. Despite the current exaggerations of the first arc of life the missing ingredients wait to be discovered in the individual heart and soul. When seen as part of life's second adventure and the inner arc of healing, the wounds and the poisons we encounter in life can become the exact opportunities for bringing out all the inner medicines and making things whole again.

The greatest remedies are often made from otherwise poisonous substances. The wonder of life and the inescapable twists of fate place the medicine of the self near where the poison dwells. Just so, the gifts always lie near the wounds, and love often appears where deep losses become acknowledged. There is no denying that we live in radical times surrounded by tasks that seem impossible. However, it is also important to remember that during troubled times the inner resources and wisdom of life move closer to the surface and become more available.

Inner Wisdom

Amidst the rush and confusion of modern life something old and wise is trying to catch up with us. When the trouble becomes so profound that no amount of knowledge can provide a solution, it is wisdom that must be found. Whereas simple knowledge tends to divide things, genuine wisdom tends to make meaningful unity possible. Wisdom involves hidden unities and uncommon knowledge. Wisdom draws upon the origins of things and can return things to their original condition. The problem with wisdom is that, like gold, finding it involves a descent into dark places.

Wisdom is always valuable because it remains hard to find; like the pearl of the self, it hides where most people prefer not to go. Unlike information that can never really add up to much and unlike knowledge that can become overly bright, wisdom combines darkness and light. Wisdom can reveal the light hidden in dark times; but it requires that we face the darkness in ourselves. People may desire pearls of wisdom, yet most are unwilling to descend to the depths where the pearls wait to be found. Wisdom involves a necessary descent into the depths of life, for that alone can produce "lived knowledge" and a unified vision.

Wisdom and true freedom are found where we submit to the way we are intended to go and surrender to the mysterious ways we are intended to grow. Wisdom involves knowing enough to be able to guide others towards the knowledge and experiences they most need. But wisdom also involves the song of life and requires learning the rhythm and song in one's heart and soul. Wisdom is not a gloomy bird; nor is it a matter of abstract ideas.

Wisdom involves both hidden truths and necessary beauties and it helps hold the two worlds together. The word *wisdom* draws upon two old roots: one carries the sense of guidance, while the other refers to a lyric or a song. Wisdom develops from finding the genuine way of one's life but also grows from learning the lyrical song of one's soul.

The inner wisdom of one's life shapes the path that must be followed; but it is also carries a song-line that runs all the way through to the end. Those who become wise become both older than others and younger at the same time. The wise may become older because the weight of knowledge makes one feel older; but they become younger as well by learning to attune themselves to the song carried in the soul and the rhythm kept by the heart. Wisdom involves a dark knowledge of the intricacies and entanglements of fate as well as the surprising thread that reveals where destiny is hiding.

Fate keeps troubling the soul and even endangering the world until people accept that some deep truths must be faced. When the time for healing comes and the wounds of life can no longer be denied, those who are closest to the wounds will be better able to face the truth and start the healing. When there's no time left for sending out for physicians or waiting for magical antidotes, the medicine must be found where it has been all along, within us. The wisdom of the world is such that each soul has something to contribute in terms of the presence of inner truth and each can offer a part of the remedy so desperately needed.

We are always close to the source of wisdom because it dwells within us; yet some fateful events are needed for the little-self to let go and wake up to the true situation. The deep self harbors the core imagination that drove our soul to life to begin with. In that sense, the exact knowledge so often sought in the outer world can be found dwelling within the soul all along. Of course, many acts of truth are required as well as the ceremonies of cleansing and polishing that remove the rotten flesh and burnish the golden presence inside each soul. Such radical rituals are needed to reverse the flow of poison once it gets into the system and becomes a danger both to the youngest part of the soul as well as the younger generation.

Meanwhile, the child of the future has already been bitten by the snake of the past. It may be our mutual fate in life to be present when the long-festering poisons that trouble the world become undeniable. The questions that everyone faces amidst the floods of change and the waves of despair are similar to those asked of the holy man and the mother and father of the fallen child: Can you face the painful issues within and make an act of truth that helps remove some of the poison from the current situation? Can you become yourself in a way that adds a blessing to the blessed roar of life? Can you loosen the stones of the inner hearth and find the gold hidden in your heart?

The same questions have always hung in the air, just as the condition of the world has always hung in the balance between the fate and destiny born within each individual soul. They are the same questions that the divine asks at the end of each life's unique adventure: In the midst of all the confusion in the great marketplace of life, did you live the life seeded in your soul to begin with? In the twists of fate that entangled you in the troubles of the world, did you find the thread of destiny intended for you? And in the end, did you become weird enough and finally wise enough to become yourself?

ACKNOWLEDGEMENTS

Many people helped to bring this book to life and to light. I am grateful to: my aunt, Florence Sullivan for the right-wrong gift of the book of myths that first opened my eyes to the world of stories; to James Hillman for advising me to value my thoughts of fate and destiny some decades ago. Jacob Lakatua gives his all to the work with stories and soul and this book could not reach fruition without him. Peter Fedofsky brought a keen eye and a deep attention to the making of this book as he does for all Mosaic work. Christina Zanfagna has been invaluable as an editor and guide and as an inspiration for the writing. And thanks to Rachel Bard for careful reading and copy editing. Thanks to Lisa Thompson for timely and artful contributions and to Rick Simonsen for many helpful suggestions. Gratitude to Jack Kornfield for cogent comments and Luis Rodriguez for encouragement and spiritual support.

Select Bibliography

Cole, Joanna. *Best Loved Folktales of the World*. Garden City, NY: Anchor Books, 1983.

Commarswamy, Ananda and Sister Nivedita. *Myths of the Hindus and Buddhists*. New York, NY: Dover Publications, 1967.

Cowell, E.B. *The Jataka; or, Stories of the Buddha's Former Births*. Cambridge: Cambridge University Press, 1901.

Greene, Liz. *Astrology of Fate*. Newburyport, MA: Weiser Books, 1984.

Hamilton, Edith. *Mythology, Timeless Tales of Gods and Heroes*. Boston, MA: Little, Brown and Company, 1942.

Hamilton, Edith. *The Greek Way*. New York, NY: Time, Inc., 1930.

Hillman, James. *The Soul's Code*. New York, NY: Grand Central Publishing, 1997.

Kornfield, Jack and Christina Feldman. *Soul Food*. New York, NY: HarperCollins Publishers, 1996.

Ramanujan, A.K.. *Folktales from India*. New York, NY: Pantheon, 1994.

Zimmer , Heinrich. *Philosophies of India*. Edited by Jospeh Campbell. Princeton, NJ: Princeton University Press, 1969.

Zimmer, Heinrich. *The King and the Corpse*. Princeton, NJ: Princeton University Press, 1948.

Related Titles by Michael Meade

Meade, Michael. *The Eye of the Pupil, the Heart of the Disciple*. Mosaic Audio, Two CD Set.

Meade, Michael. *Fate and Destiny, the Two Agreements in Life*. Mosaic Audio, Two CD Set.

Meade, Michael. *The Light Inside Dark Times*. Mosaic Audio, Two CD Set.

Meade, Michael. *The Water of Life, Initiation and the Tempering of the Soul*. Seattle, WA: Greenfire Press, 2007.

Meade, Michael. *The World Behind the World, Living at the Ends of Time*. Seattle, WA: Greenfire Press, 2008.

Index

Mohammed, 90
Moira
  meaning of, 108
Mortality, 40
Moses, 90–91
Mother
  loss of, 22
Mythology, 10, 18, 28–30, 68, 126, 132, 202
  and fate and destiny, 53
  and psyche, 18
  and Robert Kennedy, 77
  Greek, 108
  Norse, 35, 94
Narada, 177–179
  as Eisik, 182
Noah, 91
Norns, 36
Novalis, 2
Odin, 102
Oedipus, 213
  story of, 27
Old Thief, 78–85, 125, 194, 306
  as artist, 80
Open secret, 176
Oracle at Delphi, 59
Original sin, 26, 136
Orpheus, 35, 43
Otherworld, 13, 95, 103, 138, 157, 166, 168, 173, 175, 202, 205, 247, 312
  and bridge, 176
  and longing, 180
  and weird, 170
Pain, 272–274
Parents, 211, 239
  and agreements, 139
  and betrayal, 211
  and children, 121, 214
  and children's fate, 213, 281
  and gifts, 211
  and responsibility, 254
  and the soul, 132
Path

genuine, 238
Pattern
  and family, 212
  inner, 6, 9, 35, 51, 53, 93, 94, 105, 110, 130, 132, 140, 142, 148, 162, 169, 200, 235, 249
Pearls, 287–290
Perfect
  meaning of, 168
Philosophy
  meaning of, 229
Pilgrimage, 12, 91, 153–154, 160, 172, 185, 188, 243, 295
Plato, 2
Poder, 125, 145
  complex, 116
  meaning of, 111
Poison, 305–308, 314–316
  and act of truth, 316
  and longing, 306
Pollux, 43
Poverty, 20, 237, 256, 269, 277
  and Buddhism, 238
  inner, 269
  spiritual, 20
  village of internal, 292
Power, 53, 81–84, 118, 314
  abuse of, 84
  and authority, 81
  and healing, 217
  and prostitution, 282
  and the deep self, 291
  and truth, 287
Prajapati, 222–223
Prima materia, 199, 212
Prison, 78
Prostitution, 256, 282
Psyche, 35, 159, 203, 209
  origin of, 131
Rama, 238–240
Rebirth, 248
Road
  of life, 243

ABOUT MOSAIC

Mosaic Multicultural Foundation is a 501(c)3 nonprofit organization, a network of artists, social activists, and community builders. Mosaic formed to create cross-cultural alliances, mentoring relationships, and social connections that encourage greater understanding between diverse peoples, elders and youth, and those of various cultural and spiritual backgrounds.

Mosaic means putting essential pieces together; forming a whole from separate, divided, even estranged parts. The process of finding, fitting, and weaving together divergent, yet necessary pieces involves making new social fabrics from existing ethnic, spiritual, psychological, and political threads.

Mosaic events draw inspiration from the traditions of many cultures and incorporate knowledge learned in the trenches of contemporary community work. Efforts at problem solving rely on locating the genius of the situation, as the unique spirit of each individual becomes a key to understanding issues and fitting the pieces of community together in new ways.

Mosaic's nationwide youth and mentoring projects help veterans return from war, assist addicts in recovery, and inspire youth to find their way in life. Current projects involve homeless and at-risk youth, high school and college students, combat veterans, tribal communities, as well as those in detention and on probation. The practice of mentoring offers the oldest, most natural, and most effective method for awakening genius in youth, creating mentors, and developing elders.

GreenFire Press and **Mosaic Audio** are imprints of Mosaic Multicultural Foundation that serve to foster cultural literacy, mythic education, and multicultural community development. Proceeds from sales of books and recordings directly benefit Mosaic's work with at-risk youth, refugees, and intercultural projects.

For more information or to order additional titles contact Mosaic:
P.O. Box 847, Vashon, WA 98070
(206)935-3665
www.mosaicvoices.org ~ info@mosaicvoices.org

Books by Michael Meade

Awakening the Soul: A Deep Response to a Troubled World

The Genius Myth

Why the World Doesn't End

The World Behind the World: Living at the Ends of Time

The Water of Life: Initiation and the Tempering of the Soul

Mosaic Audio Recordings by Michael Meade

A Song is a Road

Alchemy of Fire: Libido and the Divine Spark

Branches of Mentoring

The Ends of Time, the Roots of Eternity

Entering Mythic Territory: Healing and the Bestowing Self

The Eye of the Pupil, the Heart of the Disciple

Fate and Destiny: The Two Agreements in Life

Finding Genius in Your Life

The Great Dance: Finding One's Way in Troubled Times

Holding the Thread of Life: A Human Response to the Unraveling of the World

Inner Wisdom: The Eternal Youth and the Wise Old Sage

The Light Inside Dark Times

Initiation and the Soul: The Sacred and the Profane

Poetics of Peace: Peace and the Salt of the Earth

Poetics of Peace: Vital Voices in Troubled Times, with Alice Walker, Luis Rodriguez,
   Jack Kornfield, Orland Bishop

The Soul of Change

Podcasts by Michael Meade

Living Myth, a free weekly podcast

Living Myth Premium, a membership-based podcast

Books edited by Michael Meade

Crossroads: The Quest For Contemporary Rites of Passage,
   edited by Louise Carus Mahdi, Nancy Geyer Christopher, and Michael Meade

The Rag and Bone Shop of the Heart: A Poetry Anthology,
   edited by Robert Bly, James Hillman, and Michael Meade